Magical Thinking and
The Decline of America

ALSO BY RICHARD L. RAPSON

Non-Fiction

Individualism and Conformity in the American Character
Britons View America: Travel Commentary, 1860-1935
The Cult of Youth in Middle-Class America
Major Interpretations of the American Past
The Pursuit of Meaning: America 1600-2000
Denials of Doubt: An Interpretation of American History
Fairly Lucky You Live Hawaii! Cultural Pluralism in the Fiftieth State
American Yearnings: Love, Money, and Endless Possibility
Amazed By Life: Confessions of a Non-Religious Believer

CO-AUTHORED BOOKS (with Elaine Hatfield)

Love, Sex and Intimacy: Their Psychology, Biology, and History
Emotional Contagion
Love and Sex: Cross-Cultural Perspectives

Fiction

Rosie
Recovered Memories
Darwin's Law
Deadly Wager and *Vengeance Is Mine* (two Kate MacKinnon murder mysteries)
Adventures of Firefly: The World's Tiniest Detective and *Take Up Serpents* (two Firefly mysteries)

For Jim & Susan –
With warmest aloha.
Dick

Magical Thinking and
The Decline of America

An Update Of "American Yearnings—
Love, Money, And Endless Possibility"

Richard L. Rapson

To order additional copies of this book, contact:
Xlibris Corporation
1-888-795-4274
www.Xlibris.com
Orders@Xlibris.com
40026

Contents

THREE: GLANCING AHEAD

POSTSCRIPTS

To my sweetheart, Elaine

INTRODUCTIONS:
FORMAL AND INFORMAL

The Crucible

PREFACE, 1988

Probably in no other society of the world can one write the script for one's life as completely as in the United States. This fact has made the nation the "promised land" for much of the world over the past two centuries. A main reason for this freedom lies in the fluid class structure which gives way to the competitive scramble we call "equality of opportunity."

The downside to the scramble for wealth lies partly in the materialism that the rest of the world has scorned and emulated. But it has also generated an exaggerated American faith in our ability to accomplish anything if only we try hard enough and have the "right attitude." The flight into endless self-improvement and innocent optimism, while it has been most recently visible during the Reagan years, has a long lineage in our past—and it is a major theme of the pages that follow.

Have we the capacity to look at ourselves and a complex world with greater intellectual and emotional honesty than we have in the past? In a poll taken by *The New York Times* in late February, 1988, Americans confessed that they no longer believed that the future would be better than the past. The results of the poll suggested that reality might be catching up with fantasy. Writing about the poll, *Times* columnist Tom Wicker said that:

> The economic power of the U.S. has declined relative to its competitors; so has its military might, and the world's wealthiest nation has sunk deeply into debt. In the daily grind of living, crises of drug abuse, education, aging, health, and the environment nag the national consciousness.[1]

Wicker thought the AIDS plague had already diminished the personal freedom some believed had been enlarged in the 1960's, and that racial and religious backlash were on the rise. After reciting a litany of national ills, Wicker concluded:

> So it's neither surprising nor dismaying if Americans . . . no longer look to the future with boundless, sometimes mindless optimism. The new realism, if sustained, is badly needed. It's better to see things as they are than through the eyes of boomers and promoters, from whose lurid pitch so much wastage and deception already has resulted.

> Besides, if Americans stop looking so eagerly to the future, maybe they can begin to look with more interest and understanding to the past—from whence, after all, they came.[2]

The disbelieving tone that marks portions of this book may have been affected by the particularly fatuous mood of the past decade, but Ronald Reagan did not create fatuousness. Much of his popularity derived from his instinct that Americans have *always* preferred to hear good news and pep talks instead of having to wrestle with complexity. This instinct toward cheerfulness in the face of anything defines a major aspect of his "Americanness."

So while this examination of American optimism appears at the end of the "feelgood" Reagan years, I do not mean it as a tract only about these times. After all, the latest rage is to bewail the end of The American Century. That decline is seen not only as a loss of military and political hegemony in the international arena, but as a crumbling from within. One writer on strategic affairs recently noted that "the problems of this country are prosaic and blatantly obvious. They are shoddy education, poor service, low productivity, excessive legalism."[3] He certainly could have added uncontrolled crime and the epidemic of drug use to his list. But even if the post-Reagan 1990's witness a darker mood than the 80's, the fact remains that there is a very long and durable tradition of national optimism. It will not be easily subdued by realism. In any event, I have tried to write a work that looks deeply into our past in order to say pertinent things not only about our present and future, but about our history as well.

Many friends greatly aided me in this enterprise. The list includes Beth Bailey, Paul Berry, Leon Edel, Marjorie Sinclair Edel, David Farber, Arthur Goodfriend, Faith Hornby, Helen Hudson, Betty Jenkins, Britt Michelsen, Marian Morgan, Donald Raleigh, Monique Schalekamp, and Rob Vrabel. My chief editor, Lizabeth Ball, is without peer. And for supports that only they can know about, I salute my daughter Kim Elizabeth Rapson and my wife Elaine Hatfield. All these friends know that even if people can't "have it all," I wish *they* could.

Honolulu, Hawaii
March 8, 1988

PREFACE, 2007

It has been two decades since the publication of my attempt to see the United States whole in American Yearnings: Love, Money, and Endless Possibility. *A large part of that book offered historical and structural explanations for contemporary developments. Since I was attempting to look at those deeper underpinnings of American society, the book was meant to stand some test of time and not simply speak to that moment in the 1980's. This book represents an effort to see how the test came out.*

The method is simple. American Yearnings *appears exactly as it did in the 1980s. No changes. Beyond correcting a typo here and there, I've not snuck in secret revisions to paper over some major blunder or hide some display of foolishness on my part. Bald. Exposed. But where pertinent, I have added comments—I call them "Afterwords." These are brief, new commentaries as I look back and reflect upon the original text from the vantage point of the 21ˢᵗ century's first decade.*

Quite a lot has happened since American Yearnings *first saw the light of day. The Berlin Wall came tumbling down. The Soviet Empire broke up. The Cold War ended. Germany was reunited. The European Union expanded dramatically, with most of its members adopting a common currency. China's economy grew exponentially, turning that huge nation into a Capitalist giant.*

The personal computer is redefining how we communicate and spend, and both cyber and biological technologies revolutionize all aspects of our lives and institutions. India's educated classes have joined China's in converting digital know-how into pockets of prosperity for the first time in centuries. Genetic knowledge and technology grows exponentially, opening up remarkable medical possibilities and posing a number of ethical conundrums.

Private lives all around the world, particularly as they relate to the lives of women, are being transformed before our eyes. Taking decades rather than centuries to unfold, arranged marriages are giving way to love marriages, women are challenging heretofore forever-entrenched male domination, divorce grows more permissive, and the subordination of the individual to family, tribe, nation and religion is giving way to rising individualism. These are aspects of globalization as much as are the spread of capitalism and technology.

On the other hand, since the initial appearance of American Yearnings, *fundamentalist Muslim terrorism has more successfully reached its murderous tentacles into all corners of the planet. Also, genocidal madness broke out in places from the Balkans to Sudan to Rwanda. Africa and the Middle East remained the holdout regions from the emerging global culture. That globalization is perhaps the major historical development of our times, bringing promises of a connected, more peaceful world, but also an array of new issues concerning its nature and who will set its rules.*

And in America, after a period of considerable prosperity and peace during the Clinton years, the election of 2000 brought into power—in my opinion—the worst Administration in the history of the Republic. There have been many bad Presidents and administrations in American history, but many of them performed dismally by being passive when action was called for, as in the years leading up to the Civil War.

But the ideological reign of George W. Bush and his team was active in bringing damage and disrepute to the United States. It lied the nation into a disastrous war in Iraq, furthering the helter-skelter growth of terrorism where it hadn't appeared before. It sent us into deep national debt, shredded the social safety net, gutted the environment, added greatly to economic inequality, breached the wall separating church and state, threatened civil liberties in the name of security, and distorted science for political and religious purposes.

It encouraged and nurtured the growth of anti-scientific, anti-intellectual, misogynistic, and homophobic tendencies in its opposition to stem cell research, abortion rights, same sex marriage, Darwin, regulations on business, universal health insurance, warnings about global warming, and checks on executive power. It smiled on religious fundamentalists with their ignorant rejection of evolution and of the value of evidence itself in favor of a medievally literal reading of the Bible as the source of knowledge.

America hence has become the laughing stock of the developed world—scorned, despised, isolated, ridiculed. It will take a long time to repair the damage done by those strange bedfellows: neo-conservative ideology and Christian fundamentalism, and the days of America as a beacon to the world may possibly be a thing of the past.

In addition to my "Afterthoughts," I've included in this updating five short "postscript" essays. "America the Ignorant" addresses some of the issues above, "New College" describes my notions of where higher education should go, and "The Psychological Revolution" hints at the changes in the world that may run deeper even than the political economic, and technological transformations that are sweeping our planet. I conclude with "America the Rightwing" and "America the Resilient?"

Of the many wise people who helped me with American Yearnings *twenty years ago, I wish to take note of the passing of two dear friends from that group: the writer Arthur Goodfriend and the biographer of Henry James, Leon Edel. I miss them both. Finally, as the new dedication attests, my indispensable partner in this book and in life remains my wife, Elaine Hatfield.*

And now, on to the dialogue with my earlier book. With all the many powerful developments over the past 20 years limned above, my question must now be addressed: do they negate, reinforce, and/or modify the analysis of American Yearnings: Love, Money, and Endless Possibility? *Let's find out.*

Monty Python and the Life of Brian
"Always Look on the Bright Side of Life"

1

The Pitfalls of Positive Thinking

I had just finished writing my final chapter. When I looked up, I saw that we had done it again. Lieutenant Colonel Oliver L. North, during the Iran-Contra hearings of 1987, boasted about the way he had lied to nearly everyone in order to further his causes. So what did we do? We instantly enshrined him as "national hero." Writing shortly after, Lewis Lapham, editor of *Harper's* magazine, observed:

> The colonel's success as witness and celebrity testified to the ignorance of a credulous American public increasingly in thrall to the fairy tales told by the mass media. Like Oliver North, the big media stage their effects in the realm of myth and dream. Their audiences lose the habit of memory and let slip their hold on the ladders of history and geography. At last count, 50% of the American population believed an accused individual guilty until proved innocent, 50% didn't know which side the United States supports in Nicaragua. 42% couldn't name a country "near the Pacific Ocean" and 40% of the nation's high school seniors thought that Israel was an Arab country.
>
> Archetypal figures come and go in enchanted theaters of the news— weightless, without antecedents—giving shape to the longing of the moment. For six days in July, it was the persona of Oliver North, inflated to the size of a float at the Rose Bowl parade, comforting the public with a world as simple as state fairs and quilting bees . . . Defying the Congress, he defied, too, the corruption of death and change and presented himself as the immortal boy in the heroic green uniform of Peter Pan."[4]

Media celebrities enter and leave the theater of adulation with some rapidity in the United States. No one can predict, by the time these words are read, whether North will be a hero, a convict, or a forgotten man. (In a society whose citizens crave attention, prison can be preferable to oblivion. Better to be wanted for murder than not wanted at all.) The cult of celebrity is a major theme of this book. So is American ignorance, especially when it comes to knowledge of the world and of the past. But beneath both celebrityhood and ignorance resides a larger subject which Lapham hints at when he uses phrases such as "credulous," "fairy tales," "myth and dream," "lose the habit of memory," "enchanted theaters of the news," "a world as simple as state fairs and quilting bees," North as "Peter Pan." Behind celebrity and innocence lie a simplicity, optimism, and innocence that define both the charm and bane of American life. What forms do they take? Where do they come from? What impact do they have on our national life? How do they shape our deepest desires?

As an historian, I must make a preliminary answer to those questions by mentioning that Americans these days read and know very little history. Though the degree of historical illiteracy has increased during the past 25 years, the fact is that Americans never have had much interest in the past. Their decisive historical experience comes from pilgrimages made to Heritage U.S.A. or Disneyworld, where they can watch a robot Abe Lincoln move his mouth or see that famous American, Peter Pan, fly.

There are at least two major reasons for this. The first relates to our nation's history itself. This was the *new* world, and it viewed the old as corrupt, decadent, and not to be emulated. The few Americans who think about history at all regard it as "bunk." But most folks are too busy constructing their presents and futures ever to think much about the past at all. *"Today is* the first day of the rest of your life." "You can be whatever you want to be." "America is the land of opportunity, the home of endless possibility." The screaming solicitations to look to the future and think positively come close to defining the American ethos. In that context there is not much to be gained from historical consciousness. "Dream the impossible dream." "Nothing is impossible"—especially success. "Winning isn't the most important thing: it's the only thing!"

A second cause for the national lack of historical awareness lies with historians themselves. With the rise over the past century of the "scientific school" of history, scholars have increasingly eschewed the big statements for small, precise monographs on delimited subjects, hoping that the accumulation of fragments rigorously described will yield up, by addition, an accurate full picture. These monographs are not designed to be read by the public, let alone the general intelligent reader. Most historians write for other historians. Their "conventional wisdom," according to Robert Darnton, "is to cut the past into tiny segments and wall them up within monographs, where they can be analyzed in minute detail and rearranged in rational order."[5]

There have been significant exceptions to this rule. In the 1950's and 1960's, some scholars thought about history in thematic ways and dealt with large sweeps of time. My mentor, Richard Hofstadter, wrote in 1956 that the ultimate historical tradition "is to try to cope with certain insistent macroscopic questions."[6] Since that time the discipline has by and large turned away from those questions, in order to illuminate the "tiny segments" of the past. Much of the "new social history" has been quite brilliant, and many of the insights derived from it have been incorporated into the pages that follow. In his presidential address to the American Historical Association in 1981, Bernard Bailyn of Harvard University noted the outpouring of specialized scholarship. While acknowledging its richness, he feared that it had produced "in modern historiography . . . shapelessness, [possessing a] . . . lack of general coherence." He said it was time to compose large-theme histories that bring about new, grander understandings and conceptual frameworks.[7] Bailyn has achieved that himself, but even his work still does not address the general reader.

This book makes large generalizations about very large topics, more sweeping, I fear, than Bailyn had in mind. It violates some of the rules I learned as a professional historian. Instead of modest, well-documented observations upon one or two themes, I am proposing some new ways of thinking about war, capitalism, sex, race, money, and marriage. I am making novel claims about the American people and commenting on society overall. Above all, in a work that seeks to include non-historians among its readers, I am raising questions about how we in the United States think.

My observations gather around the question: what, finally, do Americans want out of life? A working subtitle of this book once was *For Love or For Money?* That choice both simplifies and complicates the issue. If we are asked whether our deepest desire runs toward wealth or yearns for a "meaningful relationship," many of us will instantly respond: "yes!" Americans do not see why they should have to choose. Without missing a beat or feeling much doubt, they will exclaim in the words of another popular inspirational message of the times: "You can have it all!" They have entered the land of endless possibility.

Thoughtful people will complain that love *or* money forecloses too many possibilities. Some Americans insist that the purpose of life lies in serving Almighty God, with salvation at stake. Others claim their goal is "to leave the world a better place than I found it." One can find champions for fame, power, being good parents, for "achieving my potential," or less pompously, for having fun while you can. But even here, the most characteristic faith of this culture resists choice and still proclaims: "You can have it all."

The sad news, of course, is that you can't. I make that announcement from two perspectives. First, as a professional historian. Though my guild tends to shun explicit homilies about life, the story we have to tell is one of tentative gains rather than unmixed glory, of disappointed hopes, repeated errors, paradox, modest advances, and no little cruelty and stupidity. We write, at our best, in the tragic-comic Greek mode of pity, awe, and irony.

Second, I conclude that life has limits partly from my experience as a psychotherapist. I have talked to many people, most of them fully functioning but willing to ask tough questions of themselves and life. As much from these many sessions with "clients," as from my study of history, I know how few "have it all" or ever have. In this book, then, addressed to general readers and posing large questions, what may seem at times purely speculative also derives from substantial work in psychology as well as history.

Still I do not wish to claim too much for these reflections. Though I will try to persuade, it is in the nature of the questions posed that I can prove nothing. That may be why this genre of writing is rarely attempted; nothing can be proved definitively, and the writer exposes himself in an unseemly fashion. Nonetheless, there would seem to be some value in trying to come to grips with large ideas.

While this chapter provides an outline of the book, the introductory section of the work also includes Chapter Two, in which I introduce *myself*. This is in keeping with our cultural fixation on the individual, the personal, the autobiographical, the confessional, and, all too often, the narcissistic. Among our new magic words in this vein are "self-awareness," "self-confidence," "self-actualization," "personal growth," and "freedom." These phrases, linked with the optimism, simplicity, and innocence of "you can be anything you want to be," give form to the American mental landscape. That second chapter, "The Face Is Familiar: A 25th College Reunion," derives from a speech I gave at Amherst College in 1983. It allows the reader to see some of the influences, biases, and interests that define me and much that follows in the book. I hope to encourage the reader into partnership in a living dialogue with an actual person rather than a passive bout with yet another anonymous authority.

The work then deals with the past ("One: Looking Back"), the present ("Two: Contemporary Themes"), and the future ("Three: Glancing Ahead"). The three chapters of Part One proceed in chronological order, in a manner borrowed from the movies. Like a camera panning the whole horizon, they slowly edge in closer and closer. Though the book focuses on contemporary matters, it cannot be properly done without historical perspective. Thus Chapter Three ("Scanning the American Past, 1600-1900") looks briefly at three centuries of our history. Chapter Four moves in closer by examining aspects of the American 19th century through Henry Wadsworth Longfellow's popular poem, "The Village Blacksmith." Chapter Five treats similar issues a century later, centered on television in the 1950's. All the chapters of Part One focus directly on how Americans have tried, over time, to define "the good life." They remind us of the startling transformations that the world and its inhabitants have gone through in modern history.

The five chapters of Part Two ("Contemporary Themes") form the core of this work. They take up some of the central issues of our time and culture: the cult of celebrity, the anxieties about money, the national paralysis when it comes to thinking about the ultimate war, the conflict between marriage and individualism, and the ramifications of those two powerful, epochal on-going revolutions of this era—the movements for women's and for civil rights.

These observations are shaped into a conclusion in Part Three ("Glancing Ahead"). They return us to the private and personal concerns of the introductory section, reminding us of T.S. Eliot's lovely lines:

> We shall not cease from exploration
> And the end of all our exploring
> Will be to arrive where we started
> And know the place for the first time.[8]

My personal commentaries are serious, but I hope they will be received as neither too solemn nor narcissistic. I would like to think that I am *of* my culture, but also apart from it, and that some of the "apart" comes through in the irony and playfulness that I feel about myself, my country, and, also, about this book—punctuated as it is with grand pronouncements. I respectfully offer it up, poised somewhere between bemusement and passion, in the hope that it may expand our vision a bit.

AFTERWORD

The flight from knowledge and reality into faith and fantasy has not, I fear, abated since I wrote the words above. The "credulous American public increasingly in thrall to the fairy tales told by the mass media" that Lapham abhorred, practically defines the aspirations of millions of Americans. I fear we have not "expanded our vision" as a nation and grown smarter. I think the bad news can be summed up in six phrases or words: scientific illiteracy; "reality" TV; electing George W. Bush (twice!); religious fundamentalism; anti-intellectualism; and "whatever." They will all get some of their due in these pages.

As a start, I propose an experiment. I frequently ask my students (and I get good ones) to list all the famous living scientists they know. Their list is very short. Maybe a Stephen Hawking or two will appear. If I break the question down into component parts—how many Biologists do you know? Physicists? Chemists? Mathematicians? Geologists?—you can guess how short would be their lists. Then I ask my students how many living poets they can name. Again, a number approaching zero. Philosophers. Zero. Historians. One!! Theologians, political scientists, playwrights, anthropologists, sculptors, teachers, archaeologists, and back toward zero we head again. Even lawyers, doctors, and journalists, if they don't appear on TV, are barely known.

But ask them to name TV personalities, movie actors, entertainers, of any stripe, athletes, pop music groups—and the numbers soar. Into the scores, the hundreds, the thousands, they fly!! The point of this test is not to embarrass my students or anyone else; I truly like my students. But who and what kind of person a society knows, celebrates, and emulates tells us a great deal about that society. America may not be alone in adoring its purveyors of fantasy and ignoring its creators of knowledge, but it stands unsurpassed.

The business of America has become show business, with its worship of "stars," and the dream of being one of them, being loved by the multitude and paid in the millions is closer to the American dream in the 21st century than ever before. And so many young Americans believe that they will be stars themselves if only they can get discovered. Witness "American Idol," and its many clones.

As to one of the key new words of our time—"whatever"—we bear witness to the fact that belief is more important than "truth" or evidence. The truth is whatever you believe it to be. While "whatever" may be an expression of toleration for a variety of beliefs, it also most certainly means "who cares?" "Whatever you believe is all right with me." "It's true if you believe it to be."

This sloppy and apathetic approach to reality belongs to all ideological spectrums in America. There's Oprah touting a book called "The Secret," the newest version of "want it badly enough and it will come true." She and the authors of that silliness celebrate the notion that positive belief will:

improve eyesight . . . and work on everything from weight loss to panic attacks to getting rich to snagging the mate of your dreams or a good parking space. [As Oprah and her new gurus say:] We create our own circumstances by the choices that we make, and the choices that we make are fueled by our thoughts. So our thoughts are the most powerful things that we have on earth. And based upon what we think—and [what] we think determines who we are—we attract who we are into our lives.[9]

Reality isn't Auschwitz, or being killed in Iraq, or in curing smallpox; it's about what we think is "real." Or as Maureen Dowd added in her piece about Oprah's support of fantasy and her own powerful attacks on George W. Bush's Iraq policies:

With this [positive thinking] W. will realize that all he needs to do to change his current reality is admit that it's fake. (Similar to the wisdom of Dorothy clicking her shoes three times.) Once he stops his chain reaction of negative thought, I can stop my chain reaction of negative thought. And then there will be peace on earth and parking spaces for everyone.[10]

In falling ever deeper into positive fantasies, into general credulity, and ignoring evidence, the country has paid a high price. Our friends in the developed world are far less inclined to distinguish, as once they did, between the American government and the American people. The outside view of Americans themselves, of American culture itself, is in free fall.

I doubt whether any country in the developed world would have given an unprepared, rightwing, zealously religious, and intellectually incurious candidate like George W. Bush more than 10-15% of their vote. Americans in 2000 gave Bush almost half theirs. Though the election caused consternation in the Western world, many argued that it was an aberration, not likely to be repeated. And, after all, Al Gore won the popular vote and the election may very well have been "stolen"; the vote count in Florida and elsewhere certainly wasn't kosher. In any event, it was finally decided by five partisan, conservative members of the Supreme Court (against four moderate Justices), and hardly represented a mandate from the people.

But when Americans in 2004 voted in Bush a second time, in the face of a horrendous first term, the American people, their judgment, their intelligence, their fundamentalist religious fervor, and the triviality and retrograde nature of the culture generally came under withering attack, scorn, and ridicule from many places abroad. What was happening in America? What kind of people were we?

While the criticisms can be overdone and the simplifications are to be deplored, I happen to think these are legitimate questions. They were the topic of American Yearnings, and the concerns and criticisms I penned then remain very much in place. In fact, I feel less good about my country than I did two decades ago, and I fear for our future more than I did then.

La Dolce Vita

2

The Face Is Familiar:
A 25th College Reunion

The Date: June 3, 1983
The Place: Amherst College, Amherst, Massachusetts
The Occasion: A speech by the author at the 25th reunion of his Amherst College
                 Class of 1958
Topic: From age 21 to 46, From 1958-1983

What a privilege and what a strange feeling to see you all here. I arrived on this campus yesterday for the first time in 22 years. In 1961 I had completed a delightful teaching stint and was on my way to what would be an equally grand run of years at Stanford. My career as a professor had begun well.

When I drove on to the campus I wondered whether this "place apart" would be as beautiful as it was in my memories. Memory has played some tricks on me, but not this time. I have yet to come upon a campus lovelier than this. Yet memory remains the subject of this reunion, and I suppose it wasn't all that inappropriate to choose an historian to give its opening speech. My topic is time. I wish to reflect on the past quarter century, which historians are presumed to be able to say something about. We shall see.

Three events have recently set me thinking about what has transpired between that year 1958 when we were 21-years-old and ready to knock down the world and this moment in 1983 when we assemble here as middle-aged men. First was Art Powell's graceful anthology of the reflections of the past 25 years written by over 100 of us. The other two were somewhat more personal. My daughter Kim, who is currently a member of the Amherst class of 1985, recently snuck down to the cellar of the dormitory where I lived during my junior year, and absconded with two mounted pictures of the members of that house in 1957 and 1958. There we were, myself included, white, male, hair cut short, seemingly all assembled from the same mold. When she presented these pictures to me as a birthday gift, my thoughts went less to the ethical questions involving the receipt of stolen goods (they had, after all, been lying around unnoticed for over two decades) than to the realization that that face in the middle was really mine and those faces were really yours: serious, superficially homogeneous, cutouts from some long-gone past,

The final event came after I had been invited to give this talk. I realized that I had given a speech to this class—the Bond Prize speech—at our graduation weekend 25 years ago. It would be fun to compare what I said then with what I now believe. What *had* I said? Could I find the speech? When I rummaged through my papers, there it was, and in a few minutes I should like to share with you what I discovered.

We begin this trip in time in several ways. There were only 245 of us in 1958. Though we were not a unified class, most of us knew, at least by name, nearly all the members. There are a remarkable 150 classmates here at the reunion. Many of us have not seen each other for that 25 years. The people we remember were 21 or 22 years-old at our last get-together. We are ready to converse with someone that age. But these people today are 46 or 47. The faces are familiar, but the bodies are not. The voices haven't changed much, but the hairlines have. Some of us look like 60 year-olds: others more like 35. Some are clearly the same people we knew then, only a little older; others seem dramatically different. We are embraced by the surreal.

Surreal, yes—but poignant also. Yesterday, our president read the names of the 12 classmates who have died, leaving 30 seconds between each name. What filled those 30 seconds? For me there were often sharply-etched recollections of each person combined with disbelief and sadness that they were no more. But I also thought of mortality, of my own death, of the fact that more than a hundred of the Class of 1958 will be dead by the time of our 50th reunion. We were, after all, only 21 yesterday, when last we met. So here we are today, surrounded by time. While we are having fun, catching up on each other's lives, we simply cannot help wondering about life, about the tricks time can play.

Much of the conversation this weekend has centered on our divorces or the way many of our life-plans failed to work out as programmed back in 1958. For some this has caused grief, but for many others it has led to a positive change, an enlargement of possibilities, and an enrichment of perspectives. In this way we are much a part of what has been happening in our country. Among the major changes in our culture this past quarter-century, I would place near the top of my list phenomena that are barely suggested by the phrases: the Breakup of the Traditional Family; the Sexual Revolution; the Women's Movement. The Class of 1958, remember, was all male. I have already mentioned that my *daughter* attends Amherst today.

While driving here with Harvey Hecht, we were accompanied by his wife Gail, also a doctor and a graduate from down the road at Smith, Class of 1958. Gail remarked that her 25th Reunion was not as happy an affair as this one looks to be. The ascribed strategy for women in 1958 was to find a man, marry him, have children, do volunteer work, and provide the psychological support for her hardworking, high-earning husband. For large numbers of these women, happy-ever-after has not occurred. Many of them find themselves at age 46, single, with teenage children, and without the career that they now need to support themselves. Some belong to the new, rapidly expanding poverty class of such women in this nation. Twenty-five years later than us they are back at law schools and medical schools trying to stitch together the kinds of careers from which many of us more fortunate men are now already winding down. As some women are forced to begin, many of us are able to reach out for new activities from a position of relative financial security. The game plan may not have worked out as we expected, but most of us have made out better than our sisters at Smith who were trapped in a dramatically changing culture. My daughter's future plans bear little resemblance to that of Smith '58, and, on the whole, I think she and society will benefit by having her intelligence fed directly into the system from the start.

Not only were we all males here from 1954 to 1958; with few exceptions we were all *white* males. The cultural pluralism of American society was barely reflected in our best colleges; in the interim, the changes in ethnic relations have been astounding. The general acceptance in the 1950's of middle-class values, including those of patriotism and materialism as well as the traditional family, have been augmented by ideas that were not actively in circulation during that seemingly apathetic time. In addition to the women's movement and the ethnic movements, the culture has been shaped by the environmental sensibility, by the peace movement, by the revolution in sexuality, by the proliferation and power of television, computers, drugs and other new technologies, by America's loss of economic and political hegemony worldwide, by the opening up of space, and by a host of other transformations. Indeed, the changes have been so rapid and dramatic that a conservative reaction is certain to set in, as the election of Ronald Reagan clearly signals. Conservative, reactionary and fundamentalist religious voices will be loudly heard in the coming years, but I think the agenda of the future will be set more by the continuing march of science. Science is a self-correcting intellectual system, one in which change is assumed to be the only constant. Change, I believe, will be the major constant for the remainder of our lives.

So we have seen our tidy world of 1958 dramatically altered. But just how tidy was that world? How much, really, have the alterations affected us in our personal lives? And what might lie ahead? In the proper spirit of arrogance necessarily connected to these queries, I should like to make a few observations before I descend from the pulpit.

Let's look a little more closely at our own time here at Amherst—the so-called "apathetic" Fifties. We were homogeneous sexually and ethnically. We believed in marching straight ahead to careers and marriage; political activism was not at the top of our agenda. But it surely did *not feel* apathetic during those days. I remember it as a time of intensity, searching, excitement, not in the company of cookie-mold colleagues but intelligent, unpredictable, lively classmates and faculty. I recall apathy less than I do an appreciation for complexities. And such appreciation renders simple slogans unappealing. I recall acceptance of tradition less than I do the meaning of our required English and Physics courses: that, as words have no intrinsic meaning apart from context, we must create our own meaning.

To recollect those days more sharply I rescued two speeches I delivered in the past. One was at the inauguration of an experimental college I founded and directed in 1968-73, years exactly halfway through our period. The college was called New College; it was modeled to a great extent on Amherst as modified by the events of the 1960's, and it was part of the University of Hawaii. The other talk, which I mentioned earlier, was my Bond Prize speech of 1958. In both cases I wished to recall not only the times, but myself as well. How have we changed? What I found was not exactly what I had expected.

The speech opening New College began this way:

> In the 1950's the keywords and phrases for college students were "paradox,"
> "irony," "cool," "ambiguity," "wit," "detachment," "the tragic view of life," and
> "living with complexity." Today [1970] these words are out of fashion, though
> they may someday return. Now magic is evoked with "spontaneity," "passion,"
> "relevance," "innovation," "flexibility," "commitment," and "freedom." New
> College is to some extent the creation of young professors who went to college
> during the 1950's and who are attempting to deal with the educational chaos
> and boredom of the 1970's. The dialogue (another word of the 1970's) and
> tension (1950's) between the two periods constitute a major feature of New
> College. It is far too soon to know whether or not the mixture will produce
> a disaster or a delight.

That statement reflected how we of the silent generation had come face-to-face with an era that repudiated most of our assumptions of the 1950's. Some of us strove for a reconciliation; others, I suspect, either capitulated or, more likely, ignored the intensity of the years between John Kennedy's murder in 1963 and Richard Nixon's exit from office a decade later. Indeed, one of the interesting questions to ask this weekend is to what extent we of the placid 50's were affected and altered by the more turbulent 60's and early 70's.

But then I returned to my 1958 graduation speech. To my surprise I discovered that it was a defense of our college generation against those, including then-President Dwight Eisenhower, who were urging us to be more committed to public causes. Ike, of course, was not asking for committed zeal in the name of pacifism or civil rights; he was saying that "faith is our greatest weapon in the Cold War." He never spelled out precisely what one was to believe in, but he appealed to us to have faith in something, in anything, rather than stay detached. Faith-in-faith became the battle cry against lethargy and an awareness of complexity. Such awareness and lethargy are not the same; my speech defended the former while trying to dissociate ourselves from the latter.

I confessed that our class and, most certainly, our generation overflowed with genuine lethargics. But on the other hand I claimed:

It could be shown that many have found great satisfaction in living with and appreciating complexity. Some even have found exhilaration in discovering and understanding multiplicity and diversity. Not all men [that locution today would betray insensitivity] have felt the compelling need to devise a master scheme for satisfying all their political and cosmic doubts. Amazingly, some have not found it impossible to live with great doubts.

In 1980 I wrote *Denials of Doubt,* an overview of American intellectual history, which bewailed our national need to simplify complexity and to adopt all-embracing, pat systems of belief to deal with the world. As against those who confidently proclaim they have found all the answers, I praised those who expressed uncertainty.

So there I was, going back to my near-adolescent words of 1958, knowing that I would find out what a baby I was and how marvelously my mind had expanded since then. It was disconcerting to find that I had not grown at all in 25 years! You heard in 1958 all my best subsequent ideas. The more important discovery, though, was a general continuity between our days here in the 1950's and the years which have followed. We were not, at least at Amherst, either stereotypically apathetic or simple-minded. And the later years were not quite so revolutionary as the media have made them out to be. While some of us, perhaps, have not done much intellectual or political stretching since graduation, others have extended themselves without finding it necessary to repudiate the past. Our collegiate past provided foundations for reaching into new territories.

While it is valuable to recognize continuities, it is equally necessary to note the major changes that have also occurred in the past 25 years. These I have experienced primarily in my personal life, and for many of them I left college woefully unprepared.

The major area of ignorance was between the two sexes. For me (and, I expect, for many other men), women belonged to another species altogether. In American society in general, discussions of sex were circumspect if not taboo. The entire subject of sex, of love itself and the requirements of relationships, remained shrouded in darkest mystery. Perhaps the mystery magnified romance, but it also created rampant anxiety, unending stupidity, unrealistic expectations, warts, pimples, and a host of unfortunate marriages. Colleges, such as ours, which were single-sex, did not help matters. I am glad the all-male college, in its third century of life in the United States, has finally gone the way of the dinosaur. Some better arguments can be made in behalf of all-female schools, but their day will also soon end.

I cannot blame the times or all-male education for the ill-fated marriage I made 18 months after graduation. But I do know that at age 22, while I may have not been an intellectual infant, I certainly was a baby when it came to knowing anything about women, about relationships with them, and about what marriage meant. I know my daughter, now attending this once-male bastion and a few months short of age 20, will make mistakes and suffer heartbreak. But she won't experience them from the condition of nearly total ignorance in which her father and many of his generation found themselves in the 1950's. In this area, ignorance rarely produced bliss.

At any rate, I married while in my second year of doctoral work at Columbia. From the beginning, I realized that something was terribly wrong with the marriage, and I sensed my wife might be dealing with issues I did not understand. But I did not know. Psychotherapy in those days seemed fit only for the certifiably crazy, at least in the popular mind, so I failed to seek that possibility. Bad marriages were not supposed to occur. I confided in no one about our unhappiness; I would work things out on my own. And my thinking was almost as unsophisticated as this: I had found the kind of mate I was supposed to—pretty, intelligent, a graduate of a good college, talented. With such a mate the marriage should work.

But it did not. And divorce was also—do you remember?—nearly unthinkable in those days. In marriage, sex, and family, we have indeed gone through a revolution in these 25 years. So, through a dozen years of perplexity, I hung in there: through my teaching years at Amherst, at Stanford, and on to Hawaii. It was at Stanford, four years into the marriage, that my daughter Kim was born. When I finally divorced in 1972, I was granted custody, something practically unheard of only a decade ago. I had been a *de facto* single parent for some years, but its newly-designated official status underscored the nurturant skills I had been developing and which I would need to expand yet more dramatically in the years to come. Career came first for us in 1958, but the rigors of an unsuccessful marriage and of major child-rearing responsibilities forced on me a different balance, one with which most women and some men are wrestling these days.

A couple of years ago I married Elaine Hatfield, a distinguished psychologist, and that choice has worked out wonderfully. Neither of us is ignorant any longer about love; and while problematic relationships haunt the cultural landscape these days, we have paid dues and gained entrance to a warm place. Few conditions describe our culture today more than failed relationships and the longing for good ones. These failures represent not the failures of new knowledge and greater experience, but the enlargement of expectations. In the long run, I believe that the greater knowledge, experience, and expectations will produce happier relationships, but they will take on a dazzling array of forms, some of which have yet to gain acceptance in society at large.

My career path has followed more predictably, but even here there have been turnings that I could not have anticipated in 1958. Some of these have surprised colleagues and friends of our generation. As with many of our classmates, I moved directly without a break from graduation into a Ph.D. program at Columbia. I am not sure I ever considered the possibility of *not* going to graduate school nor do I remember ever thinking about taking a year or two in between Amherst and Columbia. I was not alone in this unyielding determination to go after a serious career. Few of the women I knew then had the same career rhythm; many married and quit school to have babies.

I married in my second year of graduate school, but never dreamed of postponing my graduate studies. So much, so typical. During that second year I received a call from Amherst informing me that Henry Steele Commager had just decided to accept a grant for a year and that someone was needed to take his place. That someone was me, and in the fall of 1960 I found myself back at *alma mater.* So I started my career at the top and have gone downhill ever since! Things began to get less typical.

When that year was up I received an offer to teach for four years at Stanford. Today that would not appear much of a decline. But I, who had never been west of the Appalachians, had at best a misty view of California. When many East coast friends, particularly at Columbia, warned me that serious intellectual work cannot be accomplished among the lotus eaters, I did not view my westward trek with quite the same excitement and anticipation that many would feel today. Since those days the country has moved west with me, and the East Coast no longer can claim a monopoly on intellectual, cultural, economic, and political power.

When those fine four years came to an end, it was clear where the expectations of 1958 would have brought me. I received an offer to launch an American Studies program at Williams College. I would return to New England, to a small liberal arts college second only in the nation to this one (I did not say that at the Williams' interview), with an extraordinary chance to be creative in my own field. Why did I not seize this perfect opportunity?

California, the Kennedy years, and the beginnings by 1965 of a new cultural matrix had already begun its work on me, making a return East look less attractive than I would have thought possible before my westward journey. Among other factors, going to Williamstown, Massachusetts, felt literally like going *back:* going back in time to a more traditional environment, going back to winter (which I had ceased to love after too many hours of shoveling snow), going back to an all-male, small-town world.

Still, I had narrowed my choices down to Williams and the Santa Barbara branch of the University of California. I returned to Williamstown for the interviews with the president and the entire history department. I was driven into the Berkshire mountains, but the time was December and the beauty had a forlorn, isolated quality. What finally tipped the scales in favor of the University of California was the letter describing the generous offer from Williams. A list of fringe benefits was included with the salary and other basics. Leading the list came the promise that if I were to go to Williams, they would give me a free cemetery plot! At age 28 I decided I was not ready to die. I stayed in California for a year, and moved out to the University of Hawaii in 1966, where I have remained since. I expect to be there for the duration.

I do not love the University of Hawaii; it is a mediocre, fairly typical large State University, located in a lovely State. But I like it enough to love my life. Some of my friends thought I had disappeared into a realm impossibly distant from creative possibilities and the real world. In fact, I had opted for a balance between career and personal needs different from the expectations of my upbringing and the culture of the 1950's. I did not abandon the work imperatives of that upbringing. I have returned to Stanford as a visiting professor. I created New College to bring some of Amherst into Polynesia. I have written seven books of history. I sailed around the world four times teaching on Semester-at-Sea and taking an active role in carrying aspects of the small liberal-arts college into the Indian, Atlantic, and Pacific Oceans, and into China, India, Egypt, and Europe. Finally, I have joined to my professorial work the career of psychotherapist. I counsel with my spouse, Elaine, and have begun to fashion my amateur fascination with psychology, which was expressed in many of my books, into a more rigorous understanding.

From some traditional perspectives my career has not ascended since my teaching stints at Amherst and Stanford. I started at the top and have worked down. But my work has been various, exciting, and I have felt a great deal of freedom to do the work I like and to project the kind of balance I like into my life. That freedom at the expense of some loss of traditional security reflects some of the cultural changes of the past 25 years. So does the experimental stretching of the meaning of "career," the interest in horizontal mobility as well as vertical, the exploration of multiplicity with only some loss of focus.

I suspect that you recognize your life more in the story of my personal experiences than in my career. While I have not taken wild and brave risks with my work (I always maintained my tenured professorial position), many of you have probably hewed more to the straight-and-narrow than I have (and with great success). The work world has changed less than that of marriage, family, sex, women's roles, and divorce in this quarter-century.

I have tried in this talk, primarily through autobiography (the most characteristic art form of these days), to evoke some of the continuities and more of the discontinuities of the years between 1958 and 1983. But I always tell my students that there are two questions to ask of their teachers more important than any others: "Oh yeah?" and "So what?" The "Oh yeah?" question you can answer today by figuring out whether my observations seem correct to you, since they carry no more real authority than would your own. If your eyes have been glazing over the past 40 minutes or if you are currently either asleep or no longer within my hearing, you may safely conclude that I failed the "Oh yeah?" test. If you are still with me, let us very briefly consider, as we approach the end here, what could possibly matter about all this.

For the "So what?" query we turn from remembrance to issues of the present and future. If I could select a single-strand of national experience over the past 150 years that seems most central and unique to American history, I would choose materialism, the chief icon of which is money. From the early years of the 19th century to the present, people flocked to these shores primarily to "better" themselves. In a society built on the aspiration toward equality of opportunity, the making of money became the signal measure by which one could judge one's achievement in the competitive New World.

In this talk today I have suggested that in the 1950's, men entered the competitive jungle, strove for material success, but spent the money earned on the family whose daily functions were maintained by a homemaker/wife. In the 15 years that followed our graduation, strong voices of anti-materialism attempted to counter the powerful bourgeois dream. This dialectic between materialism and anti-materialism, so basic to America, leads less to new syntheses than to new forms of struggle between materialism and anti-materialism. Thus, in the last decade or so since Watergate and the American defeat in Vietnam, the nation has returned to the race for money, though it is no longer a race run simply by males and in behalf of traditional families. The popularity of Ronald Reagan, I believe, is based upon his convincing Americans that the pursuit of wealth can and should be carried on enthusiastically and single-mindedly, without any of the qualms that Christianity and Humanism suggest about material greed. It is a message greatly welcomed by people these days.

There are indeed similarities between the 1980's and the 1950's, although nothing like the one-to-one equations sometimes suggested by some journalists. In temper and mood, however, these days resemble our college days more than they do the 1960's, when many people tried to temper material profits with environmental concerns, a conservation ethic, affirmative action programs for women and nonwhites, sexual freedom, the peace movement, and psychological awareness.

Given the materialism, career emphases, and the fact that we at Amherst were programmed for success, most of us here today are pretty well off financially, though we have been variably affected by the events that lie between John Kennedy's election in 1960 and Richard Nixon's resignation in 1974. Our characters are formed, our lives are shaped, and we could quite easily rest upon our laurels and simply enjoy the fruits of our hard work. Yet it takes no crystal ball to point out that while opportunities for material growth and personal freedom, based on the new information, communication, and bio-genetic technologies, have probably never been greater, so too the prospects for the end of us all have never been so imminent. Historians are usually supposed to point out that nothing is ever new, that precedents for present concerns can always be found. But this historian is equally certain that we live counterpoised between an utterly unprecedented time of potential well-being and civilized possibility on the one hand, and, on the other, a time of destruction and desolation never before dreamed or so easily attained.

In that context, resting on our laurels hardly seems a sufficient stance to assume. Fruitless to preach, but perhaps useful to suggest that being secure in success permits a more experimental and public-minded attitude than we have reason to expect from today's "yuppies." Our lives can be richer if we remain open to new possibilities and dangers while maintaining the same anchorage that plumbed deeply—at least for me—at Amherst in the 1950's. From that place of safety we were taught to avoid pat slogans and to look directly, without flinching, into the face of complicated, ambiguous, paradoxical realities. At a time of widespread ignorance, fatuous optimism, rampant materialism, and simplistic faiths, the call from 25 years ago for an intelligent awareness of complexity represents a pretty good lesson to carry forward into the next 25 years.

From this weekend, we move into preparations for our 50th in the year 2008, when most of us still alive will be 71 or 72 years old! With a little bit o' luck, I hope to meet you here. Then, through our thickened spectacles and hearing aids, we shall try to see and vaguely hear how these reflections, predictions, and promises worked out. Until then, may you fare well.

AFTERWORD

In a little more than a year, the 50th Reunion commences. I have been asked to give another talk and have agreed to do so. But the real story of this get-together will, I suspect, be unspoken: mortality. Far fewer of my classmates have died than I estimated in my 25th year speech, perhaps a small example of the congruence shown by lots of data between wealth and status on the one hand and longevity on the other. But 25 years on? . . .

It is predicted that 75 % of our class will show up for what will likely be the final big show for our group. On paper, this gathering of old guys presents a somewhat gloomy prospect! As for me, though I'm feeling healthy, I will still regard it as a supreme accomplishment to drag my living body to the Reunion. When one of my classmates was recently asked about his plans for the future, his answer was: "to have one."

ONE: LOOKING BACK

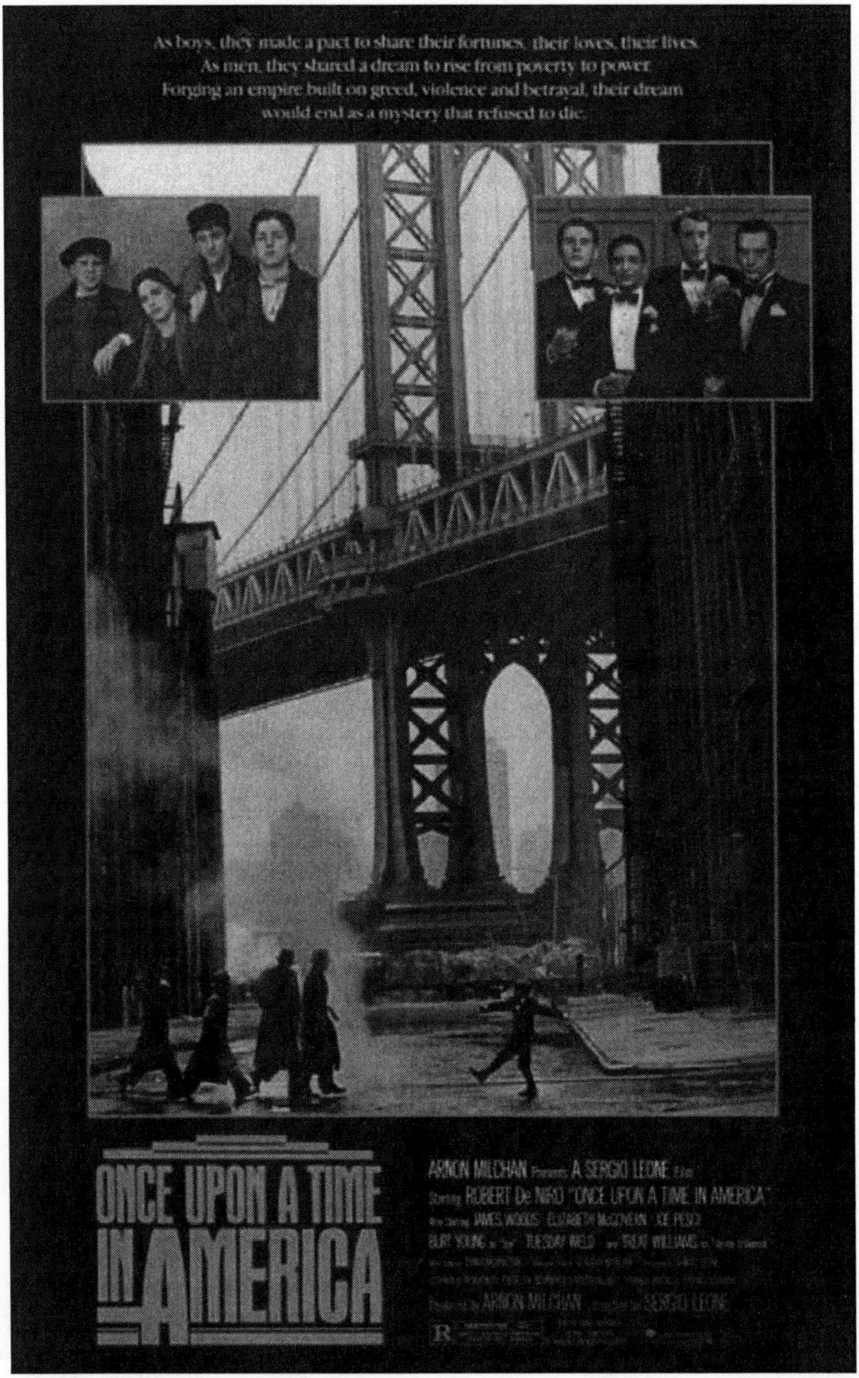

Once Upon a Time in America

3

Scanning The American Past, 1600-1900

THE RISE OF THE WEST

In the long history of the human race, no single civilization before 1800 A.D. ever came to dominate the world. Over the centuries, four cultures, more than many others, had developed the richest traditions and the greatest economic and political power. These four were what we in the West now call China (the "Far East"), India (South Asia), the "Middle East," and Europe, or "Western" civilization. The West may have been the weakest and least "advanced" of these cultures in the thousand years following 500 A.D. After the crumbling of the Roman Empire, Europe fell on barren days, recovering its classical past only with the greatest difficulty.

None of the four great culture groups ever established dominion over all the others. They tended to move on parallel tracks, intersecting at times, but generally swerving away from one another. In religion, for instance, marked differences developed between Confucianism and Buddhism in the Far East, Hinduism on the Indian sub-continent, Islam in the Middle East, and Christianity in the West. Institutions, traditions, beliefs and lifestyles had so diverged that by 1500 there barely existed even the *concept* of one world.

All that changed stunningly after 1500. The major theme in world history over the past 500 years has been the rise of the West and its conquest of the planet. Actually that mastery has taken place primarily over the past 200 years. As late as 1800, no cultural area reigned supreme. But by that date the conditions for conquest were identifiable and in a process of rapid acceleration. Profound developments that had been reshaping Europe for many centuries erupted in transformations without precedent in human history. The result was that by 1914 the West ruled the world.

Rulership, in most cases, took the form of what has come to be called "colonialism." At the time of the outbreak of the First World War the West exerted outright political and economic control over much of the non-Western world. Nations not directly made into colonial possessions of European countries and the United States were simply colonized on a subtler level with the same results: their entire societies were reshaped by Western influences. Religion, culture, lifestyle, the intellect and the arts were influenced by the West as much as were political, military, and economic affairs. This Westernizing process, though slowed since 1914, still goes on. The dialectic between Westernization and resistance to it defines much of international life today.

In our time, the 20th century, the United States has been the most powerful nation within the West and therefore in the world. Recent American history crowds around the theme of this emerging power. But certain anterior questions must first be faced. What happened to place Western civilization at the forefront of the world? How did the United States become "top dog" within Western society? In what ways did the world become "Americanized" in the 20th century? These are some of the large questions that arch over the pages that follow.

The United States was first caught up on the receiving end in these global processes, but rapidly became a leading agent for global transformations. Even before its global power was indelibly certified at Hiroshima in 1945, knowledgeable people had been talking, with some accuracy, of the years since 1900 as the American Century.

That was particularly heady stuff for a citizenry that, well before 1900, already boasted of its nation as unique and specially blessed. Such intoxication produced a faith that their society stood outside history and thus had been designated by a Manifest Destiny with the task of transforming the world. That belief has shaped much of the country's development and outlook. It has created an optimism that moved the nation to innovate and take risks on a grand scale—such as opening its shores to people of the entire world, whatever their race or culture.

Some of the risks taken have succeeded wonderfully, others have created intractable difficulties—simply because no nation *can* stand outside history. American optimism has led to the innocent, childlike, troubling belief, both on national and personal levels, that nothing is impossible, that the past neither matters nor stands in our way. That faith, perhaps more than any other, offers a metaphor for this nation's most ingratiating asset and, simultaneously, its most dangerous foolishness.

Because so much of the world in our time has been influenced by the United States, an examination of this one society carries implications for all the others. But before we can take on the uncertain propositions surrounding the phrase, "the Americanization of the world," we must gain some measure of developments that most certainly preceded it: namely, the Europeanization of America.

GOD'S WORLD: THE 17th CENTURY

The Western Hemisphere teemed with people and with a variety of cultures before 1492. Recent scholarship points to a population somewhere between 50 and 100 million at the time of Columbus' "discovery." Portions of the land were more densely peopled than parts of Europe at the same time. Two thousand different languages were spoken, and a corresponding variety of differentiated lifestyles flourished. The area now called the United States probably had a population of 10 million. The New World was hardly an empty wilderness awaiting European discovery and rescue.

The dazzling array of cultures escaped the notice of Euro-Americans, who from Columbus' day thought of this diversity as unity and named all the inhabitants "Indians." Only recently have we begun to understand and appreciate the various ways in which these societies managed to live harmoniously with their different environments. Their decimation by the incoming Europeans, whether through good intentions, deceit, arrogance, or murder, is a story of unending sadness. By the beginning of the 20th century, most of the few Indians who survived Euro-American expansionism and near-genocide had become demoralized wards of the state, quarantined on miserable reservations, often finding solace only in alcohol.

The Europeans who came to the Western Hemisphere had other things on their minds than respecting and learning from "primitive heathens." The Renaissance had introduced new ideas, new questions, the possible existence of new places; the voyages of discovery tested some of these ideas and afforded the adventurers and the royal houses that sponsored them the expectation of finding spices, trading posts—and often more importantly, gold and other riches.

Early in the 17th century the English began to send settlers to America. These newcomers possessed some motivations other than commercial. It has at times been argued that America was "born free," that the first settlers brought with them fully-realized all those beliefs that have shaped much of the modern world: democracy, freedom, individualism, capitalism, religious toleration, secularism, science, and humanism. Presumably once these seeds had been planted only time stood in the way of their inevitable flowering. Much of the history of America from 1600 to 1775 has been taught as one long prelude to the American Revolution, as though John Winthrop spawned Thomas Jefferson.

This is, of course, silly. The first white inhabitants of Virginia and Massachusetts Bay were 17th-century Englishmen, not 18th-century Minutemen. Commercial motives there were, particularly in Virginia, but at the time of the first settlements, Europe was convulsed by religious conflicts. The Protestant Reformation and the Catholic Counter-Reformation had produced the Thirty Years' War (1618-48), and the two branches of Christendom were struggling for control of the European continent. The Puritans who moved into New England in the 1630's followed directly in the line that ran from Martin Luther to John Calvin. They were, after all, Calvinists, and they demanded a stricter, "purer," religion than they had found in England. They came to establish a Wilderness Zion wherein God could be worshipped in the Correct Way, not to establish the principle of religious freedom. God forbid those worshippers who sought their own non-Puritan freedom. The Puritans did not gladly brook religion difference. Dissent would undermine that for which they had risked the perilous 3,000-mile voyage: the *right* exercise of religion.

The abiding desire of the settlers to understand, serve, and worship The Almighty may not have been as ardent in the less populous Middle and Southern colonies as in

New England, but it was powerful nonetheless. Nearly everyone in Europe and America in 1650 accepted without doubt the proposition that God existed and actively ruled the Universe. Few questioned the existence of an afterlife. For ordinary citizens on both sides of the Atlantic, the belief that one would live forever placed one's meager allotment of 30 or 40 years in a context markedly different from the way people think of earthly life today. If by serving the Lord humbly and faithfully the prospects of dwelling with God in the Heavenly City were enhanced, only the sinful or the insane—those, that is, possessed by the Devil—could possibly fail to make the effort.

The pursuit of pleasure and even, to a surprising extent, the achievement of earthly comfort were regarded as signs of sin, of placing higher value upon oneself than the Lord. The result would be certain damnation. In such a context it was only natural that people would gladly accept conditions of deprivation that we in the 20th century would find intolerable. Such acceptance was in itself looked upon as subduing pride and expressing humility before God.

Even today Christianity remains a powerful force in American life, returning in waves and new forms to an otherwise highly secularized society. Some observers, particularly of fundamentalist Protestants, see zeal, righteousness, and a belief in mission; others refer to these newer religious movements as ignorant or dangerous. The absolutist tendency that was resurrected in the 1980's in the anti-abortion movement among the evangelicals and "born-agains" and in the so-called Moral Majority, contained for many a rejection of the modern world itself, of "secular humanism," of all that has happened since 1930 and much of what has happened since 1650.

Roots of this fundamentalism lie in colonial circumstances. The colonists of 1600 were not "born free" in the modern sense. They were born into God's world, and that tradition, if no longer dominant, remains very much alive. Writers who describe the United States simply as democratic, pragmatic, and individualistic miss the equally significant strains of moralism, absolutism, and religiosity in our culture.

In America as in Europe, the scientific mode of thinking which gathered steam in the latter half of the 17th century transformed everything. Conditions for the ready acceptance of scientific experimentation were even more congenial in the New World than the Old, and the Enlightenment percolated deeper into the American social fabric than it did in Europe. Classes were less rigid, traditions less congealed. People moved more easily to new settlements in which, in order to survive the weather, the animals, and the "hostile natives," new ideas were more readily welcomed. Pragmatic adaptation to novel circumstances became almost a necessity in the New World.

MAN'S WORLD: THE 18th CENTURY

The staples of modern life—freedom, capitalism, secularism, pragmatism, democracy, science, industrialization, and individualism—emerged neither automatically nor quickly after 1650. For better or worse these values surfaced *in spite of* the European and early colonial political and religious power structure. They attained ascendancy out of conflict—a conflict that has not yet ceased. By the end of the 18th century a generation of extraordinary politician-philosophers had wrested power. These men were clearly sons of the Enlightenment; they were the nation's "Founding Fathers."

Benjamin Franklin, Sam Adams, Patrick Henry, George Washington, John Adams, Thomas Jefferson, John Marshall, James Madison, Alexander Hamilton, James Monroe and others, whatever their differences, believed that human destiny lay in human hands. Their ideas and those of their forebears had slowly formed during the 100-plus years after 1650, a century which represents something of a mystery period in the national chronicle.

College students today who take courses on their nation's history have a vague picture of Puritan life in the first half of the 17th century, but the period from 1650 to 1763 generally draws a blank. It usually gets summed up by the catchall phrase "prelude to revolution," as though five generations of colonials walked dreamily through their lives awaiting an invitation to the Boston Tea Party. Full lives were being led and profound changes were in fact in the making during the epochal period in which new lifeways were being forged everywhere.

The American Revolution and the creation of a Constitution in 1787 were only the most visible manifestations of this extraordinary century. The Declaration of Independence, whose authors endeavored to explain the reasons for the Revolution to the rest of the world, perfectly captured the spirit of the Enlightenment. In the face of injustice and tyranny, it was no longer expected that people would resignedly swallow their fate. The discontented were urged to strike back at what they saw as tyranny—and, more importantly, to struggle armed with rational thought. The revolutionaries wanted to explain logically why they had to resist George III. Thomas Jefferson and the other writers of the Declaration (including Benjamin Franklin) insisted that certain "truths" were "self-evident", namely "that all men are created equal, that they are endowed by their Creator with certain inalienable Rights, that among these are Life, Liberty, and the pursuit of Happiness. That, to secure these rights, Governments are instituted among Men, deriving their just Powers from the consent of the governed. That, whenever any form of Government becomes destructive of these ends, it is the Right of the People to alter or to abolish it, and to institute new Government . . ."

The words are so familiar that many readers just now no doubt skipped quickly over them. But they are amazing, revolutionary words, challenging in every phrase the accepted wisdom of the world since the death of Jesus. They proclaim the responsibility of human beings, not God or some church, to define life's purposes. They insist that people possess rights just by dint of being human. They conceive of political authority as servant to these rights. Servants can and should be replaced when they no longer perform the services expected of them. The world turned upside down—rationally. Human destiny resting in human hands . . .

The lives led by Franklin and Jefferson exemplified the Enlightenment. These two men, who along with Abraham Lincoln, are the three pre-20th century Americans most cherished by the world, devoted themselves to improving life *on this earth*. Franklin sought to make daily life happier, easier, and nobler for himself and his fellow citizens—for ordinary people, not just a self-designated elite. In a little more than 25 years, a period *preceding* his greatest public renown, Franklin accomplished with each single good deed enough to justify an entire life. Taken together the list takes on amazing proportions. Even though some innovations may look mundane, it is in their very ordinariness that Franklin's achievements become archetypal of the genius of the Age of Reason.

1731	Franklin founds the Philadelphia Library.
1732	He publishes the first issue of "Poor Richard's Almanack." [The Almanack, which went on for 25 years, with his witty, worldly-wise, common-sense sayings, played a major role in forging a united American "character" from the diverse types who lived in the colonies.]
1736	Chosen clerk of the General Assembly; forms the Union Fire Company in Philadelphia.
1737	Elected to the Assembly; appointed Deputy Postmaster-General; plans a city police.
1742	Invents the open, or "Franklin" stove.
1743	Proposes a plan for an Academy, which is adopted in 1749 and eventually develops into the University of Pennsylvania.
1744	Establishes the American Philosophical Society.
1745	Publishes a pamphlet, "Plain Truth," on the necessity for disciplined defense, and forms a military company; begins electrical experiments.
1748	Sells out his printing press business; is appointed to the Commission of the Peace, chosen to the Common Council and to the Assembly.
1749	Appointed a Commissioner to trade with the Indians.
1751	Aids in founding a hospital.
1752	Experiments with a kite and discovers that lightning is an electrical charge.
1753	Awarded the Copley medal for this discovery, and elected a member of the Royal Society; Yale and Harvard both grant him the M.A. degree; appointed joint Postmaster-General.
1754	Appointed one of the Commissioners from Pennsylvania to the Colonial Congress at Albany; proposes a plan for the union of the colonies.
1757	Introduces a bill in the Assembly for paving the streets of Philadelphia; publishes "Way to Wealth"; pleads the cause of the Assembly against the Proprietaries (he does this in England).

It was at this point that his *Autobiography* broke off. Still to come were his manifold Revolutionary activities, his work in helping to compose the Declaration of Independence, his diplomatic accomplishments (as the European emissary) in making and keeping the peace in the post-Revolutionary years, his role in the framing of the Federal Constitution, and countless other activities.

Did the secular, earth-bound preoccupations of Franklin and his colleagues signal a reaction against Christianity? Was faith in the Christian God significantly eroding in the minds of 18th-century philosopher-kings? The answer is yes and no, but mostly yes—particularly when it came to intellectual and political leaders. Franklin and others of his time propounded a religious and moral system called Deism. The Deists had "advanced" well beyond the Arminian dissent of the previous century. Franklin, for example, writing Deist pamphlets as early as 1728, was very unusual, a precocious loner for the most part. Even Jefferson never went as far.

For the Deists, God was the Great Clockmaker who originally wound up the Earth, but then abandoned it to run on its own thereafter. Deists read the Bible metaphorically; for them miracles were scientifically explicable. Earthly morality was important for its own sake and for the good of society. Franklin's rather glib religious principles evoked a sensibility that John Calvin would have despised:

- That there is one God, who made all things.
- That he governs the world by His Providence.
- That he ought to be worshipped by adoration, prayer, and thanksgiving.
- But that the most acceptable service of God is doing good to man.
- That the soul is immortal.
- And that God will certainly reward virtue and punish vice, either here or hereafter.

Though later critics such as D.H. Lawrence mercilessly attacked this creed as being insufferably smug, anti-religious, weak, and hypocritical, they did not recognize Franklin's deeper concerns and his genuine contributions to social liberation and moral living. The Enlightenment was grounded upon a very deep concern with morality.

That moral concern connected closely, however, with practical matters. When segments of American leadership grew alarmed at what they deemed to be financial and political instability following the American Revolution, they instigated the characteristic Enlightenment strategy. How to build a nation? Answer: Assemble in one place the most reasonable, intelligent men (always men). Let them think, debate, compromise. Have them submit to paper the results of their deliberations. Have them write a Constitution that will lead the way to a brighter future.

Linked in this chain of ideas are some astonishing, arguable, hopeful, revolutionary assumptions about the world. Whether sanguine or not, the authors of the Constitution participated in a remarkable act. They planned for the generations to come. They believed that stately, orderly progress would continue as long as mind ruled passion, as long as restraint prevailed over excess. They resisted popular clamor because of their reverence for reason.

The opponents of the Constitution, also children of the Enlightenment—and this includes Thomas Jefferson—attacked it with papers and later with amendments, not with bullets. Americans disagreed with one another, often bitterly, on the worth of the Constitution, remembering that debate is the legitimate offspring of respect for reason. Federalists and Anti-Federalists alike agreed that human beings could better their world, and they did not flinch when they recognized themselves as the responsible parties in that enterprise.

THE WORLD OF THE PEOPLE: THE 19th CENTURY

In the endeavor to "explain" that elusive, sometimes discredited, entity called The National Character, American historians have developed a rough consensus. The American "type" has been portrayed as self-reliant, pragmatic, ruggedly individualistic, optimistic, down-to-earth, energetic, and unimpressed by artificially-drawn distinctions. He is unsophisticated in manners and intellect. This masculine type (and that this ignores the feminine represents a serious conceptual shortcoming) displays raw, aggressive, violent, boastful characteristics, but is also friendly, bluff, open and cheerful.

His history has culminated in democracy, equality, free enterprise, prosperity, individualism, materialism, violence, informality, and the belief in progress. It has also led to a society not known for restraint, tradition, knowledge of or respect for history, intellectuality, serenity, gentleness, high culture, or the tragic sense of life.

Despite internal contradictions in this portrait, it stands as the classic representation of the American and his country. Anyone reading a list of these nouns and adjectives would attach to it the label "American" more readily than "English" or "Chinese" or "German" or "French" or "Samoan." These are the characteristics so many historians have been trying to account for, whether by frontier theses (Frederick Jackson Turner), or by the absence of feudalism in the New World (Louis Hartz), or by ways in which the English heritage mixed with abundant land and plentiful resources (David Potter).

This classic picture does not describe the 17th-century Puritans or today's suburban American. It depicts *some* people and it is a picture conjured up by those bidding us return to simpler times. That rugged, ebullient American actually had his day primarily in the 19th century. There he was most sharply etched for that long moment running roughly from 1815 to 1920.

In the 19th-century egalitarian age, when moral idealism and the pursuit of wealth were seen as complementary, no boundaries were large enough to gird the vision of average Americans. No prose, for that matter, was sufficiently expansive to express adequately the extravagantly boastful optimism of the time; the grandiose feeling, anthem-like phrasing, naiveté, sloganeering, and unbounded enthusiasm cascaded through the society.

Americans would be rich, very rich. They would bow down before no one. They would reach out, grow, conquer. Theirs would be the grandest, the most powerful, the wealthiest, the most humane nation in the history of civilization. All its children would receive the world's finest education. All its churches would reach out to The Almighty in their own ways, and all its people would be free to worship as they wished. All persons would be allowed to vote. Injustice, slavery, and privilege would be abolished for all time.

Transcontinental railroads would be built. Magnificent cities would rise phoenix-like from the ground. Wild land would be tamed. The United States would span the Oceans. The nation would harbor all the tempest-tossed souls who sought refuge on its shores.

Its artists painted landscapes which stretched toward the space of infinity. Its poets enshrined the divinity of the individual. Its philosophers transcended the conventional boundaries of traditional philosophy. Its businessmen took gargantuan strides towards control of endless resources and vast amounts of money. Its soldiers knew no limits to their bravery. Here then unfoldeth the epic age of American history.

Everything expressed yearning for the stupendous, the monumental, the grandiose. This was a truly Revolutionary era in which all persons felt certain they too would "rise" in their own personal revolutions. Nineteenth-century Americans had not repudiated the Enlightenment; they had appropriated it. The gentlemanly Rationalism, limited democracy, latent revolutionism had been transmuted by masses who had only dimly understood what Locke, Voltaire, Montesquieu, Franklin, John Adams, Jefferson, and Madison were driving at. In the language of intellectual history, Rousseau had replaced Locke, transforming the Enlightenment from a philosophy into a passion. Romanticism had replaced Rationalism in European arts and letters. In Old World politics, power still resided with an elite, but in the New World, the masses sought to take charge everywhere. They carried on the original spark of the 18th century, but they fanned it into a fire that would have seared Montesquieu and Alexander Hamilton, alike.

In the Age of Faith in God, the 17th century, the man of greatest talent (until the 20th century, always the man) went into the *ministry*. In the post-Newtonian American Enlightenment of the 18th century, in which faith in Mankind challenged fealty to God, the man of greatest talent went into *politics*. In the Egalitarian Age of the 19th century, the man of talent, imagination and ambition found most room for his energy in *business*. The abstract faith in Man was superseded by a faith in the powers of the people, of virtuous hardworking individuals driven to achieve ends not foretold by the circumstances of their birth.

In God's world of the 17th century, fulfillment arrived upon entrance into the Heavenly City. The skeptical-optimistic leaders of the Rationalistic 18th century believed it would be realized on earth, not in some possible afterlife. That better day, however, would not come during the lifetime of the participants; they were laboring for 'posterity,' for future happiness, for their grandchildren, for future generations yet unborn.

The people of the 19th century could not wait that long. They might have to work enormously hard for many years, postponing immediate gratification, but they labored in the hope that sometime during their *own* lifetime they would reap the rewards that virtue and hard work brought. For some that reward might be a feeling of satisfaction or justice or purpose, but for most, it was supplemented with money. Money became the measure of success in a competitive achievement-oriented society. Money seemed less important for what it purchased than for what it said about how well one had done in the competitive scramble.

Americans of the 19th century were buoyed by the faith that they would not have to die in the same circumstances into which they had been born. By a combination of hard work, virtue, and character they could (in phrases which today can look like clichés) "rise," change their lot, make something of themselves, improve their circumstances, outstrip their parents, live the American dream. We may nowadays take these phrases and the ideas that lay behind them for granted, but that one's condition at birth should not dictate life was a revolutionary notion. It literally was the *American* idea. It cast the United States as the symbol of freedom in the 19th century and it induced tens of millions of men and women around the world to uproot themselves in order to start a new, better, freer, more prosperous life in the New World. "Freedom" may have been the word most associated with the United States, but equality of opportunity formed the largest part of what people meant by it. The promise of equal opportunity, more than any other factor, was what made the New World truly "new," and it is still the major lure for those people in the rest of the world who today consider emigrating to the United States.

THE REAL AMERICAN REVOLUTION

The reality fell far short of the rhetoric, of course, but the special genius of the 19th-century American experiment lay in the nation's ability to translate a significant portion of the theory into reality. This was accomplished by incorporating egalitarianism into major institutions. Americans have grown so accustomed to these institutional breakthroughs that they hardly realize what went into making them possible and how far-reaching have been their consequences.

When comparing the entire course of American history with that of other nations, one would be justified in regarding America's as a remarkable success story (the glaring exception would be in matters relating to race). From a powerless colonial possession less than 400 years ago the nation has grown into the most *powerful* country the world has yet to see. Some citizens regard that power as a decidedly mixed blessing, asserting that it has engendered a habit of aggressiveness, a thirst for dominion, and a propensity toward reckless, impulsive violence. Evidence can be adduced, however, for the proposition that the awesome power has also been used to maintain peace, rebuild devastated countries, and combat injustice.

The first colonists had to scratch for survival against the rocky, stubborn soil and harsh climate of New England and the swamps and mosquitoes at Jamestown, Virginia.

Less than four centuries later (not a long time in human history), Americans had built the *wealthiest* nation the world has ever known, and its people now enjoy material comforts that in many ways surpass those of kings, popes, and sheiks of the past. Some citizens believe the wealth has produced avarice, cupidity, materialism, and the exploitation of nature. But the wealth has also made its way into the homes and lives of people whose efforts would otherwise have been exhausted on endless, unrewarded meniality. These rewards have, perhaps, made possible the release of considerable intellectual and creative energies that might never have found expression.

Some 20th-century Americans, when assaying the significance of the great wealth and power of their homeland, have found in it as much to dispraise as to cheer. They forget, as do many others, that in addition to being the wealthiest and most powerful nation ever known, their country was for much of its history, especially in the 19th century, the most *idealistic.*

At the heart of her brave dreams lay not merely the egalitarian faith itself, which even on paper looked good to millions of people, but more important by far the serious endeavor to transform that promise into daily routine. The institutional transformations occurred in all the basic cultural domains: family life, education, religion, politics, and, less consistently, in the opportunities afforded women. Discussions of these authentic American revolutions of the last century take us to the end of this chapter.

The Egalitarian Family

The transition from the Old World authoritarian, patrilineal, extended kinship clan to the egalitarian, conjugal, child-centered family has a long history which scholars are avidly exploring. These changes began in the European middle classes, but as the United States developed in the 19th century into the world's first middle-class society, a larger proportion of the population than elsewhere participated in this far-reaching social change.

Pressures on the traditional family had mounted with particular intensity in the 17th-century American colonies as children and young people adapted more easily than their elders to the novel demands of the wilderness. The colonial families could not maintain discipline. They became unsteady about the locus of authority. Respect for father and tradition declined, instability set in, and many families floated rudderless. At their best, the evolving families loved more, showed more appreciation for mothers and daughters, displayed more flexibility and intimacy, and encouraged greater self-confidence among children. Most foreign observers characterized the children as spoiled, arrogant brats, precocious beyond belief, totally lacking in respect or discipline. Only a few managed to find some charm, intelligence, and promise in that precocity.

What these European visitors failed to see is that by the second quarter of the 19th century, the elements of what we now call the modern family were all in place in the New World. The historian Carl Degler saw four such elements:

One. The marriage which initiated the modern family was based upon affection and mutual respect between partners, both at the time of family formation and in the course of Its life. The woman in the marriage enjoyed an increasing degree of influence or autonomy within the family.

Two. The primary role of the wife was the care of children and maintenance of the home. Furthermore, the wife, as the mistress of the home, was perceived by society and herself as the moral superior of the husband, though his legal and social inferior. The organizational basis for this relationship was that woman's life was physically spent within the home and with the family, while the man's was largely outside the home, at work. The ideological justification of this division of labor and activity will be referred to as "the doctrine of the two spheres."

Three. The attention, energy, and resources of parents in the emerging modern family were increasingly centered upon the rearing of their offspring. Children were now perceived as being different from adults and deserving not only of material care but of solicitude and love as well. Childhood was deemed a valuable period in the life of every person and to be sharply distinguished in character and purpose from adulthood. Parenthood thus became a major personal responsibility, perhaps even a burden.

Four. The modern family on the average is significantly smaller in size than the family of the 18th and previous centuries, a change that has major consequences for women as well as for the family.[11]

Before the 18th century, European and colonial families were primarily economic units. Domestic privacy rarely existed, emotional relationships were remote, children and women were low in the hierarchy, families were large, and marriage for love seemed a frivolous idea. Because early death was the norm, people may have been unwilling to make emotional investments in one another. Though the evidence is still coming in, some scholars have described pre-modern families as little more than utilitarian associations of replaceable surrogates. Whether or not that characterization is an exaggeration, it remains true that the emergence in the past two centuries of the "modern" family—formed by marriage for love, held together by affection, child-centered, domesticated, smaller than before—constitutes a change of major historical proportions.

While the family in the second half of the 20th century also appears to be re-forming itself in remarkable ways, it can nonetheless be argued that the four lineaments of the early 19th-century family listed by Degler have remained substantially in place for well over a century, and have not disappeared from today's unsettled, but exciting scene.

Public Education

The potential of children flowered in the institutional invention that impressed the foreign observers most forcibly—free, compulsory public education. The travelers may not have liked the children, but they were enthusiastic about packing them off to school.

Through public schooling, Americans were testing the most optimistic, consequential, and perhaps arguable doctrine of the Enlightenment: that every person, especially every child, was educable. Born free of original sin and other impairments, the infant would grow up in direct concordance with the experiences to be written on the blank slate. Render those experiences positive, moral, and humane, and the infant would become a morally-developed, intelligent child and, as an adult, a responsible citizen. The school system intended that not only would all children learn to read, add, and write, but that they would learn to be virtuous citizens through the inculcation of moral values. So great was America's faith in this process of public education that they devised a system whereby all children would be able to go to the common schools free of charge—and they would also be *compelled* to do so.

Some socio-biologists today question the validity of this basic premise, often arguing that much of intelligence and even character lies in the genetic wiring. If so, education can achieve only marginal gains. Other critics question the value of public education, and especially its latter-day extension into higher education, even when they believe that nurture outweighs nature. But in the second quarter of the 19th century faith in education was the cornerstone of the hopeful, future-oriented, idealistic society. As long as children went to schools, tomorrow would inevitably be better than today. Foreign observers were impressed by this national commitment and by the zeal that went into its development. If the United States accomplished nothing else, they felt its noble experiment in schooling would be enough to earn the nation an honorable place in history. In later chapters we shall take a harder, closer look at how things have come out with the egalitarian family and the public schools.

Voluntary Religion

European visitors to the New World were horrified by the next attempt to institutionalize equality—the disestablishment of official religion—which they saw as the emasculation of religion and a certain invitation to atheism and social chaos. Jefferson, the Deist as religious reformer, neither anticipated nor desired that his fellow citizens would abandon the worship of God. Most reformers believed that freedom of worship would enhance chances for authentic faith as long as disestablishment was accompanied by public education with a strong moral bent.

They were, by and large, correct. The proliferation of churches in the 19th century testified to the fact that people would continue to worship God—but in their own way. The European visitors still doubted that ordinary folk could be trusted to make such profound decisions on their own, and they feared that the loss of religious authority spelled doom for the exercise of religion itself. Moreover, they never stopped predicting that when religious faith weakened, the foundations of civilized society would crumble as well. Accustomed to this kind of criticism from abroad and, to a lesser extent, at home, Americans never looked back after disestablishing the Anglican Church. They fashioned hundreds of modest denominational parishes throughout the land in which motley associations of people could worship comfortably.

Many British visitors changed their minds about the quality of religious worship in the United States after they attended some actual church services. Though uneasy at first with the informality, many of them eventually began to complain about the pomposity and dustiness of St. Paul's in London and other authorized Anglican sanctuaries. After participating in a few Congregational services in Springfield, Massachusetts, in which standing room only was the rule, the English traveler Morgan Phillips Price reported:

> I noticed on other Sundays also that the churches were far fuller than in England. I was particularly struck by the number of young people I saw there. Another thing that impressed me was the fact that the method of conducting the service was in the full sense of the word popular and even unconventional. The preacher began his sermon with an address to the children. He brought an alarm clock into the pulpit, informing the children that he had picked it up on a rubbish-heap, and that the clock had told him that it had been thrown away by its owner because it did not go off when required, was unreliable, and did not speak the truth. He had taken pity on it, and had decided to give it a fresh chance. He had set it to go off at just that moment. Would it mend its ways and be reliable? The whole congregation sat as still as mice. One could have heard a pin drop. As the silence continued, and it became clear that the clock would not speak the truth, a titter was heard, then a guffaw, and then a real peal of laughter, until finally the whole congregation rocked and the church re-echoed with mirth. I saw then why the churches in America are full on Sundays. [12]

Though Price told that story in 1936, similar tales abound in 19th-century descriptions of American religious observances. Religion, far from dying in the New World, achieved an egalitarian spirit and a popularity that was never matched in Great Britain. Hundreds of denominations turned into thousands by the 20th century. Religious worship remains popular in the United States, though one could make the case that the true contemporary national religion ritual on Sundays, far surpassing church-going, is watching professional football. Grander today than Easter Sunday is the epiphany of Super Bowl Sunday.

Mass Suffrage

Almost as alarming to the Europeans as voluntary religion was the adoption of mass male suffrage, which was a logical consequence of the foregoing reforms. If children rose in prominence in the family, if all persons were educable, if they therefore were compelled to attend schools, and if these educated citizens could be trusted to worship God in their chosen way, it was but a short step to empowering them to elect the President, the Congress, and the rest of the government.

Americans hardly paused to ask the question that had tormented political philosophers from Plato on down: Could the people be trusted to govern themselves? Rather, there occurred in the first half of the 19th century a quantum change in political consciousness. Numerous factors precipitated political democratization: new states in the West; greater availability of land, which multiplied the number of property-holding (and thus eligible) voters; greater interest in politics because of economic issues and the question of internal improvements; political romanticism; the demise of the disinterested Whig politician of the Revolutionary generation.

The election of Andrew Jackson to the Presidency in 1828 symbolized the altered political climate. Though he had no right to claim humble origins, he still descended from a different social class than had his predecessors. For the nation's first four decades as a Republic, all the Presidents had come from the upper-classes. In fact, for 32 of the nation's first 36 years the United States was ruled by *Virginia* aristocrats: George Washington (1789-1797), Thomas Jefferson (1801-1809), James Madison (1809-1817), and James Monroe (1817-1825). During this same period the judicial branch was led by another member of the Virginia gentry, John Marshall (1801-1835). The Virginia Dynasty in the Presidency was broken only by the two four-year terms of John Adams (1797-1801) and his son, John Quincy Adams (1825-1829), both of whom came from one of the leading families of Massachusetts.

Government of and for the people had been written into the Constitution, but those leaders of the Age of Reason feared rule *by* the people. To overcome mobocracy and the rule of passion, ordinary people would have to be educated. Once that process commenced, mass suffrage could then follow. In the surge of early 19th-century reform, mass suffrage constituted nearly an inevitable cornerstone of egalitarianism.

The term "mass suffrage" was, however, misleading. The "mass" excluded both women and black men. In many ways, the "New World" was well on its way to living up to its name. One glaring exception was the existence and countenance of slavery in a society committed in other ways to equality of opportunity. Nothing could more powerfully give the lie to egalitarian claims than the treatment of human beings as chattel. This chilling hypocrisy contributed mightily to the American Civil War. Large portions of society truly felt that "all men are created equal." In an age when moral concerns were taken seriously it is certain that the moral issues surrounding the question of slavery in an otherwise egalitarian society were among the major causes of the Civil War.

That last sentence may seem banal in its obviousness, but for a century after 1865 many historians scrambled to find other "causes" for the Civil War: the rabble-rousing of abolitionists, the breakdown of the political parties, "cultural" differences between North and South, a staggering array of economic factors. Anything but slavery, which many southern historians disingenuously labeled "the peculiar institution." Such a neutral euphemism sounds better (and more defensible) than slavery. The fact is that while the North won the Civil War on the battlefields, the South often won it in the history books.

Black men received the vote after the Civil War. The surprising fact about the institution of mass suffrage was neither that it happened nor that black men were eventually included as much as that it took until 1920 for the Republic to grant the same franchise privilege to its women.

Equality for Women?

One of the major themes repeated by many of the early investigators into the once-neglected subject of women in U. S. history has been female oppression in a male-dominated society. The term "oppression" is not particularly apt for the case of women as compared, for example, with slaves. Women, nonetheless, did not receive equal treatment with men. The instance of suffrage represents just one of countless indignities, often under the guise of chivalry, which prompted the female battle-cry, "Up from the pedestal!"

These inequities, now being documented by scholars, tell a true but fragmentary story. Less studied today is the phenomenon that found European travelers, upon meeting American women, struck by their self-confident carriage, candor, intelligence, and *esprit*. The observers tended to generalize about emancipated ladies, about the freedoms and scope accorded them (by the men!). Henry Latham was "astonished at their touching without reserve upon all manner of topics which English ladies would ignore,"[13] and Alexander Mackay, writing in 1849, noted:

> A young girl in America is in every way a freer agent than her European sister; the whole course of her education is one habitual lesson of self-reliance—the world is not kept a sealed book to her . . . She soon acquires a strength of character, to which the young woman of Europe is a stranger, and acts for herself whilst the latter is yet in leading strings.[14]

One can easily resolve the apparent contradiction between the accurate assertion that women were denied equal opportunity with these paeans to their independence. The visitors compared the condition of American women with the even worse conditions of *Old World women* and concluded mistakenly that the Americans had achieved emancipation. Those who wrote of female oppression compared the opportunities open to women with those available to *American men*. The same shifting of perspectives, often done without awareness, explains how some can think of the 19th-century New World family as authoritarian (the standard of comparison the 20th century family), while those who compare it with the European family of the same period can characterize the Americans as undisciplined egalitarians.

The women's movement as an international phenomenon has for more than 150 years derived its greatest impetus from the United States, where women appeared already to have achieved substantially more freedom and respect than had their sisters elsewhere. This reminds us that revolutions are rarely begun by those teetering on the edge of despair. The hopeless, oblivious to brighter prospects, generally resign themselves to their bleak situation. Those who have moved some distance upward can see the heights; those with some freedom desire as much as those with more; those with some hope foment revolutions. Most of the revolutions of modern times have been generated from the rising middle classes rather than from the streets. Because American women have a tradition of freedom greater than that of most of their sisters elsewhere, one may expect them to continue to be leaders in the campaign for complete equality of opportunity, a cause very much in the mainstream of American belief.

The transformations in the role of women, in family life, education, religion, and politics were accompanied by the institutional breakdown of other traditional preserves: law, medicine, and the clergy. This resulted, naturally, in more egalitarian access (and also resulted in an increase of quacks, frauds, and incompetents in the professions). Since the making of money was the major sign of success in the egalitarian scramble, there were unseemly, corrupt aspects to the egalitarian revolution. But the reign of the Almighty Dollar even at its crudest also served to add excitement and optimism to the times.

With the transportation, cultural, religious, and socio-political revolutions of 1800-1850, most of the traditional fixities were lost in American life. The cornerstone of the New World experiment of the 19th century was exactly as Alexis de Tocqueville described it in 1830 in the first two paragraphs of his masterwork, *Democracy in America:*

> Among the novel objects that attracted my attention during my stay in the United States, nothing struck me more forcibly than the general equality of condition among the people. I readily discovered the prodigious influence that this primary fact exercises on the whole course of society; it gives a peculiar direction to the laws: it imparts new maxims to the governing authorities and peculiar habits to the governed. I soon perceived that the influence of this fact extends far beyond the political character and the laws of the country, and that it has no less effect on civil society than on the government; it creates opinions, gives birth to new sentiments, founds novel customs, and modifies whatever it does not produce. The more I advanced in the study of American society. the more I perceived that this equality of condition is the fundamental fact from which all others seem to be derived and the central point at which all my observations constantly terminated.[15]

The success or failure of the United States as a civilization depends upon the extent to which the rhetoric of the experiment in equality of opportunity is matched by the reality. ("Equality of opportunity" is closer to Tocquevllle's intent than his misleading phrase "equality of condition.") Lives were lost in the Civil War and in many other instances to keep that experiment going. The experiment continues today, and millions of people in the United States and elsewhere differ on the results. Much that follows in these pages seeks to assess the consequences of the egalitarian effort. The dialectic between egalitarian promises and realities will tell us a great deal about the life-desires of ordinary Americans.

AFTERWORD

Historians tend not to be conventionally religious. This may be one reason that Americanists, myself included, have insufficiently recognized the importance of religion in American history, particularly after the "Great Awakening" of the early 18th century. But with the growing power of the Christian right wing in these last decades and their outsize influence on national politics— baleful and destructive, in my view—we are reminded that America remains the last and most religious nation left in the developed world. It would be foolish to pooh-pooh its significance. (There are, of course, many Christianities, a religion that has survived in part because of its creative adaptability. One very important strain of Christianity has been its Social Gospel wing, emphasizing the message of Jesus to help the poor and lift up the meek. That strain is alive in America, particularly among African-American parishes: alive, but not quite kicking, when compared to the Christian right.)

In a spate of polls, the vast majority of Americans have expressed their beliefs in the existence not only of a God, but also of Heaven, Hell, Satan, and angels. Far fewer Europeans and others in the developed world accept those beliefs, and several polltakers have been too embarrassed even to as ask Europeans whether they believe in the existence of angels!

In a USA Today/Gallup Poll in 2007, respondents were asked: ". . . If your party nominated a generally well-qualified person for president who happened to be [see below], would you vote for that person?" "Catholic" received only a 4% "no" vote. Negatives for blacks were only 5%, Jewish 7%, a woman 11%, a Hispanic 12%. Below 50% were Mormons, people married 3 times, a 72 year-old, even a homosexual. The only category to receive a more than 50% vote disqualifying that person for the presidency was for an atheist.[16] I doubt whether this dismaying result would turn up anywhere else in the developed world.

Perhaps religious belief is the major element today in American exceptionalism. Given its importance historically and contemporaneously, we need to know more. First, we need to make some distinctions. As in the rest of the modern world, even in America we are witnessing a decline in traditional religions: "mainstream" Protestantism (Episcopalians, Methodists, Unitarians, Lutherans, et al) and Catholicism. Catholicism has increasingly become a Third World religion for the poor.

The heart and soul of the growing Christian right goes under names like Fundamentalists, Evangelicals, Pentecostals, and Southern Baptists. They are not interchangeable. Fundamentalists emphasize a literal reading of scripture as the only source of truth. Others focus on feeling ecstasy at large, charismatic church gatherings or in their emotional connection with their god.

But, by and large, most adherents don't make these distinctions and, in fact, share a set of opinions that have provided the engine of their political potency. Most "evangelicals" oppose

Magical Thinking and The Decline of America

abortion rights, same sex marriages, sex education (except abstinence education), homosexuality, stem cell research, assisted suicide, the separation of church and state, and an atheist as President. They generally doubt the principles of The Enlightenment, are dubious about science, reject Darwin, distrust "the outside world," and like neither women's nor sexual liberation. I believe fear of those latter two "liberations" to be cornerstones of their faith and sense of urgency.

It would be a mistake to assume unanimity in the positions of evangelical Christians. There is plenty of division, lots of internal debate, and more clearly waiting on the horizon. But there is also enough unity, if perhaps only temporary, to render it vital that we understand the true nature of evangelical American religion.

There is no question that belief runs deeply in the channels just described, and that there is at work a powerful and deep rejection of the modern world altogether. On the other hand, it may be the case that this religion is far shallower and more superficial than that. In fact, evangelical Christianity may be more in step with very secular American themes than is often recognized.

I have in mind here, for one, its optimism, which is a major theme in this book's general description of "the American philosophy," perhaps the major theme. In traditional fire-and-brimstone evangelical Christianity, nearly everyone, believer or not, was headed straight for hell and everlasting torture when they died. But all surveys today show that modern believers, practically to a person, are certain they are headed to Paradise after they die. They seem certain they have guaranteed a sure inside track to Heaven, an idea not devoid of American optimism!

Further, there seems a strong congruence between religious belief and becoming monetarily rich. Nothing is more American—and secular—than that faith. When I was a therapist with my wife, we saw several clients who went to a Pentecostal church, most of whose adherents were Amway salespeople. Naturally, Elaine and I named it (to ourselves!) the Church of the Amway.

Finally, the ecstatic experience of going to church—a long, continuing tradition derived from tent revivals going back to John Wesley—has the aspect not only of renewing optimistic faith but also of being entertained and having fun. Surely some of the appeal of the TV evangelists derives from their showbiz talents.

So optimism, moneymaking, and entertainment may account for much of the appeal of evangelical religion, and these are very American, very secular traits. This may weaken the argument that the evangelical faith directly rejects modern, secular values. But that rejection may actually be central, with modern techniques simply being employed as the means to catalyze a deeper, more pre-modern faith. Or we've an example of "cognitive dissonance" at work.

What it really means, however, is that we historians who wish to understand America must factor in the importance of religion more than we've done heretofore and must try to figure out what's really going on when a majority of Americans rule out Darwin and a Presidential hopeful who doesn't adhere to god-belief. And we mustn't ourselves as scholars and people rule out the possibility that what we're seeing isn't just ignorance pure and simple.

The scientific illiteracy of many, if not most, Americans surely plays a major part in this sad story. Nonetheless, I conclude that, without pre-judgment, we historians and other disinterested parties need to study this focus on faith more than we do and understand it better than we do. We need more fully to comprehend why, in an increasingly secular and knowledge-based world, the one major developed nation to continue to embrace religious belief is the U.S.A.

55

A HELL OF A PLACE
TO MAKE YOUR FORTUNE.

A NEW SERIES

DEADWOOD

MINERS SUPPLY & PROVISIONS

PREMIERES SUNDAY, MARCH 21, 10PM HBO
IMMEDIATELY FOLLOWING 'THE SOPRANOS' AT 9PM
Subscribe online at HBO.com AOL Keyword: HBO

Deadwood

4

The Village Blacksmith:
The 19th Century

The inner life of a people in a society striving to be egalitarian does not reveal itself through the declarations of its elites. In the last 50 years, a visitor to the United States would learn less about the desires and attitudes of its population from official statements than from looking at advertisements on television, attending movies or sports events, or listening to popular songs.

For earlier eras such as the 19th century, before the advent of mass media, the problem of gauging the private concerns of the people raises thorny strategic problems. What to do? For the TV-less 19th century, sources revealing the preferences and sensibilities of the inarticulate majority are rare. Personal diaries and artifacts that can in significant ways recreate the view of life of ordinary citizens are scarce and not always easy to interpret correctly. Among the best items available are those known to have been popular and important. Once identified, these data deserve very close scrutiny.

One very good artifact for the 19th century is Henry Wadsworth Longfellow's poem *The Village Blacksmith*. This poem, memorized by generations of Americans, may rank as the best-loved poem, the most revered conception of goodness in American popular cultural history. Because in its carefully wrought images it brings together a picture of what the good life was supposed to be like, not only in 1837 (when it was first published) but for decades thereafter, it would be valuable to take a close-up, detailed look at how and why it worked so effectively.

Our response to the poem (do we find it laughable? moving? mawkish? perceptive? banal?) will probably reveal as much about ourselves as they provide an adequate aesthetic commentary on the poem itself. We can also learn something about the directions in which the nation has moved since the poem lost popularity. Though some common citizens and intellectuals of Longfellow's time saw *The Village Blacksmith* as an exercise in sentimental tripe, far more Americans—intellectuals as well as schoolchildren of the era—were touched, gladdened, moved to tears, even changed by its sentiments.

First, I ask the reader to go through the poem, to respond to it in whatever way comes naturally, and take note of that response.

THE VILLAGE BLACKSMITH

1.   Under a spreading chestnut-tree
     The Village smithy stands;
The smith, a mighty man is he,
     With large and sinewy hands;
And the muscles of his brawny arms
     Are strong as iron bands.

2.   His hair is crisp, and black, and long,
     His face is like the tan;
His brow is wet with honest sweat,
     He earns whate'er he can,
And looks the whole world in the face,
     For he owes not any man.

3.   Week in, week out, from morn till night,
     You can hear his bellows blow;
You can hear him swing his heavy sledge,
     With measured beat and slow,
Like a sexton ringing the village bell,
     When the evening sun is low.

4.   And children coming home from school
     Look in at the open door;
They love to see the flaming forge,
     And hear the bellows roar,
And catch the burning sparks that fly
     Like chaff from a threshing-floor.

5.   He goes on Sunday to the church,
     And sits among his boys;
He hears the parson pray and preach,
     He hears his daughter's voice
Singing in the village choir,
     And it makes his heart rejoice.

6.   It sounds to him like her mother's voice
     Singing in Paradise!
He needs must think of her once more,
     How in the grave she lies;
And with his hard, rough hand he wipes
     A tear out of his eyes.

7. Toiling,—rejoicing,—sorrowing,
   Onward through life he goes;
   Each morning sees some task begin,
   Each evening sees it close;
   Something attempted, something done,
   Has earned a night's repose.
8. Thanks, thanks to thee, my worthy friend,
   For the lesson thou hast taught!
   Thus at the flaming forge of life
   Our fortunes must be wrought;
   Thus on its sounding anvil shaped
   Each burning deed and thought.

Now for a look, stanza by stanza, at Longfellow's myth-making craft, so taken to heart by generations of Americans.

The title: *"The Village Blacksmith."*

Rather than follow the long tradition of the central character in poetry as mythic figure, god, military warrior, great statesman, or member of royalty, Longfellow places at center stage an ordinary person, dramatizing the age's new conception of heroism. This glorification of the common man is akin to romanticism as it is, of course, to egalitarianism. The homespun hero also lives in a village rather than in a city and plies a trade that involves physical work.

Stanza #1, lines 1 and 2:

"Under a spreading chestnut-tree
The Village smithy stands . . ."

The blacksmith works in an appropriate setting for a 19th century American hero, under an abundant, growing tree, close to nature and not surrounded by the four walls of a city factory, Nineteenth-century writers made the countryside and the rural life synonymous with goodness, purity, and innocence. The cities by contrast were regarded as cesspools of corruption, wickedness, and sin. One can only speculate whether these attitudes affected the actual depressing fate of American cities from the 19th century until our own day.

A traveler in Europe, even in the last third of the 20th century, could move from one remarkable city to the next, cities which have been livable, beautiful, safe, designed as reminders of the passage of time, repositories of pride, places to which rural inhabitants still dream of someday escaping: Oslo, Stockholm, Helsinki, Leningrad [now St. Petersburg], Moscow, Copenhagen, Edinburgh, London, Paris, Amsterdam, Brussels, Berlin, Warsaw, Prague, Budapest, Vienna, Munich, Zurich, Berne, Geneva, Venice, Florence, Rome, Lisbon, Madrid, Barcelona, Athens, Istanbul, and scores more. Although

Richard L. Rapson

many of these cities face serious threats from Americanization and its chief agent, the automobile, they are still individual in ways that Philadelphia, Newark, Pittsburgh, Detroit, Cincinnati, Indianapolis, Cleveland, St. Louis, Dallas, Houston, Phoenix, Los Angeles and dozens of other standardized, car-bound American cities simply are not.

Europeans have had love affairs with many of their cities. They have planned their development, investing money, emotion, energy, and artistic creation. *The Village Blacksmith* illustrates the American love affair with the (tamed) countryside. Contemptuous depictions of cities in New World literature may be a factor behind the indifference toward urban planning—an indifference which has resulted in ugly, dirty, and dangerous urban landscapes. Except for San Francisco, portions of Manhattan and Washington, D.C., New Orleans, Boston, Chicago, and Seattle, the excitement of traveling in America focuses on the great parks of the western third of the nation.

Stanza #1, lines 3 through 6:

> *"The smith, a mighty man is he*
> *With large and sinewy hands:*
> *And the muscles of his brawny arms*
> *Are strong as iron bands."*

The hero is not described in intellectual or spiritual terms; his immediate attribute is physical strength, a quality available to all people regardless of birth. Indeed those of humble birth are more likely to work outdoors with their hands than are privileged professionals. Doctors, lawyers, and merchants, (not to mention kings, queens, lords and ladies of the manor) do a lot of sitting and standing, activities that infrequently bring forth muscles as strong as iron bands.

Stanza #2:

> *"His hair is crisp, and black, and long,*
> *His face is like the tan:*
> *His brow is wet with honest sweat,*
> *He earns whate'er he can,*
> *And he looks the whole world in the face,*
> *For he owes not any man."*

Lines one and two elaborate the physical characterizations of the previous stanza, and they remind us that outdoor work and the tan skin brought on by it do not fix disrepute on the worker. In Europe, white skin conveyed status because it indicated its possessor did *not* have stoop to manual labor. Longfellow stands the European definition of "class" on its head.

These first two lines also introduce the reader to an image which has become more fully fixed in the American mind than practically any other: "His brow is wet with *honest*

60

sweat" succinctly sums up much of the meaning of the so-called Protestant or Puritan work ethic. While fewer signs of that coupling of religious virtue and hard daily work appears in the writing of the first generation of 17th-century New England Puritans, it became a favorite theme in most popular 19th-century literary and religious writing.

The concept of the work ethic functions especially well in the Longfellow homily because of the phrase "honest sweat." "Honest" pertains to morality. "Sweat" is purely physiological. So linked in the mind are these two ordinarily disparate associations that it would sound ludicrous to utter *"dishonest* sweat," though it is no more illogical than its famous opposite. Hard work can be virtuous; it can also serve unsavory purposes. Or, most likely, moral judgments would be irrelevant to the job being done. But for Longfellow's readers, sweat signifies goodness.

The blacksmith also embodies egalitarianism. Because he was a good worker and, by inference, a good person, *no one* could "lord" it over him. He carried no burden of shame, bore no debt, financially or spiritually, to any person, no matter that person's birth claims, wealth, or power. Clear-eyed and guiltless, he epitomized the humble classes who refused to bow down obsequiously before foreign visitors. The "arrogance" of those commoners often brought chagrin to the upper-class sojourners who were used to more respectful treatment at home. The lines illuminate the blacksmith's essential dignity and a special kind of New World nobility: he could look *anyone* in the eye.

Stanza #3:

> *"Week in, week out, from mom till night*
> *You can hear his bellows blow;*
> *You can hear him swing his heavy sledge,*
> *With measured beat and slow,*
> *Like a sexton ringing the village bell*
> *When the evening sun is low."*

Long, hard days ran into weeks, months, and years in a steady round. There was no talk of a 40-hour week, time-and-a-half overtime, or paid three-week vacations. Here hard work invokes religious simile: the blacksmith's labors are redolent of the ringing church bells in the small village. Longfellow subtly introduces religion into the mosaic of the "good life," a theme which he greatly expand in the fifth verse.

Stanza #4:

> *"And children coming home from school*
> *Look in at the open door;*
> *They love to see the flaming forge*
> *And hear the bellows roar,*
> *And catch the burning sparks that fly*
> *Like chaff from a threshing-floor."*

The next tile in the mosaic of "goodness" consists of children. The nation idealized the young, carriers of innocence and purity (like the countryside) and unlimited potential. Children were the chief instruments of human perfectibility and the mainstay of the democracy. More than anything else, they symbolized the happy future of the land. They attended school, which would make moral individuals and responsible citizens of them all, and they learned from paragons of virtue such as the blacksmith. With his door wide open in welcome to the passing youngsters, they would be schooled in the values of simplicity and diligence.

Alternative visions of childhood as something other than wholesome have existed and continue to do so. William Golding's post-Darwinian *Lord of the Flies,* where the young in a state of nature turned into fearsome, ghoulish cannibals, replaces the 19th-century idyll with a nightmare. Today, as doubtlessly then, anyone passing a schoolyard during recess would note as many instances of cruelty as those of sweet innocence. Children, like adults, are in fact complicated creatures.

The last four lines of the stanza introduce an element of industrialization to the poem. Because it is firmly located in a village and within a moral context, the industrial picture is made acceptable. The poet's taming of the industrial monster replicates the highly popular, decorative 19th-century poster in which a train (the archetypal industrial machine) steams its way through a pastoral setting.

In like ways, Longfellow softens the threat of industrialization. The factory images of flaming forges and roaring bellows occur in a place more like a barn than a factory. The burning sparks are compared to wheat chaff, and the whole scene rendered as enjoyable and inspirational to the children who loved to "look in at the open door." This reminds one of the romantic appreciation of the organic and of nature's sympathy for man. Here is idealized even the smithy's dirty yard, bellowing with smoke and acrid smells, littered with scraps—a vision of what large-scale industrialization would bring. There is some irony in the idealization of this particular type of pre-industrial metalworking man laboring under a doubtlessly sooty chestnut tree. Nature still loves him.

In general, the attempt to reconcile industrialization with the pastoral would eventually allow Americans to pursue dollars while still feeling like virtuous Jeffersonian yeomen. Before long the industrial revolution would utterly destroy the world of the village and its blacksmiths, but the myth has survived the Reagan years. Millionaire capitalists strut around wearing cowboy hats on their heads and spurs on their boots, talking nostalgically of family, God, simple values (like "free enterprise"), and the good old days. Stanza #5:

"He goes on Sunday to the church,
And sits among his boys;
He hears the parson pray and preach
He hears his daughter's voice,
Singing in the village choir,
And it makes his heart rejoice.

The first two lines make the religious component of idealized life explicit. Religion in this same mythic village in the 17th century was everything; now it stands *among* other elements of life, important but not everything. The fourth and fifth lines inform the reader clearly that the blacksmith is a family man ("boys" in line two contains certain ambiguities), introducing the family for the first time into this compilation of goodness. The sixth line betokens a capacity for tenderness in the manly blacksmith, a broader conception of masculinity than entertained in most popular 20th-century fictions. This sets the stage for the most dramatic, moving moment in the poem in the ensuing stanza.

The word "rejoice," partly religious in tone, partly a sign of substantial emotional range, helps to enlarge the "soft" side of Longfellow's hero. Yet there remains a suggestion of a division of labor and sentiment for the sexes. The little *girl* sings in the choir, not the boys. Religion belongs more to the sphere of women than to men. Women of the age were supposed to cultivate the spiritual, men the physical. These lines evoke something of that idea of man the doer, woman the pacifier, softener, and culturizer.

Stanza #6, lines 1 through 4:

> *"It sounds to him like her mother's voice*
> *Singing in Paradise!*
> *He needs must think of her once more,*
> *How in the grave she lies;"*

Such a literary use of death was another romantic convention. The pathos grows with the recognition that the blacksmith is a widower, alone carrying on the family. He remembers his beloved wife, but is consoled by the certainty that her goodness gained her entry into Heaven. The existence of an after-life still commands belief. And *we* are reminded that on this earth we can find One Perfect Love: the blacksmith will not fall in love again.

Stanza #6, lines 5 and 6:

> *"And with his hard, rough hand he wipes*
> *A tear out of his eyes."*

The first four lines of stanza six, if not the entire poem, prepare the way for this emotional bombshell. No couplet in American poetry has caused the shedding of more tears. The dramatic highpoint of this poem, a permanent image graven into the national mind, it works for the most part because of the contrast between the blacksmith's "hard, rough hand" and the tear in his eyes. It is a touching, poignant moment because tender grief is deepened when we are made to recognize its tough, manly source. In order to cause this strong man to cry, hurt must have run deep.

Some people respond warmly to this moment because modern-day masculinity has been so debased as to preclude tender feelings. Perhaps it tells us something of modern life to realize how tough and unemotional are our heroes: the cowboys, policemen, spies, lawyers, private eyes, and military men who emerged triumphant by the 1940's, and who, by and large, continue to furnish the heroic image in countless TV shows and movies. Imagine Charles Bronson-Dirty Harry-Rambo-James Bond-the Marlboro Man crying—or, for that matter, "rejoicing."

The contemporary hero, square-jawed, muscled, cynical and Caucasian (though new black "studs" now stalk the screen), has little of the tenderness of the blacksmith. Nor do the new female heroes. The offspring of Charlie's Angels don't whimper much. They are feline, lean sexy, hard-on-the-outside, and only slightly softer-on-the-inside. Although the "hippie" movement of the 1960's may have broadened the definition of masculinity to include such things as flowers in the hair (long hair like the blacksmith's?—Stanza #2, line 1) and some gentleness, many men still think that if they are not macho they will be thought of as wimpy.

Modern readers, along with some of Longfellow's contemporaries, might find the 6th stanza's epiphany corny. Such a judgment, though doubtless not without aesthetic validity, tells us as much about the judges and their cultural climate as it does about the Aesthetics of Poetry. In assessing the poem, it is equally revealing that millions of 19th-century Americans and many in the 20th century cried a lot over this stanza. They share a romantic sensibility, "romanticism" being a term that can as properly be applied to 19th-century popular American taste as to the more exalted concurrent outpourings of European music, poetry, art, and literature coming from the pens and brushes of Schubert and Beethoven, Byron and Keats, Dickens, Goethe, and Turner.

Stanza #7:

> *"Toiling,—rejoicing,—sorrowing,*
> *Onward through life he goes;*
> *Each morning sees some task begin,*
> *Each evening sees it close;*
> *Something attempted, something done,*
> *Has earned a night's repose."*

After the theatrics, Longfellow lets the reader ease up. The poem settles into the steady, rhythmic patterns of life. We have met the blacksmith at work, in joy, in grief, *"Toiling,—rejoicing,—sorrowing,/* Onward through life he goes . . ."* The rest of this verse drives home the point that such a simple, universal life is rife with meaning and purpose. Each day, the blacksmith begins something and by day's end completes it. This accomplishment contrasts with that great film image of work in the 20th century: Charlie Chaplin on the assembly line in *Modern Times,* demonstrating that, like existence itself, a man's labor constitutes a long, Sisyphean exercise in absurdity.

The day's toil satisfactorily completed, the blacksmith receives literal and metaphoric reward of great significance: an untroubled, good night's sleep. "Earned a night's repose" works like "honest sweat." "Earned" carries moral meaning to a physical activity, "repose." Generations of people, many remembering Longfellow's lines, climb into bed after a hard day's work, comforted by this literary tradition, secure in the knowledge that they deserve and will get a peaceful, conscience-free night's sleep. Whether that sleep corresponds to a peaceful death and the appropriate heavenly rewards is conjectural.

Stanza #8:

"Thanks, thanks to thee, my worthy friend,
For the lesson thou hast taught!
Thus at the flaming forge of life
Our fortunes must be wrought;
Thus on its sounding anvil shaped
Each burning deed and thought."

In this redundant, gratuitous ending, Longfellow reminds his readers of the lowly blacksmith's wisdom. He also insists upon the universal application of the story. Like much popular, edifying, didactic literature of the day, *The Village Blacksmith* concludes with "the moral." It might have been better, from an aesthetic point of view, to finish the poem at stanza seven, where the poet put the blacksmith to a serene sleep.

Taken together, this tale captures the belief of the age that life had purpose, that it made sense. Most persons were sure that selfish, slothful, sensuous, and greedy individuals, despite whatever short-term pleasures they experienced, would eventually suffer earthly and, worse yet, eternal punishment. The blessings of this life and the hereafter would accrue to the simple, decent, toiling individuals whom the new egalitarian democracy honored. Most Americans found in this a reassuring formula.

Today many Americans look longingly backward to these simpler times, though in reality, and nostalgia notwithstanding, they probably never did exist. However, the myth survives. It has a reality of its own which continues to exert a force even in the industrialized, urbanized, technological world which, not long after 1837, removed the blacksmiths of the nation from their villages and deposited them into the factories of Pittsburgh and Cleveland.

AFTERWORD

The rural nature of the Blacksmith's world puts me in mind of the 2000 Presidential election. After George W. Bush was named President by the Supreme Court over Al Gore, a map of North America gained very wide circulation on the Web, based on the dramatic divide between Republican Red-State America and Democratic Blue-State America.

The map showed vividly that the "blue" states were bunched into a highly populated but relatively small area on the West coast, the Northeast coast, and the upper Midwest. But the map added all of Canada to the blue states and called the new nation that arose from this linkage "The United States of Canada."

The rest of the United States, the less densely populated but vast land masses of nearly the entire interior of America—the Republican "red" states"—was named "Jesus Land." The South, Southwest, Mountain West, and lower Midwest were seen as the new, expanded home of H.L. Mencken's famous "Bible Belt."

The obvious point was not only to demonstrate the existence of a gigantic chasmatic cultural divide within the United States between the secular, modestly progressive blue states and the religious, very conservative red states. That seemed clear. But because the blue states seamlessly shared basic values with Canada (and, it could be argued with just about the whole "rest of the West"—Europe and the old British dominions of Australia and New Zealand), "Jesus Land" was really an isolated aberration in the modern world.

Thus red state vs. blue state American entered the common lexicon. It is a distinction that, I believe, obscures more than it reveals, since many of the red states gave more than 40% of their votes to Gore and many of the blue states gave more than 40% of their votes to Bush.

I do believe there is a significant cultural divide within America, though how permanent it is and whether a "vital center" will regain dominance is not yet known. The Congressional elections of 2006 (that returned control of both houses of Congress to the Democrats) suggests that the politics of polarization may soon run its course. But given the gigantic cultural disparities that truly do obtain in America, I'm not sure where the center would reside or whether the cultural divide can disappear.

Rather than the red vs. blue geographical model of division, I have come to believe that a far more useful paradigm distinguishes rightwing religious rural America from the more liberal and secular urban concentrations. Since the red state areas are more rural than the blue, we may have deceived ourselves with the red-blue metaphor. I think the rural-urban distinction works much better.

Though the village blacksmith (or his creator Longfellow) would probably never have dreamed of voting for someone like G.W. Bush, the poem reminds us of the power of rural mythology in our history and its active power down to the present day. Just look at how our recent Presidents have presented themselves. From "the new frontier" of John Kennedy, to cowboy-hatted Texan Lyndon Johnson, to "peanut farmer" Jimmy Carter, to Ronald Reagan's cowboy outfits and strutting boots, to Bill Clinton's evocation of "the man from Hope [Arkansas]," right on through to Connecticut-reared, Yale educated George W. Bush with his heavy Texas twang and Crawford ranch barbeques, we see the continuing power of the mythology of the small town and open land.

This mythology, which may be helping America increasingly become something of a backwater in the economically advanced world, lingers and exerts outsize influence on our politics. This is the case despite the fact that America is mostly urban and suburban. Such a flight from reality cannot be a good thing. Still, there it is: "Under a chestnut tree the village smithy stands." He could be standing in Crawford, Texas or Hope, Arkansas, but definitely not in downtown Boston, Cleveland, or Los Angeles.

Happiness

5

Advertisements, TV, and The Good Life at Mid-20th Century

In the previous chapter, we scrutinized an artifact from the 19th century, Longfellow's *The Village Blacksmith,* in order to get a glimpse at the aspirations of ordinary Americans. The parallel effort for recent times can be made more easily because of the centrality of the mass media.

Television, particularly, furnishes a fecund source for looking into the popular mind. This is true not simply because the average American spends seven hours a day in front of the tube, but also because of the way programs are selected for viewing by the three major networks. CBS, NBC, and ABC are not primarily interested in entertaining or enlightening the population. Like all other businesses they are out to make money and they do so by having others pay for advertising. In turn these advertisers choose when to run their commercials by sponsoring the programs that garner the largest audiences. (Audience size is measured by other businesses like the Nielsen Company.) If the ratings for a program are low, the networks generally drop those programs and produce others that will be watched by more people.

Hence all incentives push toward programming aimed at the masses. Ten million viewers watching Shakespeare—a remarkable figure—cannot compete with 25 million people watching "I Love Lucy" or "Dallas" or "Miami Vice." So Shakespeare does not get shown commercially; "Dynasty" does. The common denominator gains the airwaves. Most of the sitcoms, car-chasing shoot-'em-ups, soap operas, and quiz shows on the three networks are interchangeable. They tend to be uncontroversial, written by formulas and committees for the mental level of 13-year-olds. They attain the largest audiences and therefore the greatest advertising revenues.

Tocqueville's "tyranny of the majority" is clearly, classically at work here more than a century after the appearance of *Democracy in America* in 1830. But despite alternative approaches to financing, and thus to program selection—the BBC comes to mind, for instance—my interest lies not in easy, righteous indignation. American television—its programs and its commercials—opens large windows into the national mind precisely *because* its makers fix themselves so totally on reading that mind. They put on the screen what they think Americans wish to see; the chosen programs and ads in turn reinforce those national pre-occupations. The match-up may not be that perfect, but it certainly comes close enough to suggest that a look at American television may tell us something instructive about Americans during the second half of the 20th century.

To aid in mapping changes and making comparisons with current developments, I would like to focus this analysis on the decade 1955-65. Television had advanced beyond infancy in those years, and had yet to face substantial challenges from public television and, later, cable TV and video recorders.

The programs and pictures that flashed from the TV sets in that decade were received by viewers in widely differing degrees of consciousness, which ranged from dumb stupor to wonder. There is no reliable way to estimate the effects of the programs and only inadequate ways to gauge the influence of advertising. The consequences for children and adults derived from the long parade of violence, for example, is the subject of much study and speculation. No definite conclusions have yet emerged, though the evidence suggests that the exploitation, enjoyment and unrelenting repetition of violent acts teaches us, if not to perform them, at least to expect and accept them. People may not approve of mayhem, but they get used to it. It is easier after a while to become numb to violence than repeatedly to recoil in horror at each mugging.

Despite the absence of "hard" data, it seems reasonable to assume that television has had a powerful impact.[17] It may also be persuasively argued that the program material on commercial TV has been largely filler for the industry's real preoccupation and revenue source—the advertisements. The images used in commercials to induce consumers to purchase products they usually did not know they needed can tell us much about how society defined the "good life" at mid-century.

The quality of the ads is not at issue here. It should surprise no one that more dollars per minute go into the making of the advertisements than into the programs themselves; from a production standpoint, the commercials are frequently much more interesting than the banal shows. TV connoisseurs derive great aesthetic pleasure from the technical, entertainment and production values of the best of these artistic soufflés. Many have charm and wit, others do not, but all must pass the test, in the long run, of selling products.

I am also not focusing on whether the advertisements are honest. Commercials only rarely provide accurate information about the product or service being promoted; practically every one of them fudges the truth. Nor do I wish to get into the claim sometimes made by advertisers that their work furthers prosperity and advances society, except to note that vast revenues go into promoting cosmetics, alcohol, and (until the government belatedly stepped in) cigarettes—all of which are of questionable social value. The moral problems of advertising are fundamentally related to the moral problems of capitalism in itself, a topic slated for discussion in the 6th chapter.

The question we face here is more technical and in some ways further reaching than that of advertising morality. A person composing advertising copy or making a film about a commodity has one overriding objective: to sell the product. If we want to learn about the merits and liabilities of a Chevrolet, we should read *Consumer Reports*, not the ads for the car. The advertising writer sells a service or commodity by surrounding it with a set of images that viewers connect with the way they long to live. If, subconsciously or consciously, viewers link a product with that style of life, they may choose it over a competing product, though more often than not the two will differ little except in name and packaging.

The advertising writers do not invent these visions of how to live. They write what they think will strike chords "out there." But the constant repetition of the ad on television, radio, billboards, in magazines and newspapers, and in catchy jingles composed specifically for the purpose (with the full panoply of marketing studies behind them) can redouble the impact of that vision. Whether cultural predispositions create the commercials or whether the commercials instill the values really does not matter; beliefs may be strengthened through mutually reinforcing processes. To analyze advertising as an index of the popular definition of "the good life" does not presuppose a conspiracy on the part of Madison Avenue. The advertising industry creates visions of the good life no more than did Longfellow in The *Village Blacksmith*. Yet in many ways, advertising has come to replace the literary moralizers, the churches and the schools as shapers and reflectors of modern values. The historian David Potter has noted:

> In contrast with [churches and schools], advertising has in its dynamics no motivation to seek the improvement of the individual or to impart qualities of social usefulness, unless conformity to material values may be so characterized. And, though it wields an immense social influence, comparable to the influence of religion and learning, it has no social goals and no social responsibility for what it does with its influence, so long as it refrains from palpable violations of truth and decency. It is this lack of institutional responsibility, this lack of inherent social purpose to balance social power, which, I would argue, is a basic cause for concern about the role of advertising . . . . What is basic is that advertising, as such, with all its vast power to influence values and conduct, cannot ever lose sight of the fact that it ultimately regards man as a consumer and defines its own mission as one of stimulating him to consume or to desire to consume.
>
> If one can justifiably say that advertising has joined the charmed circle of institutions which fix the values and standards of society and that it has done this without being linked to any of the socially defined objectives which usually guide such institutions in the use of their power, then it becomes necessary to consider with special care the extent and nature of its influence—how far it extends and in what way it makes itself felt.[18]

The figures who peopled the commercials of the 1950's and 1960's were usually young. Rarely did one see people who appeared to be middle-aged, let alone elderly.

The women were mostly in their 20's, the men in their 30's. Immediately we confront a cultural stereotype of the era: yes, to older men with younger women; no, to older women with younger men. Since women have a life expectancy approximately seven years longer than men, logic would dictate an exact reversal of the American stereotype. We see the beginnings of such a reversal today among women with successful careers. Their incomes often attract younger, pretty men who take care of domestic chores, lend psychological support to wives who are out competing in the tough world, and who willingly become decorative sex objects for their successful mates.

In the commercials around 1960, the featured actors looked attractive, but in specific ways. The women were generally tall and lean (though not as thin or even anorexic as the clotheshorse fashion models of *Vogue* or *Harper's Bazaar*). Some psychologists believe the fetish for thinness has contributed to the appearance (or recognition) of anorexia, bulimia, and other eating disorders. In any event, no amply-constructed Rubens beauties for modern America, though society has honored changing body types and styles of physical beauty throughout its history (including the Rubens-Lillian Russell look). After the beehive style of the earlier 1950's, women's hair began to hang long in the "natural look," the result of many hours of work (and special products).

The youngish-looking man who was older than she was usually in his late 20's or in the full maturity of his 30's or early 40's. If in his 40's, he looked much younger than his years so that his sophistication, when combined with his healthy, good looks, made him irresistible to the much younger girls of the commercials.

The man's handsomeness also displayed itself in a peculiarly American way. He looked very "masculine": square-jawed, heavy-chested, ruggedly athletic but still smooth enough to order the finest wines in a chic French restaurant. He epitomized the term "manly" in the narrow New World sense of that word. This deep-voiced, tough but clean-cut male did not look particularly kind, gentle, intellectual or spiritual. He matched his streamlined, good-looking, efficient female counterpart. There was a sense of self-centeredness in these "mod" figures. They were also the detective heroes, cowboys, and spies who starred in movies and TV programs.

The message promoted by these professional models possessed charming simplicity: if you were a man who bought the product being promoted, chances were you would also come to possess the alluring woman, who would be thrown in as a bonus. It worked in reverse for the woman, though male sex objects appeared less frequently than female until the next phase of the women's movement reasserted itself in the mid-1960's.

The youth, the attractiveness and fun-loving qualities of these heroes were largely come-ons for that great modern American obsession—sex. Material articles that had nothing to do with sex were sold with the unstated, yet unmistakable promise that their use would make the buyer irresistibly attractive to members of the opposite sex. When a man applied Noxzema shaving cream to his face, the husky, female Scandinavian voice in the background cooed: "Take it off, take it *all* off." Squeeze the tube of Brylcream shampoo and out came a beautiful woman. Buy a Serta mattress, and the girl lying on it, Joey Heatherton perhaps, cuddled up next to you.

Richard L. Rapson

Let the woman buy the right detergent or can of coffee, and the man would be won. Let the frowsy school-teacher purchase a Mustang and she would be instantly transformed into a sexy swinger sought by every male. Anything that touched the body in any way automatically made the buyer sexier: mouthwash, toothpaste, breath mints, underarm deodorant, perfume, cologne, shaving cream, after-shave lotion, pre-shave lotion, stockings, underpants, brassieres, athletic supporters, shoes, shirts, bathing suits, eye shadow. hair dressing, hair coloring, wigs and toupees, tennis rackets, bowling balls, aspirins, iron pills, coca cola, diet foods, whisky, cigarettes, pipes, cigars, cigarillos, beer.

Ingenious ways were devised to bring body and product together, against all odds. Copywriters actually tried to make people (businessmen in particular) believe that when they traveled by airplane, they really flew on (or in?) a woman's body! "Hi. I'm Nancy. Fly me." Additionally, for decades, the airlines hired only good-looking young, white, unmarried women to serve drinks, advise passengers of flight arrival times, reassure the queasy, and make men drool. The definition of acceptable beauty—racially (Caucasian), physically (very pretty, in the particular ways described above), maritally (not yet), and with regard to age (mostly in their 20's)—expressed national preferences on these matters.

Airlines were newcomers compared to cigarettes and automobiles in the business of sex. In movie after movie, especially those of the 1930's and 1940's, the very act of lighting up a cigarette was laden with sexual innuendo. When Lauren Bacall or Bogart lit the other's cigarette, they were really lighting one another up with erotic suggestions, smoky bedroom looks, Freudian phallic gestures. Eventually a woman who smoked epitomized the worldly, sophisticated *femme fatale*. When the teenage girl lit up her first cigarette, it symbolized for her the transition to womanhood; it became the New World puberty rite. The boy, sneaking behind the barn for his first draw and puff, similarly grew to manhood during that act. Smoking would soon be followed by his first attempt at sexual intercourse, which proved beyond a doubt to him that his boyhood days were over. Confirmations and bar-mitzvahs were no competition for tobacco and sex in making men out of boys and women out of girls.

When Madison Avenue took over the cigarette fetish from Hollywood, there was no possibility that they would fail to exploit the sexual gambit. Even to the final days of television advertising, Silva Thins for lean, threatening-looking macho men and Virginia Slims for lean, confident, liberated women touted the sexual powers of smoking. The suggestive commercial left no doubt that one could offer a Tiparillo to a lady. To top things off, the Silva Thin man wore Brut, Hi-Karate, or English Leather on his wind-hewn face, products which did not bring out his sensitive side, while the Virginia Slims temptress went about her predatory ways wearing Ambush or Tigress or My Sin.

Most of all, it was the automakers who, with great success, transformed their steel-and-chrome vehicles from articles of transportation into symbols of status and sexuality. Originally the automobile actually did perform a functional role in the emerging sexual revolution at the beginning of the century. Young men and women

72

could escape from the threatening glances of the ubiquitous chaperone; in the back seat of a Model T they could "neck," "pet," and occasionally "go all the way."

Long after the automobile had contributed to new sexual mores and had begun to disperse the population into ever-more remote suburban ghettoes, it achieved importance in the world of symbols. The owner of a new Packard gained not only mobility, but status and power as well. As the years passed, a newly gained sexuality completed the package. Purchase the right car and a desirable woman would hop into the front seat as you drove off. Yesterday she had disdained you in your ordinary sexless machine.

Women in advertisements lounged on the hoods of cars or beckoned the man to come inside the open, inviting front door, into experiences hitherto only dreamed. At automobile shows, the newest chrome-plated model often sat on a revolving pedestal surrounded by six or eight long, slinky female models. The male patron looking at a car could not be sure, consciously or unconsciously, whether he gazed at the women or at a machine; the symbols intertwined.

As long as men were the main purchasers, the cars were baited with women, but as the Mustang commercials of the early 1960s indicated, autos could make women buyers attract the right men as well. Money once purchased virtue. Then it bought power. Now it promised sensuous experiences as well.

All kinds of other products were promoted for their sexual value. The sex, the youth, the attractive men and women provided the ingredients for a rather coherent picture of the Good Life. The people were usually neither old nor plain. The activities they engaged in while using the advertised goods were not associated with work. The scenes they inhabited bore no relation to the intellectual or the spiritual realm. Instead, the people always *played*. They ran through green woods, sailed on blue waters, gorged themselves at picnics, frolicked at the beaches. They entertained guests at home, ate out at fine restaurants, went on long drives (rarely through cities), and edged always toward the boudoir.

Utopia was a leisured world. Its inhabitants were sporty, happy, affluent, and frivolous. In the American Good Life of advertisements one needed to be young, fit, beautiful, well-dressed, smooth, cool, and strong. And with these attributes one made love (off camera), and played, and played—and was unrelentingly happy. The products were represented as bringing that sort of sappy happiness closer. Consumers who did *not* possess the right goods, who did not engage in The Endless Party, probably ended up wretchedly. Pursuit of life's manifold other possibilities seemed pointless. What were those other possibilities anyway? None came readily to the national mind. The advertisements offered few alternatives. They conscientiously excluded elements of life such as work, struggle, aesthetic pleasure, doubt, aging, thinking, creating, truly loving, spiritual questing, or just quietly listening to music or curling up with a book.

There was only one alternative to the "fun" life. It appeared in the TV *dayime* ads, and its themes have shaped the expectations of most Americans during the past century. In our time, marriage and family have been the primary objectives in the American pursuit of meaning. Family values have ruled the daytime airwaves almost from the moment television entered the nation's living rooms. Housewives were spoken to explicitly by the pitchmen whose companies paid for the *soap* operas and quiz shows that were supposed to keep the women entertained.

Sexual and other themes were not excluded altogether. Just as the Coca-Cola bottle had been designed to suggest a woman's body, a bottle of Mr. Clean subliminally evoked a bare-chested man. The ad itself was also fairly direct. Other cleaners, like Comet or Ajax, were anthropomorphized into knights on white horses riding into the dull routines of the housewife. They transported her, as if in a fairy tale, from drudgery into enchantment. The homemaker became a princess rescued from a lonely tower by a dashing young prince. Many messages promised quick freedom from household chores through the use of this detergent or that floor wax, so that the wife might have more time and energy to take on the role of sexy, playful woman, ready to excite and hold her man when he returned home from an office filled with pretty, young, single, available secretaries.

The more fundamental word sent out by Corporate America to the housewife dealt less in fantasy than with making her over into an unquenchable consumer. In order to fulfill her role as a housewife or mother, she simply had to buy a dazzling myriad of products. If she did not, her neighbors would have cleaner floors, better-adjusted children, tastier coffee, fewer headaches, and whiter clothes. In that circumstance, she would have failed in meeting her responsibilities. Advertising writers helped to fix the role of women as homemakers during a time when society and the economy had begun to offer her other choices.

Proctor & Gamble drove home the message that happiness came from buying dozens of household commodities. All detergents may have been the same, but capitalism invented dozens of different names for them, and for the sake of prosperity many of these indistinguishable brands had to make it in the marketplace. There were strong economic reasons for reducing millions of homemakers into a class of "crypto servants," a phrase coined by John Kenneth Galbraith. Rising standards of consumption, when combined with the demise of the menial personal servant, created the need for someone to manage that consumption. A new social virtue was ascribed to managing the household. Galbraith further explained:

> The virtuous woman became the good housekeeper or, more comprehensively, the good homemaker. Social life became, in large measure, a display of virtuosity in the performance of these functions—a kind of fair for exhibiting comparative womanly virtue. So it continues to be.
>
> She must cook and serve her husband's meals when he is at home: direct household procurement and maintenance; provide family transport; and, if required, act as charwoman, janitor and gardener. Competence here is not remarked, it is assumed. If she discharges these duties well. she is accepted as a good homemaker, a good helpmate, a good manager, a good wife—in

short, a virtuous woman. Convention forbids external roles unassociated with display of homely virtues that are in conflict with good household management. She may serve on a local library board or on a committee to consider delinquency among the young. She may not, without reproach, have full-time employment or a demanding avocation. To do so is to have it said that she is neglecting her home and family, i.e., her real work. She ceases to be a woman of acknowledged virtue.

The conversion of women into a crypto-servant class was an economic accomplishment of the first importance.[19] As to the home itself, commercials conjured the ideal image. Americans knew where they wanted to live. In thousands of depictions of cozy domesticity, few ads placed the people in an urban high-rise apartment, or a cabin in the country, or a townhouse condominium with communal landscaping. The American dream came true only in the single-family home. The "American Dream" *was* a single-family home of one's own. The house stood somewhere in Suburbia. Its kitchen invariably contained all the modern appliances. The warm living room had some older-looking, comfortable furniture. A lawn fronted the house, surrounded often by that nearly symbolic, protective picket fence, walling off a vaguely threatening outside world. Inside, three children and a dog cavorted, sometimes around a private swimming pool. In the garage there were always two cars. An American dream: a house of one's own, a picture-book family, the two automobiles. As the United States entered the final third of the 20th century, it seemed as though the dream of the single-family home might have to be abandoned. The home, especially, cost too much; high interest rates on already immense mortgages made buying a home prohibitive for millions of young people entering middle-class adulthood. Would the families themselves disappear as well?

Other images cropped up in the ads to supplement the aspirations of mid-century Americans. One must be careful about ascribing the fetish for whiteness in the ads (teeth, clothes washed whiter than white, Ivory Snow) with the sterile, antiseptic, and even racist qualities many Europeans observed in American life. After all, Americans also had to be tan, though only healthy, outdoorsy, sporty Caucasians could get a true tan. Tan skin, in a historical reversal, came to be associated with leisure and the money for tropical vacations. (The Blacksmith's tan was a sign of work, an activity valued in the American 19th century, but previously despised in the Old World as déclassé.)

The tan was also associated with a larger perennial theme—romance. At the conclusion of most commercials, movies, and radio and TV programs, whether they were of the detective, adventure, or love genre, boy and girl either were locked in one another's arms or else walked away together hand-in-hand. Affluence was always desired; a scrubbed toughness always valued; virtue (though no longer "Puritan") still usually rewarded. Happy endings sold. Anything less than happy ranked as depressing, even un-American. In a world increasingly devoid of public meaning, private happiness became the *sine qua non*.

At the end of Bertolt Brecht and Kurt Weill's angry modern classic, *The Threepenny Opera,* the anti-hero Mack the Knife sings the song which comments upon the play's bitter, mock "happy ending":

> *Happy Ending, nice and tidy,*
> *It's a rule we learned in school,*
> *Get your money every Friday,*
> *Happy endings are the rule.*

In the face of a clouded universe, 20th-century Americans, in and out of advertisements, turned inward to private worlds, convinced, without irony, that happy endings would occur in their own lives, no matter the mess in which the world might find itself.

Television's images of the "good life" bore little resemblance to those in *The Village Blacksmith.* Hard work had given way to play, asexuality to nearly obsessive sexuality, the village to suburbs and cities, pious folk to good-looking young people spending money and having fun. Some themes, however, lingered: a sense of family, forms of egalitarianism, a certain physicality.

The differences stand out more powerfully than the similarities, especially were we to bring our content analysis of advertising imagery up to date. With or without such updating, however, one additional belief continues to hang on. Both the worlds of Longfellow and of Madison Avenue are orderly and purposive. Causes for this wishful thinking have been outlined in the third chapter, and consequences will constitute a major theme in the ensuing pages.

Most aspects of the cheerful national faith simply refuse to go away: namely the propositions that things work out, that the good are rewarded, that happy endings are the rule. They remind us that among all the people of the industrialized world, Americans are nearly the last optimists, the holdouts against the "tragic view," the lingering innocents, the most certain "positive thinkers," the believers in Heavenly rewards. Beneath their propensity toward violence there is something disarmingly, even eerily, sweet about Americans—sweet and, perhaps, willfully resistant toward reality.

AFTERWORD

I must confess that I have done my best to avoid watching or hearing advertisements these past years. But that's not easy. Ads appear unasked everywhere: popping up on my computer screen, glaring at me from the chest-high fronts of tee-shirts, from bumper stickers, license plates, billboards, jarring me from my complacency at movie theaters, and of course jumping at me at high volume on radio and TV. I try to get to the movies just before the actual feature begins, and I record nearly everything I watch on television, enabling me to fast forward through the endless commercials.

I've done what I can to keep them out of my life as much as possible, and with some success. Besides sparing me from commercial overload, the major outcome of my efforts, however, has been to *render me incapable of analyzing and deconstructing current advertisements as I once did decades ago.*

So here I appeal to my reader to answer some questions. We know that, by definition, the main effort of advertising is to define us as consumers and entice us to buy the products being shilled (this is why advertising exists, after all) and to make us feel that our life is lessened if we don't possess this or that commodity. But has the content of the appeals changed from what I've described above? If so, what might that reveal about a changing (or static) culture?

I suspect that the main themes probably remain: sex, leisure, getting-ahead, getting the girl (or boy), private matters, and—selling oneself, the ultimate commodity. I imagine that the tone remains relentlessly upbeat if slightly more ironical. Is that right?

In the area of change, my guess is that there are more funny commercials, more non-whites in them, and a reduced distinction between "women's products" as promoted on daytime TV and prime-time male-oriented commodities. If so, that would say something about changing attitudes toward race, gender, and how to make us laugh.

But I don't know if that's correct, either. Having offered in this chapter some thoughts about the content of ads in an earlier time, we may have a basis for a longitudinal examination of changes in American culture as reflected over time. I don't have the will (or masochism!) to do this myself, but maybe over the head of someone reading this, a bulb will light and a great, revealing study will result. Now there's a valuable product!

TWO: CONTEMPORARY THEMES

King of Comedy

6

Heeeeeerre's America:
The Showbiz Culture

The date: the Fourth of July, 1987. The refurbished Statue of Liberty will soon be unveiled. The show commemorating this event has been on network TV for several days now. And what a show it has been! Am I dreaming? Have I, between the thousands of ads showing Lady Liberty drinking a Bud, driving a Chevy, and chomping on a Big Mac, have I *really* seen the all-American superstars I think I've seen—talking, dancing, mugging, singing, and looking patriotic?

Was that Barbara Walters interviewing Sylvester Stallone and Rodney Dangerfield about the meaning of the Declaration of Independence? Look, there's Johnny Carson talking to Henry Kissinger about Hank's newest movie, and Hank's going to sing us his hit song from the film, "The Realpolitik Rag." What a dance routine: dressed up as drum-and-buglers and doing a tap dance are Michael Jackson, Howard Cosell, Joan Rivers, Arnold Schwarzenegger and William F. Buckley.[20] Singing the Bill of Rights in close four-part barber shop harmony are—can it be?—Luciano Pavarotti, Dr. Ruth Westheimer, G. Gordon Liddy, and Madonna. Jane Pauley is moderating a debate between Richard Nixon, Jimmy Swaggart, and Dr. Joyce Brothers on whether the Washington Redskins will go all the way again. Tricky thinks the Redskins will take it all because they always give 110%, play with great concentration, and have lots of integrity. Dick is still running for ex-President, and he's making a fine comeback in the ratings.

Lots of other folks have shown up for the show: Alexander Haig and Tina Turner, Tiny Tim (haven't seen him for a while) and Wilt the Stilt, William "the Refrigerator" Perry doing a *pas de deux* from "Swan Lake" with the aerobics dancer Jane Fonda. There are Joe Namath, Elton John, Carl Sagan, Princess Di, Molly Ringwald, Lee Iacocca (who put this show together) all chatting amiably with David Letterman. Arthur Schlesinger, Jr. is debating Tammy Faye Bakker about national fiscal policy. That's John McEnroe singing a trio with Norman Mailer and Gomer Pyle written specially for the occasion by Mick Jagger. There are lots of other stars, but the star of all stars of this show is

81

Richard L. Rapson

America Herself, dressed up as Lady Liberty (played by Liza, Barbra, and Uncle Miltie in drag). And the Master of Ceremonies for the whole performance—and who could ever do it better?—is none other than Ronnie Reagan himself.

And who is this Ronnie Reagan? Is he an actor? a President the United States played by an actor? an actual President of the United States? a football player in the movies? a real football player—Dutch Reagan? a baseball play-by-play announcer? a soldier? a comedian? a patriot? a television star? Is he make-believe or real? Is *America* make-believe or real? Fantasy Island or global superpower? Are those waving, giggling, hyped-up citizens being interviewed by Dan Rather real people or TV extras? Is this whole show just an excuse for the networks to get huge advertising revenues?

Questions cascaded down upon me. I didn't know the answers. I no longer knew what was showbiz and what was real. My head was spinning when, mercifully, I awoke. I sat up, reassured only when I saw that the television set was still in its place. I needed to find reality. I grabbed my *TV Guide* and saw that a program was coming on about the Declaration of Independence. Tom Jefferson's words would straighten me out, so I rushed to turn on the TV. There it was.

The following document is brought to you by E-Z Flow Tomato Ketchup, Achilles Tennis Shoes ("Tending more tenderly to tense, tired tendons"), Rub-a-Dub Hot Tubs and by Japasone, "The motorcycle that gets you there in one piece every time." And now, our sponsors proudly bring you a declaration:

"When, in the course of human events, it becomes necessary for one people to dissolve the political bonds which have—"

Quickly now, because we only have a second left in this segment, What's the next word?

"—connected—"

Human events . . . connected . . . those are great ideas, ideas that built this country, but it takes more than great ideas to make a nation great. It takes a great beer like Suds, and great chewing gum like Cud's artificial-flavor-packed Ginger Mint ("never sticks even to loosest dentures, but adheres easy to the bedpost"). Suds and Cud's are proud bring you this declaration, along with Mercutio Canned Pork and Beans, Glaze Shampoo, Father William Clerical Collars and Copperfield's Tick and Flea Powder. For over a century, when your dog cried out for fast relief from ticks and fleas, Copperfield's was there.

Now back to our declaration.

"—them with another, and to assume, among the powers of the earth, the separate and equal station—"

Equal has never been good enough for Kafferdiddler's, the ice cream so superior, so expensive, yet so irresistible that paupers kill to get it. Rush right out . . . [21]

I turned off the TV, hoping to escape yet another nightmare. But America itself seemed to have become the nightmare: a land of mass idiocy, a frivolous, trivial citizenry, a value system reducing everything, even the self, to a commodity. So many celebrities were no more than manufactured personalities, hardly different from Suds and Cud's and Bud. Capitalism, sports, entertainment, politics, advertising, patriotism, television, and the showbiz personality had become so intertwined that reality could no longer

82

be identified. What was this phenomenon? Where had it come from? Where was it taking this society?

The phenomenon itself, call it the showbiz culture or the cult of celebrity, has a power easy to underestimate because of its absurdity. For many citizens living in this competitive society, no sign of success can be surer than being invited to appear on the Merv Griffin Show or making the cover of *People* magazine. The key seems less achievement than instant recognition. In America, as Daniel Boorstin once remarked, one is well-known for being well-known, not because one is talented. Talent matters little without having it marketed. One can become famous most easily by doing things that television likes to cover: by being an athlete or an entertainer, for example.

Ask nearly any group of Americans to list their heroes, and the great majority of those listed will fall into the two categories. But not any athlete or entertainer will do. They must have a personality and style fit for the media and be well-promoted. Muhammad Ali makes the list of heroes, but Larry Holmes does not; Magic Johnson and Julius Erving do, Moses Malone and Alex English do not quite make it; Pavarotti does, Samuel Ramey does not; Boy George does, George Winston does not.

Moreover, versatility that allows one to flit from one media activity to the next helps immensely. Sinatra acts in movies and makes political pronouncements as well as sings. Is Joe Namath a football announcer, a football player, or a prominent actor in advertisements? Jane Fonda is a fine actress, a best-selling promoter of fitness, an author, and a political spokesperson.

As I write, leading candidates for the Presidency of the United States in 1988 include former football player, Jack Kemp, and a TV evangelist, Pat Robertson, while an ex-basketball star, Bill Bradley sits on the sidelines along with other telegenic types. Harry Belafonte has been discussed a candidate for the U.S. Senate in New York, and who would wish to run against Robert Redford, Charlton Heston, Bill Cosby, Clint Eastwood (recently elected Mayor of Carmel, California) or Paul Newman should they ever throw their hats into the ring? "Personalities" such as actor George Murphy, known for little more than being well-known, have made it into the Senate. But no one, of course, epitomizes this interchangeability of roles more than President Reagan.

Celebrities can manipulate images of the self with such facility that they can make themselves seem credible in a wide variety of roles and professions. Before Reagan became President, John Lahr wrote:

> Visibility is now an end in itself . . . . Renown comes from having a job, not from being good at it. Politicians become newscasters; newscasters become movie actors; movie actors become politicians. Celebrity turns serious endeavors into performance. Everything that rises in America must converge on a talk show.[22]

The cult of personality is a flamboyant and telling example of culture turned in on private egos. When non-entertainers make celebrity lists, they too seem to have "personalities" or to have fabricated them. Think today of American business, and one thinks of Lee Iacocca. How many other corporate CEO's can Americans name? How many academics are known besides Leo Buscaglia and Indiana Jones? How many scientists other than Carl Sagan and Dr. Strangelove? How many doctors other than Dr. Joyce Brothers and Marcus Welby?

Barbara Goldsmith noted that "at a recent Manhattan dinner party, the celebrity guests included a United States Senator, an embezzler, a woman rumored to spend $60,000 a year on flowers, a talk-show host, the chief executive of officer of one of America's largest corporations, a writer who had settled a plagiarism suit, and a Nobel laureate."

Goldsmith went on: "The line between fame and notoriety, has been erased. Today we are faced with a vast confusing jumble of celebrities: the talented and untalented, heroes and villains, people of accomplishment and those who have accomplished nothing at all, the criteria for their celebrity being that their images encapsulate some form of the American Dream, that they give enough of an appearance of leadership, heroism, wealth, success, danger, glamour and excitement to feed our fantasies. We no longer demand reality, only that which is real seeming."[23]

I wish to propose briefly two interconnected ways of understanding the nature and the origins of this fixation upon celebrity. The first is economic. I shall mention it here and expand upon it in the next chapter. The second hypothesis is psychological.

The economic component can be stated baldly. The business of Americans is making money. Whatever concerns pop up in the body politic from time to time—moral discussions of slavery, the creation of Utopian societies, fear of immigration, civil rights issues, feminist concerns, environmental preoccupations, or peace (or war) movements—merely distract from the business of getting ahead, though these issues, too, have an economic base.

Once that obsession with material success or at least upward mobility is understood, many aspects of national life fall into place. What makes the Reagan years so revealing, this argument continues, is that the mask has been ripped off. Americans no longer feel the need to disguise, out of embarrassment, their material drives. The President has unleashed those appetites, and Americans can strive for the main chance in an all-out, guiltless manner. Madonna established her celebrity status by proudly proclaiming she's a "material girl," just as Marilyn Monroe sang out a generation earlier that "diamonds are a girl's best friend."

The best way to get ahead is to sell something that someone stands willing to pay for. This does not have to be a socially desirable product; it requires no redeeming social values; it has nothing to do with justice; the sales item can even be your self. Women, traditionally denied entry into business, often had few recourses but to sell themselves—not just in prostitution, but in the far larger enterprise of finding a husband. Selling goods to women to help them market themselves has been one of the nation's major commercial activities.

Magical Thinking and The Decline of America

In the early years of the industrial era during the first half of the 19th century, a period less prosperous than ours, the major items for sale were usually tangible products of some sort: shoes, guns, food, buildings, clothing. To be sold they had to be manufactured in the first place, and a value system which here, for shorthand purposes, we can label the "work ethic," helped shape the upward economic aspirations of millions of 19th-century Americans.

In the more prosperous 20th century, products continue to be made, but citizens can now afford items that would not have been classified as necessities in the previous century: technological "toys," hula hoops and pet rocks, trips abroad and fancy, upscale brand-name products. Even more importantly, the United States has moved from being a product-oriented society to a service-oriented society. Entrepreneurs offer a myriad of services that are marketed as precisely as the tangible products of earlier days had been. Instead of manufacturing horseshoes, one can now make more money packaging and marketing horse races—or dog races or dog cemeteries or funeral services or séances or a religious program or a detective shoot-'em-up or a crime syndicate (the *Godfather* movies were so on-target because they correctly saw the Mafia as a metaphor for family life and for American economic enterprise) or a drug dealership or a detoxification clinic or a pop psychology cult . . . The creative American will come up with some service that people will purchase. That is really the only criterion involved: *will enough people pay enough money for my service/product that I can turn a profit?* One does not generally have to find any other justification for the activity and America prides itself on throwing up few obstacles in the way of such enterprise.

In the showbiz culture, the ultimate product *is* oneself; the ultimate goal is the attainment of celebrity, of being well-known. That requires the same marketing techniques as in selling cars, soaps, E.T. dolls, E.S.T. (or E.S.P.) training, movies, and dating services. Where everything can be reduced to its dollar value, where everything is seen as a commodity, there is nothing inconsistent with the packaging of self, whether one is an entertainer, a politician, or an assassin of politicians. We see capitalism at work. The business of America may be business, but that includes *show* business as well.

It would be easy to wax indignant over all of this, and some indignation seems in order. But this material society has changed lives begun in poverty and degradation into lives of decency. Material comfort does not make the good life, but material comfort can make the good life possible, and America has afforded unparalleled opportunities for that basic material dignity. Furthermore, America may not be noted for its elevated, sophisticated, philosophic values, but it is a nation of energy, informality, novelty, new beginnings, and considerable freedom. I should like to address the moral equation of American capitalism more fully in the next essay. For now, suffice to point out the connection between the economic system and the showbiz culture.

The other cause for the emergence of the cult of celebrity, though psychological in nature, connects closely with the economic realm. For this argument I am in debt to the cultural historian Warren Susman. Central to his thinking is a dialectic between two American social orders of "cultures." "The older culture" he defined as "Puritan-republican, producer-capitalist." It "demanded something it called 'character,' which stressed moral qualities; whereas the newer culture insisted upon 'personality,' which emphasized being liked and admired."[24]

These terms sound much like those made famous by David Riesman, Nathan Glazer, and Reuel Denney in *The Lonely Crowd* back in 1948. Riesman postulated a transformation from a 19th century character type he called "inner-directed," to an emerging middle-class type in the 20th century that he named "other-directed." The inner-directed person was guided by an internal gyroscope and bore some resemblance to the morally-certain entrepreneurs who abided little opposition and who gathered so much power and wealth in the last third of the 19th century. The new other-directed types wore metaphorical antennas out their ears, trying discern how others perceived them. Once they received the signals as to their "images"—am I well-liked?—they would adopt new behaviors so that they could fit in and be popular. Riesman described something like a movement from individualism to conformity, though the terms are too general to suit his arguments precisely.

The Lonely Crowd was enormously influential, but then fell it eclipse in the 1960's when individualism appeared not only to be back, but running rampant. There were other problems with the book. The authors looked for causal explanations for the cultural transformation in population trends that, in fact, seemed to have little to do with the changes they were describing. Also their demographic data were wrong. Their character types were felt by some to be too loosely defined so that readers wouldn't quite know where to place themselves.

Historians argued that, compared to Europeans and Asia in the 19th century, Americans of the early Victorian era were even then profoundly other-directed. Many of these scholars faulted Riesman's history and used Tocqueville, a favorite of Riesman, to prove the *other*-direction of American life in the 19th century.

Finally, critics pointed out that if one were tracing characterological changes between the 19th and 20th centuries insofar as *women* were concerned, one would have to argue a movement in a direction quite opposite from that proposed by Riesman; women, the critics rather persuasively pointed out, have been moving in the direction of increasing independence and individuality. When compared to their 19th century sisters, 20th-century women appear to be moving from other-direction toward something closer to inner-direction.

Despite these telling criticisms, *The Lonely Crowd* has had staying power. By dealing with some of these problems, Susman has given new life and terminology to the Riesman position. For example, when trying to explain the movement from "character" to "personality," Susman poses possibilities that are historical, economic, social, and psychological. Pitted against his Puritan-republican, producer-capitalist culture, he posits "a newly emerging culture of abundance. If twentieth-century American politics," he said, "rarely carries the burden of ideological conflict, there was nonetheless a significant and profound clash between different moral orders. The battle was between rival perceptions of the world, different visions of life. It was cultural and social, never merely or even centrally political."[25]

Even when abundance ceased during the Great Depression of the 1930's, the rhetoric of the day filled the air with the new words of the new middle classes: *plenty, play, leisure, recreation, self-fulfillment, dreams, pleasure, immediate gratification, personality, public relations, publicity, celebrity.*

Everywhere buying, spending, and consuming were emphasized. Advertising not only sold products but offered "a vision of the way the culture worked: the products of the culture became advertisements of the culture itself. "All this," said Susman, "seemed to stand in opposition to those words and ideas associated with the more traditional Puritan-republican, producer-capitalist culture that envisioned a world of scarcity (or at least one of significant limits), hard work, self-denial, sacrifice and character."[26] Unlike Riesman, Susman insisted upon the tenacity of the older moral order.

> It did not, it would not, disappear; the culture would have to be understood by its particular conflicts rather than by a consensual order. Moreover, the traces, expressions, causes, consequences, and environment of the culture of abundance were inter-related and ubiquitous. The new environment in which people worked and lived included more than the urban manifestations of factory and city street.
>
> The electric light could actually change the nature of night and one's sense of time. Chemically produced colors made possible a world of color never seen before. Photography and new methods of printing flooded the world with images, the effects of which we are barely beginning to understand.[27]

Many inventions spanning the transitions from the 19th to the 20th century created new kinds of sounds: the telephone, the phonograph, the radio, the talking pictures. Historians have intricately, analyzed the effects of moving from societies that communicated orally to a new literate world of print. "But what are the consequences," Susman asked, "of a new world of oral communication developing within a literate culture dependent on print? What is the result of all the visual images bombarding the eye . . . and of the new means of producing and transmitting sounds to the ear?"

In order to enlarge his questions and to suggest some answers, Susman listed the elements of the new culture of abundance that together accelerated the transition from character to personality (and its ultimate expression: celebrity). They included "a new interest in the body itself: physical culture, health, diet, food and its preparation, 'eating out,' nutrition and vitamins, obesity." The body was pampered by fashion and cosmetics and a new array of institutions arose designed to foster pleasure: department stores ("palaces of plenty") restaurants, hotels, bathing beaches, swimming pools, amusement parks, planned suburbs. New professions, such as interior decorating, were created along with new kinds of music, new rhythms, new dances, and an altered sense of music's cultural role. Said Susman:

Indeed, a multitude of cultural forms native to this period developed: the comics, the poster, the photograph, the phonograph, the telephone, the radio, moving pictures, advertising, pulp magazines and with them certain genres of fiction and nonfiction stories, and, perhaps most centrally, the automobile. We have, of course, had many studies of these phenomena but seldom in terms of their consequences for a definition of a culture and its ideology.[28]

To this list we would now have to add airplanes, television, TV satellite dishes, Walkmen, space ships, personal computers, compact discs, camcorders, video recorders, music videos, and a host of new forms which continue to reshape the culture of abundance. But what does it mean? What are the consequences for society of a world of synthetic imagery? The question is not easily answered. There is nothing intrinsically evil about lots of people being entertained (mass culture) or buying things or even buying psychological help (the term "the therapeutic society" is in vogue.) "The culture of abundance," argues Susman, "was not largely the result of evil machination to control and distort human life."[29] Many seers indeed prophesy a golden age of freedom and individualism, derived from the power of information available to ordinary citizens who possess their own computers.

Some critics, however, particularly those who focus on celebrity, are greatly alarmed by the new powers of image manipulation available in the culture of abundance. Goldsmith contends that "image is essential to the celebrity because the public judges him by what it sees—his public posture as distinguished from his private person. Entertainers are particularly adept at perfecting their images, learning to refine the nuances of personality. Indeed, the words 'celebrity' and 'personality' have become interchangeable in our language. Public-relations people, who are paid to manufacture celebrities for public consumption, are often referred to as imagemakers. Celebrities are invariably accepted as instant authorities. Advertising takes advantage of this, fusing the celebrity with the product to be sold. Robert Young's long association with a physician role on television helped solidify his image as a medical authority, adding credence to his endorsement of Sanka."[30]

Christopher Lasch, whose major metaphor for society's ills is "the culture of narcissism," believes that narcissists have the best chance of obtaining celebrityhood. They often possess charismatic personalities and have "no compunctions about manipulating people or their environment, and no feelings of obligation toward truth."[31] Any celebrity list of the past 25 years would have to include Lee Harvey Oswald, Charles Manson, Bonnie and Clyde (who is real, who is fictional?), Jim Jones, Sirhan Sirhan, Gary Gilmore, the Godfather, John De Lorean, John David Chapman, John Dean, G. Gordon Liddy, John Mitchell, Oliver North, Jean Harris, Claus von Bulow, John Hinckley, Jr., and Roy Cohn.

One of the most searching studies of celebrity and its social consequences is Richard Schickel's *Intimate Strangers: The Culture of Celebrity*. Schickel fears that the major effect is nothing less than "the corruption of rational thought." He thinks of celebrity "as the principle source of motive power in putting across ideas of every kind—social, political, aesthetic, moral. Famous people are used as symbols for these ideas, or become famous for being symbols of them." Institutions then use these figures for more than advertising a product. Celebrities are made to represent larger, vaguer longings; they are used to turn complex moral and spiritual matters into simple slogans; they are used to undermine reasoned discussions in all areas of civic life, including politics:

> Most important, they are both deliberately and accidentally employed to enhance in the individual audience member a confusion of the realms (between public life and private life, between those matters of the mind that are best approached objectively and those that are best approached subjectively), matters that are already confused enough by the inherent tendencies of modern communications technology.

Schickel takes these arguments one frightening step further.

> The result of all this is a corruption of that process of rational communication on which a democratic political system and reasonable social order must be based. Indeed, I have come to believe that those appalling acts of irrationality that have so shocked and disturbed us in the last two decades—the assassinations and the attempted assassinations of public figures—are far from being aberrations, given the workings of the celebrity system in our time; I have come to believe that they are, instead, the logical end products of that system and that those who perpetrate these dreadful acts may have a clearer perception of certain aspects of our shared reality than it is comfortable for the rest of us to acknowledge." [32]

It may seem stretching a point to blame celebrity, which is derived from abundance, for the national decline of rationality, democracy, "a reasonable social order," and for truth itself; to connect it with crime and political assassination. Worship of the stars seems, on the face of it, an innocent pleasure. And when I looked at those American faces on television when they were celebrating the centennial of the Statue of Liberty, images that set off the thinking behind this chapter, they seemed like happy faces in a happy, abundant land. Fantasy or reality? Performance or actuality? Personality or truth? Television or real life? America or Disneyland?

History may have to yield to psychology for those answers. I should like to try that by reflecting upon some of my experiences as a psychotherapist. Couples who come to see me and Elaine Hatfield (my wife, who is a "well-known" psychologist—after all, she has been interviewed on TV by Phil Donahue, Barbara Walters, Hugh Downs, David Hartman, and . . .) often suffer from a common affliction. Many of their marriages and relationships have been based on performances. They have been actors and actresses pretending to love one another, playing the roles of happy spouses, saying they enjoy sex, and faking their orgasms. Like many Americans, on and off the public stage, they have been taught to appear cheerful and to think positively. They have also been led to believe that everyone else is happy, that other people have "normal" families. "Why not me? It must be my attitude. It must be my fault."

Upbeat thinking sometimes can encourage people successfully to overcome obstacles that the resigned might not attempt. A belief in oneself not quite justified by hard-boiled self-evaluation can be beneficial, But *unwarranted* optimism, so common in the land, when combined with the performing mode fixed in our minds by TV, often denies—with awful consequences—reality. People convince themselves that one's attitude, that wanting something badly enough, that dreaming the impossible dream will make their dreams come true. When that strategy fails, as so often it does, then despair sets in. Most of those sunny, feel good Americans who believe "you can have it all" are in for greater suffering than if they had faced the future with more realistic expectations.

Emotional depression roots more deeply when it follows facile hope. Instant, enthusiastic religious conversion leads to unrelenting helplessness or anger when the promises of faith are not delivered. And those couples and individuals in therapy who deluded themselves as well as their friends with their chipper performances of happiness almost have to begin re-conceiving the world from scratch and to consider meeting it with honesty and common sense.

I see those giggling, childlike faces on TV game shows and at media events like the Statue of Liberty celebration and I feel a shock of sadness for them and for the country. They are so good on television. They would light up "Good Morning, America." They have nice personalities. But will they perform competently in the workplace? Will they be intelligent and patient enough to examine personal and public issues in a complicated, well-informed, mature way? Will they be as good in relationships, as parents, and in life as they are before the cameras? I do not know, but I am worried.

But enough of all this gloom. It's time to sign off and, anyway, tomorrow's a brand new day, a new beginning. Thank you all for reading this. You have been *such* a lovely audience. I hope you have a truly *wonderful* day—I *really* mean that. I love you all!

AFTERWORD

Some of the names have changed, but the blurring of the line between fantasy and reality has hardly diminished. In fact, it has grown immeasurably over the years. The cyberspace technology has advanced into realms of manipulation barely conceivable only 20 years ago, with even more astonishing technological advances still to come.

Individuals can sit at their laptops and doctor photos on iPhoto, present false personae in chat rooms like MySpace.com and Match.com. There have been a lot of dates from Hell in the past few years. Walloping surprises, too!! As Randy Cohen writes: "Not every six-foot guy with a head of rich luxuriant hair would be recognized as such. Not in person. Not by his wife. (He's married?

That liar! That tiny, bald liar!)[33] Anyone can post false information on the Web. Politicians and their hired guns in Public Relations can invent fanciful stories to slander opponents and justify wars that lead to the slaughter of thousands. Future historians will sit in bewilderment at how the war hero, John Kerry, was turned into a coward and traitor in the 2004 Presidential election, while his combat-shirking opponent strutted before cameras as the latest incarnation of John Wayne.

Movie and television celebrities hire image manipulators who convince the public that the images so created are more real than reality. Children sit at the beach, heads down, playing Aliens vs. Predator 2 without ever looking up at the ocean. Cyber and media stars are more "real" to many people than their friends and families, and the technology of manipulated reality will only become more amazing.

This retreat from reality into fantasy and from verifiable knowledge into belief is no longer news. But that doesn't make it any less true or alarming.

OFFICE CHIEF OF POLICE
SAN FRANCISCO, CALIFORNIA

WANTED

$1000.00 REWARD

JOHN "DOC" McTEAGUE

Whose photograph and description appear hereon, is wanted by this department on suspicion of murder and burglary.

On December 24, 1922, Trina McTeague, the wife of the above was brutally murdered and robbed of $5,000.00 in the City and County of San Francisco. The above was seen in the vicinity of murder on this date.

Description: Age 37, height 6-2, weight about 200, eyes blue, hair light yellow, complexion light. Has short, heavy blonde beard.

Keep a sharp look out for this man and if located, arrest, hold and wire me and I will send officers with proper papers for him.

The above reward of $1000.00 will be paid by me for his arrest and detention or for any information leading to his arrest.

For further information see Erich Von Stroheim's "Greed" adapted from Frank Norris' classic American novel "McTeague."

A Metro-Goldwyn Picture coming to the Peoples' Theatre, starting March 14

D. J. O'BRIEN, Chief of Police.

Greed

7

Capitalism, Socialism, and
The American Love of Money

I am an American who loves to travel to Europe whenever I can manage it. I recently returned from a trip to Tuscany after having had a fine, dulcet time. And though it's always good to get back home, America seemed somewhat pinched. Why? America's spaces are infinitely grander than Europe's. Personal freedom, too, stretches further than that in the more class-bound, traditional Old World. I do not wish to *live* in Europe; my friends, family, home, work, habits, hobbies, sports teams, cultural memories, and language are all American. Yet my country continues to disappoint me, attempts to cage me—and time in Europe enlarges me in ways that vacations elsewhere fail to do.

This past trip came in 1986, with Reaganism in full flower and my country's shortfall thereby clearer. Embarrassingly, it had something to do with that old hoary accusation that the Old World had been hurling at the New for nearly two centuries, the one about American materialism. Embarrassing because it seems such a cliché, because it is based so considerably upon envy and the world scrambles so resolutely for just those monetary riches that it professes to scorn.

But I could *see* it in a new and more complex way that spring afternoon as I sat outside having lunch in an Italian hill town built in the 15th century, looking down upon the vineyards, hills, green meadows, and spring flowers of the Tuscan countryside all around us. Partly it was the town itself, half a millennium old, and unchanged from the way it looked in the paintings of Bellini and Da Vinci. *We* tear down our buildings when they cease to be cost-efficient. Partly it was the unaccidental and utterly serene harmony between man's works and nature visible in that timeless, rolling, lived-in landscape. Outside of New England, it is difficult to find that special kind of harmony in the American landscape. But mostly it was in the sitting there, just the sitting. Long, slow meals, leisurely conversations about everything (with only passing reference to the latest interest rates), looking at people, sipping the wine which came from the vineyards around us, going no place.

It was then that I could realize that it is not simply American materialism that is at issue; it is the matter of time as well. And when the use and meaning of time enters the picture, we move closer to essential and existential matters in our understanding of American life.

To a significant degree, time really *is* money in America. America's contribution to world cuisine is fast food. Leisure time is linked with work—at parties with one's co-workers, on the golf course "finalizing" that deal, in the exercise parlors toning up to make that good impression; doing business at the "power breakfast"; shopping for clothes in order to dress for success, speed-reading Dostoevsky or Dale Carnegie for efficiency, or attending time-master seminars. And Ronald Reagan smilingly assures his countrymen that the business of America is making money and that they should stop feeling guilty about it. Three more points on the Gallup Poll.

One can hear echoes of the famous diatribe of D.H. Lawrence against Benjamin Franklin, that allegedly essential bourgeois epitome of America:

> Oh, Franklin was the first downright American. He knew what he was about, the sharp little man. He set up the first dummy American.
>
> At the beginning of his career this cunning little Benjamin drew up for himself a creed that should 'satisfy the professors of every religion, but shock none.'
>
> Now wasn't that a real American thing to do?
> *'That there is One God who made all things.'*
> (But Benjamin made Him.)
> *'That He governs the world by His Providence.'*
> (Benjamin knowing all about Providence.)
> *'That He ought to be worshipped with adoration, prayer, and thanksgiving.'*
> (Which cost nothing.)
> *But*—'But me no buts, Benjamin, saith the Lord.
> *'But that the most acceptable service of God is doing good to men.'*
> (God having no choice in the matter.)
> *'That the soul is immortal.'*
> (You'll see why, in the next clause.)
> *'And that God will certainly reward virtue and punish vice, either here or hereafter.'*
>
> Now if Mr. Andrew Carnegie, or any other millionaire, had wished to invent a God to suit his ends, he could not have done better. Benjamin did it for him in the eighteenth century. God is the supreme servant of men who want to get on, to *produce*. Providence. The provider. The heavenly storekeeper. The everlasting Wanamaker.
>
> And this is all the God the grandsons of the Pilgrim Fathers had left. Aloft on a pillar of dollars.[34]

I linger on Lawrence as a reminder that while his theme might be valid, his judgment and tone betray an astonishing narrow mindedness. We know that Franklin was a far more complicated and elusive American type than Lawrence imagined. We know that the upside of materialism is opportunity—an opportunity that the Old World only recently began to offer ordinary people. The chance to rise proved so attractive that millions sailed to the strange new world in hope of a dignity that most of them actually managed to achieve. We know that the pragmatic Yankee mentality can be seen in more ways than one.

E. L. Doctorow, in his popular mixture of fiction and history, *Ragtime*, imagined Sigmund Freud's trip to the United States in 1908. Doctorow described the hurly-burly energy and chaos of New York City, all of which was too much for Freud:

> He had not really gotten used to the food or the scarcity of American public facilities. He believed the trip had ruined both his stomach and his bladder. The entire population seemed to him over-powered, brash and rude. The vulgar wholesale appropriation of European art and architecture regardless of period or country he found appalling. He had seen in our careless commingling of great wealth and great poverty the chaos of an entropic European civilization. He sat in his quiet, cozy study in Vienna, glad to be back. He said to Ernest Jones, America is a mistake, a gigantic mistake.[35]

But for others it was a thrilling place. What for Freud was "overpowered, brash, and rude" could be seen just as easily as equality a work—energetic, vital, spontaneous, open-ended. The quiet, cozy Viennese study might stand for class stratification and stagnation rather than peace and order. Peter Gay's perspective is helpful:

> From Alexis de Tocqueville in the 1830's to Sigmund Freud eighty years later, critics saw the United States as the quintessential bourgeois society, an incarnation, whether promise or threat, of the middle class culture toward which European societies seemed to be irresistibly traveling. The United States was a country in which, as Stendhal and Dickens and countless other observers noted, the bourgeois appetite for material things, lack of higher ideals, and incompetence in love was most perfectly realized and most blatantly displayed.[36]

The moral ambiguity of a middle-class society was elegantly captured by Tocqueville in his *Democracy in America* (1835). Three decades later Anthony Trollope made the same point in direct, uncomplicated fashion. The English novelist acknowledged that he liked living in Great Britain. He was sure he would prefer it to living in the United States. In England he belonged to the upper one-tenth, which was a privileged class. He lived a privileged life, as did Freud, in Vienna. But he could also appreciate the blessings of an egalitarian society wherein:

If you and I can count up in a day all those on whom our eyes may rest, and learn the circumstances of their lives, we shall be driven to conclude that nine-tenths of that number would have a better life as Americans than they can have in their spheres as Englishmen.[37]

The American model of egalitarianism, in theory, was remarkably simple and, as is only appropriate, rather well understood by the citizenry. Visualize, if you will, life as a running race. The American idea insists: a) that everyone must run the race; and b) that all should be lined up evenly at the starting line. The thrust of social legislation, in its purest form, aimed to remove artificial, inherited privilege, and to aid those artificially underprivileged. We are talking theory here, but the nation did eliminate titles of nobility, it did create a system of universal, compulsory public education, it did eventually declare "separate but equal" unconstitutional, it did pass programs of affirmative action. American egalitarianism meant the effort to attain equality of opportunity.

Once each lifetime race commenced, it was assumed that some would win, some would lose, most would be bunched in the middle. Yankee equality bore little resemblance to Communist egalitarianism wherein all citizens would presumably receive equal shares of the pie throughout life. If the American system were functioning correctly, those who won would *deserve* to win: they supposedly worked harder, possessed more talent, character, and virtue than those who slipped behind. And those who lost would do so only because they were lazy or lacked virtue; hence the aversion toward welfare.

And what was the measure of victory in the race? Not to put too fine a point on it, it was money. In this competitive, achievement-oriented society, material success was the index that measured one's character, ability, and diligence. The result?—a middle-class culture marked by "the bourgeois appetite for material things, lack of higher ideals, and incompetence in love."

The question to ask, then, is: *how* does one make it in this competition? In *Ragtime*, Doctorow created a character, a Jewish emigrant from Latvia generically named Tateh, who opposed the capitalist system. He joined the Socialists and enlisted in the struggle to upend the system and substitute in its place one based on a more equitable distribution of wealth and also based presumably on principles of social justice. He found it unconscionable that a few could live in such endless, obscene wealth and have the power to exploit the lives of millions of struggling, diligent laborers who toiled endless hours in unsafe conditions for a few pennies an hour. For his efforts, Tateh got nothing except knocks on the head and brushes with death. Socialism found no home in the United States.

One day, quite by accident, a novelty store owner paid Tateh $25 for a "cartoon book" in which, merely for a hobby, Tateh drew pictures of an iceskater in different phases of figure-eighting. This moment, based upon a frivolous skill, constituted the turning point in Tateh's life as he moved from being a Socialist fighting for principles toward becoming an American financial success:

Thus did the artist point his life along the lines of flow of American energy. Workers would strike and die but in the streets of cities an entrepreneur could cook sweet potatoes in a bucket of hot coals and sell them for a penny or two. A smiling hurdy-gurdy man could fill his cup. Phil the Fiddler, undaunted by the snow, cut away the fingers of his gloves and played under the lighted windows of mansions. Frank the Cash Boy kept his eyes open for a runaway horse carrying the daughter of a Wall Street broker. All across the continent merchants pressed the large round keys of their registers. The value of the duplicable event was everywhere perceived. Every town had its ice-cream soda fountain of Belgian marble. Painless Parker the Dentist everywhere offered to remove your toothache. At Highland Park, Michigan, the first Model T automobile built on a moving assembly line lurched down a ramp and came to rest in the grass under a clear sky.[38]

    Tateh, the artist (he had been proficient in the ancient art of silhouette), decided to join the system, to "point his life along the lines of flow of American energy." (Doctorow employed a metaphor out of physics). Tateh capitulated to the American Way rather than continuing his efforts to replace capitalism. In doing so he became an entrepreneur just like the sweet-potato seller, Phil the Fiddler, Frank the Cash Boy (Phil and Frank were characters out of Horatio Alger, Jr.'s fictions), Painless Parker, and Henry Ford. These men all offered something for which someone else might pay money. The potato vendor would only earn pennies; Henry Ford would make millions, but the idea was the same. It did not matter whether the product "advanced" society or not; it mattered that someone might wish to buy it. If it could be mass-produced, more people would by it. Nor did "it" have to be a "product" in any traditional sense. Phil the Fiddler offered fairly low-level musical entertainment, while Painless Parker provided a not-so-painless service. Tateh also entertained while Ford and the potato chef turned out tangible products. Provide something someone else will purchase . . . and if you come up with a really good gimmick that can be infinitely reproduced anywhere, like soda fountains, automobiles, or McDonald's hamburgers, the earnings might be grand indeed.

    The strategies could modulate with time. Benjamin Franklin in the mid-18th century outlined bookkeeping techniques with which one could develop the requisite virtues of a self-made man. A century later, Horatio Alger's heroes, including the fiddler and the cash boy, relied on a combination of pluck and luck.

    In *The Great Gatsby,* first published in 1925, F. Scott Fitzgerald described much more than the flamboyant aspects of the Jazz Age; he portrayed some of the late 19th-century cultural anguish. Fitzgerald used the Ben Franklin-Horatio Alger story to portray, in Gatsby's character, a man made wealthy through means that neither Franklin nor Alger would have approved. After Gatsby's death, his boyhood "schedule," dated September 12,1906, was found. It read:

Rise from bed... 6.00 a.m

Dumbell exercise and wall scaling... 6.15-6.30 a.m.

Study electricity, etc.. 7.15-8.15 a.m.

Work .... 8.30-4.30 p.m.

Baseball and sports .... 4.30-5.00 p.m

Practice elocution, poise and how to attain it......................... 5.00-6.00 p.m.

Study needed inventions... 7.00-9.00 p.m.

GENERAL RESOLVES

No wasting time at Shatters or (a name, indecipherable)

No more smoking or chewing

Bath every other day

Read one improving book or magazine per week

Save $5.00 (crossed out) $3.00 per week

Be better to parents[39]

Gatsby made his way with Franklin's help. But his early innocence was warped by an era in which the World Series and golf matches were rigged, when everyone was bored by ethics, life, God, and honest works. Among the characters in the novel, only Gatsby, the crook, has any of the wide-eyed optimism and wonder left. He was a bit like a perverted version of the village blacksmith. Also featured in the text were the city, the automobile and the new sexual mores. Fitzgerald introduced his readers to 20th-century culture and to a new people suffering from it, "boats against the current, borne back ceaselessly into the past."[40]

The chance to make money has offered hope unavailable to millions of immigrants who had no such opportunity in the old worlds of Europe and Asia. That opportunity to rise materially has carried with it a rise in dignity, energy, and happiness. The United States, for over 150 years, has become the model for the world. No movement of people in history has matched those millions who came to the New World in the past century. And if all inhabitants of the globe today were free to choose where they would most like to live, can anyone doubt that the United States would far outdistance any other nation? Add to these thoughts the unquestioned realization that in less than 200 years the United States has become the dominant political, economic, military, and cultural force on the planet, and one has a pretty strong case for the superiority of the American system.

Yet, serious questions about material egalitarianism remain. The speculation, by no means limited to the Marxists, that the American version of capitalism places a premium on greed, cannot be pooh-poohed. The democratic socialist dismay at the inequitable distribution of wealth accords increasingly with the facts. Is it really right or useful that the rich few should be *so* rich and have so much power, while the majority, most of whom work hard and believe in "decency," should have to labor so strenuously just to try to make ends meet? Or that this rich nation should allow such huge numbers of its citizens to live with poverty, despair, drugs, violence, and humiliation?

Here is another set of questions, posed through a little story told by John Kenneth Galbraith in *The Affluent Society* (1958). Galbraith described a domestic Sunday ritual of his day.

> The family which takes it mauve and cerise, air-conditioned, power-steered and power-braked automobile out for a tour passes through cities that are badly paved, made hideous by litter, blighted buildings, billboards, and posts for wires that should long since have been put underground. They pass on into a countryside that has been rendered largely invisible by commercial art. (The goods which the latter advertise have an absolute priority in our value system. Such aesthetic considerations as a view of the countryside accordingly come second. On such matters we are consistent.) They picnic on exquisitely packaged food from a portable icebox by a polluted stream and go on to spend the night at a park which is a menace to public health and morals. Just before dozing off on an air mattress, beneath a nylon tent, amid the stench of decaying refuse, they may reflect vaguely on the curious unevenness of their blessings. Is this, indeed, the American genius?[41]

The Affluent Society was ironically titled. The signs of wealth are apparent throughout the tale above: the family drives in a fancy car; their food is extravagantly packaged, they own a portable icebox, an air mattress, and a nylon tent. Few families in few places in the world in 1958 could have possessed such luxuries. But, on their tour they witness a dirty city, billboards, a filthy stream, an unsafe park. Galbraith distinguishes between private affluence and public poverty, and poses the problem of social balance. An adequate sewage system, a well-staffed police force, and decently maintained cities are severely lacking. The multi-millionaires of Beverly Hills may possess gorgeous swimming pools, displayed on the spacious front lawns of their extravagant mansions, but they still have to breathe the filthy, smoggy air of Los Angeles along with the Chicanos, blacks, and less well-off white folks all around them.

In a later book, *Economics and the Public Purpose* (1973), Galbraith argued that the spending imbalances and problems of priorities that he believed scarred America were integral to the structure of the economy, bound up in capitalism itself. Socialism supplies public social services more fully than capitalism, but is ours a capitalist economy? Just what is the American economic system?

If by capitalism, we mean free and open competition combined with a free market in which wages, prices, and production levels are set by the laws of supply and demand, we know that such conditions operate only fragmentally in this economy. Instead, major economic decisions, including the setting of prices, wages, and production quotas, are most often made by the combined power of four massive forces: Big Business, Big Labor, Big Government, and the Military. Galbraith called this the Planning System and found much fault with it.

The language commonly used to describe economic issues, particularly in political campaigns—capitalism *vs.* socialism, business *vs.* the people, the free market *vs.* big government spending (Ronald Reagan has, of course, hugely outspent all other presidents, chiefly to fund the military, though he has staked his reputation on opposition to the "big spenders")—bears little resemblance to the realities. We need a new vocabulary. We need to recognize which parts of the economy function in the classical capitalist mode, which function in the traditional socialist mode, which huge chunks of economic life resemble the Planning System, and which portions are best described with a language which recognizes the *many* economic models which sometimes incongruently co-exist. Since the New Deal, the question of big government *vs.* little government when asked by politicians has always smelled like a red herring. Big government is here. A better question, perhaps, is what do we want government to do?

When the vocabulary begins to come into line with the reality we then might ask even more of these interesting questions about the economy. In what enterprises might the free market be the most productive and just? What areas are *not* essentially profit making, but perhaps necessary to a well-functioning society? When that is determined, we can then ask just how willing we are to invest. Precisely how important to us are clean air, the public schools, affordable health care, clean and ample water supplies, police forces, the military, low-cost housing, a balanced transportation network, open spaces, public radio and television, cultural activities in general such as theatre, dance, opera, scholarship, and scientific research? Other than the military, most of these activities receive significantly more generous public support in the other nations of the industrial world than in the United States.

What then is the proper balance between the profit motive and public spending? between domestic and military spending? Are Americans imbalanced in their lives? Too greedy? too materialistic? too narrow? too focused on money? Would too much domestic governmental spending make us dependent on Big Daddy? too soft and lazy? too undisciplined to compete in the world? And, finally, what kind of gap between the very rich and the very poor makes moral and practical sense?

That gap is adjusted through taxation and spending policies all the time, but how often do we ask if we can maximize both profit incentive, innovation, and hard work on one side with justice, fairness, and the humanistic-Judaeo-Christian ethical creed which we claim as our own?

We can, on the basis of some hard data, ask the psychological question as well: just what is the correlation between wealth and personal happiness? A plenitude of studies already suggest that once a modest plateau of material comfort is reached, there is very little correlation between additional wealth and the happy life. Where precisely is that plateau and how should that information be translated into social policy? Moreover, all these questions must be asked within the context of a global economic reality. If there exists just *one* powerful, competitive, profit-oriented nation, all other nations may be forced to compete just as fiercely if they are to survive. Questions of fairness can easily fall by the wayside when assaulted by this real-world, unsentimental competition.

In the face of these difficult questions I would like to round out this essay by assuming, on the one hand, that economic preoccupations are here to stay, that the Marxists and the Reaganites (who agree on this point) may be correct. Let me also assume that the good life consists of more than material decency, but that it must be based upon that material decency. I regard it as a sign of progress that larger numbers of the peoples of this earth do not have to spend all of their few, precious days cadging the next meal, wandering in search of shelter, relying on magic to ward off diseases which science has now rendered curable. Humans can take up exploration of their other capacities and advance beyond other species when not constantly obsessed with the issue of material survival.

If, then, material competition forms a cornerstone of American life, on what basis can we determine whether the nation is on or off course? In such a middle-class society, one decisive standard of national success or failure depends upon whether the middle class is expanding.

Given our nation's history one would have to argue that overall we have done well on that score. "Rags to riches" may border on the mythic, but by and large (though there is, perhaps surprisingly, substantial scholarly debate on the point), people have improved their material lives in the past two centuries. There exists a substantial middle class, and many millions at least rose from rags to respectability. One could argue that the industrial revolution has done that, not America's kind of proto-capitalism, and that the advance has been international. In the final quarter of the 20th century, other nations with substantially different systems from our own have registered remarkable material accomplishments, countries such as Sweden, West Germany, Switzerland, Norway, Japan, Canada, Denmark, and The Netherlands. But the evidence seems strong that the mantle of leadership in the material advance of humanity, first worn by Great Britain as it pioneered the Industrial Revolution, has been carried, since the middle of the 19th century and until recently, by the United States.

The "until recently" raises problems. Between the end of World War II and the mid-1970's economic inequality declined in the United States. But in about 1977 the country, in the words of Barbara Ehrenreich, "lurched off the track leading to the American dream." The rich began to get richer, the poor more numerous, the middle smaller in numbers and doing less well than before. According to a 1984 report by Congress' Joint Economic Committee, "the share of the national income received by the wealthiest 40 percent of families rose to 67.3 percent, while the poorest 40 percent received 15.7 percent (the smallest share since 1947); the share of the middle 20 percent declined to 17 percent."[42]

"The change is particularly striking when families with children are compared over time," wrote Ehrenreich.

In 1968, the poorest one-fifth of such families received 7.4 percent of the total income for all families; in 1983, their share was only 4.8 percent, down by one-third. During the same period, the richest fifth increased its share from 33.8 percent to 38.1 percent. The result, according to the Census Bureau, is that the income gap between the richest families and the poorest is now wider than it has been at any time since the bureau began keeping such statistics in 1947.[43]

The reasons for this growing disparity between the rich and the poor are various, and hopefully they suggest only a temporary reversal of the downward redistribution of wealth. The major tax overhaul of 1986 might contribute to a reversal of that trend. But the trend grows from factors fundamental enough to make me dubious. They include the baby-boom in the work force after the Second World War; the policies and rhetoric of the Reagan administration which led to a reduction in taxes for the rich accompanied by cutbacks in social spending for the poor; the increase in divorces which created a new poverty class of single mothers; the changing pattern of marriage which reduces it as an agent of upward mobility for women ("today the doctor marries another doctor, not a nurse"); the globalization of the economy, wherein American jobs are lost in those industries where we become less competitive, e.g. making automobiles and steel; and, finally, the technological revolution which finds computers, for instance, replacing many mid-level occupations—middle managers, department store buyers, machinists—as well as traditionally low-paid occupations such as bank tellers and telephone operators.

If the United States continues to move toward a two-tier society, Marxists predictions of class struggle between an avaricious bourgeoisie and a vast, angry proletariat, which have been foiled by the emergence of a massive middle class, could conceivably come to pass. I doubt that will happen; Americans don't even know how to talk about class struggle let alone have one. We all still think of ourselves as members of the middle class. "In fact," says Ehrenreich:

> From the point of view of the currently affluent, the greatest danger is not that a class-conscious, left-leaning political alternative will arise, but that it will not. For without a potent political alternative, we are likely to continue our slide toward a society divided between the hungry and the over-fed, the hopeless and the have-it-alls. What is worse, there will be no mainstream, peaceable outlets for the frustration of the declining middle-class or the desperation of those at the bottom. Instead, it is safe to predict that there will be more crime, more exotic forms of political and religious sectarianism, and ultimately, that we will no longer be one nation, but two.[44]

My concerns about the United States in an economic context are several. We ask for trouble if we allow the rich to get richer and the poor to get more numerous. The decline in public spending for enterprises which are not money-makers—good air, good schools, affordable medical care, and the like—suggests a serious loss of perspective, especially as we pour dollars into the military arena instead. Empires collapse when their military obligations outstretch their capacity to pay for them. And our national fuzziness about just what kind of economic system we have dooms us to ask the wrong questions, to mouth slogans, and to continue a pathetic political discourse.

These are serious matters, but they are theoretically correctible. Because they are solvable, I should like to return to my most serious concern, the one that takes me back to Tuscany. And that is that the United States, driven above all by material concerns, is a powerful but trivial place. The middle-class fascination with money has yielded the mixed results described above.

Whether one likes a society so shaped is, ultimately, a matter of personal taste. But let me say it and then be done with it: I wish more Americans loved education for its own sake and not primarily for its practical advantages. I wish they were more cooperative and less competitive. I wish they were less in a hurry. I wish they rewarded their artists and scholars as much as they do the go-getters and celebrities. I wish they were more thoughtful and informed. I wish they liked Mozart as much as Madonna, Shakespeare as much as Stallone. I wish they were less provincial and knew more about and cared more about the rest of the world.

I will continue to live in the United States: it has been my home for five decades of habits, words, work, memories, friends, passions and hope. I frequently do not love it, but I do not wish to leave it. One of its best qualities is that I am free to say these kinds of things here. Another is that there is no place on earth where I am freer to write the script for my life. But I do nonetheless look forward to my next trip to Tuscany.

AFTERWORD

In the previous chapter and afterword I discussed the fantasy world inhabited by so many Americans. Consider this mass delusion as it relates to money. In a Time *magazine survey after the 2000 election, Americans were asked: "Are you in the top 1 percent of earners? Nineteen percent of Americans say they are in the richest 1 percent and a further 20 percent expect to be someday."[45] That is, 39% of Americans believe they are or about to be in the top one percent of moneymakers.*

One can see from this why people hardly blink when tax breaks go to the rich at the expense of the middle and working classes, or when regulations for corporations are gutted at the expense of the environment or worker safety, or when the disparity between the rich and the poor grows, as it has dramatically these past two decades. Americans identify with the rich because they believe they will be one of the very wealthy any day now. They don't want to be overtaxed or regulated when that day comes, especially for the benefit of the lazy poor! What a sales pitch, brought off brilliantly by Republicans, business interests, and conservatives generally. What a story! Only in America . . .

I never thought capitalism and the desire for wealth would gain such a complete triumph as it has in this country. Even evangelical religion offers wealth as one of its great promises for belief.

Once upon a time that promise of wealth made America the country to which all non-Americans wished to move. Until recently it was axiomatic that if all inhabitants of the globe were free to choose where they would most like to live, the United States won hands down. In that sense America was, in a very telling way, the world's best hope.

I would bet that most Americans today still believe that the world continues to view America as "the promised land," and if foreigners could leave their own nation they would flock to American shores. The truth, quite surprisingly, is different, more complicated, and more interesting. In 2005, the Pew Research Center asked nearly 17,000 people from 16 countries: "Suppose a young person who wanted to leave this country asked you to recommend where to go to lead a good life—what country would you recommend?"[46]

No more than one in 10 people in the other nations said they would recommend the United States! Canada and Australia led the popularity contest. Canada was chosen by the Germans, Chinese, French, and the Dutch. The Dutch also chose Australia (a tie with Canada), which was the first choice also of Germans (another tie), Canadians, and the British. Poles and Spaniards chose Britain, Russians and Turks chose Germany, Lebanese chose France, Jordan picked the United Arab Emirates, Pakistanis favored China, Indonesians went for Japan, and the people of India named the United States.[47]

I do not wish to over-interpret these findings. America remains a vital, productive, diverse, and resilient society. Popularity comes and goes, and the promise of upward mobility and considerable freedom continues to attract immigrants from around the world to America. But America's dog-eat-dog competitiveness and its minimal social safety net, more pronounced these days than ever, seem less attractive to some than the different balances in life offered by Canada, Australia, and a host of European nations. Not everyone gets the time or money for an idyll in Tuscany or the south of France. The social systems of Scandinavia and New Zealand aren't very open to immigration. But the ideal of a more leisurely, less competitive, and more balanced life than that afforded by hard-driving America exerts an ever growing appeal and pull.

Dr. Strangelove
Or: How I Learned To Stop Worrying and Love the Bomb

8

America's Cheerful View of War

Americans find it difficult to believe when they hear it, but from many quarters, hear it they do: the United States is the most dangerous nation in the world. Many nations, not just the Soviet Union, feel that the United States could start World War III. Some of that fear derives from the image of America as a trigger-happy society that celebrates violence and commits violent acts in staggering quantities.

The reputation is not made out of whole cloth. No other industrial society even approaches the epidemic of crime that so terrorizes the United States. In 1986 the F.B.I. released statistics revealing that the chance of an American citizen getting murdered in his or her lifetime is an incredible one in 153. One out of 28 non-white males will have his life terminated by murder! Most Americans will be victimized by serious crime during their lifetimes and fear is an ever-present fact of the nation's life. Those who are persuaded that the American experiment has produced a failing civilization drowning in drugs and despair, greed and anomie, violence and fear, need hardly go beyond the statistics above.

Despite them and beyond all reason, in no industrial country can anyone so easily purchase a firearm. This may be *machismo* taken to the grotesque, yet each new generation proclaims its right to bear arms, remembers the fabled days of the Wild West, talks tough, and proclaims its readiness to fight. Youth gangs roam the streets of big cities carrying automatic weapons possessing firepower substantially in excess of the local police. Instead of banning arms, people tend to feel their only protection lies in purchasing their own guns. Lots of Americans think of themselves as tough hombres, whether they wear a sombrero, a uniform of the U.S. Marine Corps, or a thug's outfit. And much of the rest of the world, including many a frightened American, gazes upon this spectacle uneasily.

Add to this portrait the emphasis on competition so basic to the capitalist system, and one can see why many Americans view the world as a bruising football game in which we have to come out on top. Richard Nixon in fact loved to use football metaphors to describe politics and foreign policy. He often quoted football coaches like George Allen and Vince Lombardi, both of whom talked tough. ("Winning isn't everything; it's the only thing!")

There are historical bases for worrying that the United States is, in some ways, a reckless, trigger-happy nation that could launch a first-strike nuclear assault. In addition, we have had a unique relationship to war throughout our past, indeed a happy one, lending some credence to the idea that we do not fear it in the way Europeans and Asians (Russians included) do, and that we could go off half-cocked.

This is no funny matter, but America's sometimes adolescent, innocent approach to foreign policy and our competitive model of the world has an aspect of the ridiculous. Garrison Keillor entitled one of his essays, written during the Nixon years (1971):

U.S. STILL ON TOP, SAYS REST OF WORLD

'America today is Number One in the world . . .'
—President Nixon

The White House is very, but unofficially, elated over America's top finish in the 1971 Earth standings, announced yesterday in Geneva. The United States, for the twenty-eighth straight year, was named Number One Country by a jury of more than three hundred presidents, prime ministers, premiers, chairmen, elder world statesmen, kings, queens, emperors, popes, generalissimos, shahs, sheikhs, and tribal chieftains who hold voting memberships in the Association of World Leaders.

"The White House issued a brief statement acknowledging the honor and calling for 'renewed dedication to the principles that have made us great,' but in the West Wing, behind doors that were kept locked to reporters for forty-five minutes after the news broke, complete bedlam prevailed. Presidential assistants, special assistants, counselors, and secretaries jumped up and down and raced from suite to suite embracing each other and shouting at the tops of their voices, according to inside sources. Stacks of papers, some marked 'Top Secret,' were thrown from windows in jubilation, and several well-known advisers were pushed fully clothed into showers, though not for attribution . . . .

"It was the forty-fifth title win for the powerful industrial state since it first copped the prize in 1917. Except for some lean years in the twenties after it turned its back on the Versailles Conference, then the big-money circuit, the U.S. has dominated the world scene in this century, though it still trails the Roman and British Empires and the Mongol Horde in total wins . . . .[48]

The American Century probably did symbolically begin in 1917. Western civilization found itself stuck in the mud of the First World War, which participants—at first thinking of it as "the war to end all wars," called the Great War. With the Russians pulling out to pursue their revolution, the war might still be going on had not the United States entered the fray three years after Sarajevo. That participation tilted the balance, and the American side won within 18 months. They came out of the war powerful, prosperous, and confident.

With eerie symmetry, a very similar pattern took shape a couple of decades later. The United States kept its distance from the Second World War. But the moral imperatives were clearer this time, and as the Allied Forces fell beneath the onslaught of the Nazi *blitzkrieg*, neutrality could not be maintained as easily or for so long as Woodrow Wilson had held on to it. Franklin Roosevelt could sigh in relief when the Japanese pulverized the Naval Fleet at Peal Harbor in 1941. The news was horrific, but the result silenced the America First-ers. The United States was now in the war, and Roosevelt had command of a unified country. More slowly this time, but inevitably, the American entry spelled doom for Hitler. The moat of the Atlantic Ocean protected America's awesome industrial capacity from bombing. And, by 1945, after the dropping of two atomic bombs, the Allies had triumphed. More particularly, the United States had triumphed and emerged from this conflict with a global dominance that even the nation's most fervent boosters could never have anticipated.

War had once again confirmed America as #1. Despite the hardships and deaths, the experience of war at the deepest levels of feeling were doubtless profoundly different for Americans, and more benign, than they were for the English or the Russians, Germans, French, or Japanese. In fact, America's experiences with war may be far less awful than for any major society in the world in modern times.

Go back even to the American Civil War, where on the face of it the patterns would seem so different. Not so different, however, if one looks at the Civil War from the *northern* perspective. In David Kennedy' s words:

> America has had a peculiar, even peculiarly happy, experience with war. The argument is especially compelling if one directs attention to the victorious North, where the Civil War embodied all the features that were typify every subsequent American military engagement.
>
> First, from the Northern point of view, the Civil War was fought somewhere else. It was fought on other people's soil. There were no major military engagements that deeply penetrated the industrial, populated Northern heartland. Second, the war ushered in an era of immense economic growth for the North, and strengthened the hold of certain Northern elite groups on American political and economic life. Third, and perhaps most important, quite simply, the North won. Victory confirmed, for Northerners, the myth of national righteousness and omnipotence. It nurtured in the minds of Northerners a powerful impulse to self-congratulation, creating what Robert Penn Warren has called a "treasury of virtue" on which the North and indeed the nation as a whole would continue to draw for generations.[49]

The pattern for most of the nation' s history was encapsulated by the Northern experience. It was fought elsewhere. The lives of women and children were spared. The economy prospered. The war was won. But what of the South, where the battles *were* fought and where families *did* die; where the economy was decimated, the war was lost? Two points stand out. First, the South *is* different. History impinges. Southern literature understands tragedy and its people often seem shadowed by doubt. Arnold Toynbee once told this anecdote:

> I remember watching the diamond jubilee procession myself as a small boy. I remember the atmosphere. It was: Well, here we are on top of the world, and we have arrived at this peak to stay there—forever! There is, of course, a thing called history, but history is something unpleasant that happens to other people. We are comfortably outside all that. I am sure, if I had been a small boy in New York in 1897 I should have felt the same. Of course, if I had been a small boy in 1897 in the Southern part of the United States, I should not have felt the same; I should then have known from my parents that history had happened to my people in my part of the world.[50]

The South has often seemed a different nation within the United States, particularly *after* the war, when it became more conscious of itself as a separate region than during the ante-bellum period. Travel south of the Mason-Dixon line today, and one will see the Civil War still going on, still celebrated at the battlefields which line the landscape, still remembered at half-time during college football games when the Confederate flag waves in rhythm to the anthemic sounds of *Dixie*.

This suggests the paradoxical second point: that while the South may have lost the War on the battlefields, it found a way to win it in its cultural structures and in the history books. Though both North and South adhered to the ideal of equality of opportunity, the major difference before the War between the two regions was the existence of slavery—an institution repugnant to that ideal.

After the War, and well into the middle of the 20th century, many reasons other than slavery were adduced for the War by Southern historians and Southerners in general. Slavery was euphemistically renamed "the peculiar institution," and Northern abolitionists and other "rabble-rousers" were blamed for the War. The breakdown of the political parties, an array of economic causes, the existence of a Southern romantic, chivalric culture at odds with the crass industrial North—all these were trotted out to explain the War. Defending slavery on moral grounds was hardly possible, though even there its so-called "sweet paternalism" was emphasized over its cruelty by some Southern historians and citizens.

Southern soldiers and military leaders were apotheosized as larger than life, brave and benign heroes. Robert E. Lee assumed the robes of Christ, paralleling Lincoln's passage to heaven in the North. In these and other ways, the South softened the loss and eventually could share with the North a certain innocence about warfare.

That innocence, in either section, did not diminish with the Spanish-American War of 1898. It, too, augmented the national experiences with war. It was fought elsewhere; it bolstered the economy; America won. Victory—gloriously brief and wondrously triumphant—freed Cuba, opened an American Empire in the Philippines, embarrassed Catholic Spain, and further confirmed America's romantic, heroic mythology of war.

Much of that mythology derived from nothing more than geographical luck. From the beginning of our history we were protected by the 3,000-mile moat of the Atlantic. The United States, therefore, did not have to divert its economic resources into maintaining a large, standing military establishment, as did the Europeans. America was not subject to the continual conflicts of the Old World or the fear of these conflicts. It could pour its monies into developing its economy, much as did Japan after the Second World War. The United States achieved the same enormous economic successes during the 19th century as Japan and Germany have since 1945. True, the American Revolution and the War of 1812 were fought on American soil, but they were crowned with success (or at least not defeat), and they ushered in periods of sustained growth, security, and national confidence (as did America's aggressive Mexican War).

But it took the two world wars of this century, the most horrendous wars ever fought, to bring the lineaments of America's peculiarly fortunate experiences of war to fullest expression. Ten million Europeans died in the First World War and another 21 million were wounded. It was a war so devastating that most scholars mark it as a watershed in modern history. It ended West Europe's dominance in the world; it sent into steep decline those social classes that had gained the most from the hegemony; and it precipitated profound cynicism about the ruling ideas of the 19th century.

In that same war 100,000 Americans were killed. The number is not small, but it amounts to one percent of European deaths. Moreover the war boosted America's economy, brought about the boom of the 1920s, and made the nation the world's financial top dog. Most important, the rapid victory that followed America's intervention confirmed the nation's myth of invincibility.

The same pattern characterized the Second World War. This time 30 million Europeans died, half of whom were civilians. The industrial plants of Europe and the Soviet Union were decimated. The war ended with 16 million people struggling to survive in refugee camps while some of the heavily bombed cities were left with practically no homes in which people could possibly live.

America lost 400,000 lives—a terrible toll, but only slightly more than one percent of European deaths. Civilians were not killed nor cities bombed nor people left homeless. While European and Russian industrial production and GNP were reduced to less than half the pre-war total, the United States achieved a doubling in both those categories. And for almost three decades after the war, America assumed the mantle of the world's top economic, military, and political power. World War II confirmed not only the global hegemony of the United States, but gave Americans reason to think of themselves as the world's moral guardians as well.[51]

People of other nations may not have pieced these arguments together when they think of the United States as being dangerously innocent about the terrors of war and therefore innocently capable of launching the final war. Similarly, in their relative ignorance about history, many American presidents and foreign-policy makers have used recent history to justify aggressive diplomacy. They focus on the events leading up to World War II to argue that "history shows" the dangers of appeasement, of weakness, and of compromise in dealing with one's foes. The image of Neville Chamberlain promising "peace in our time" after he caved in to Hitler at Munich has been used time after time to justify military intervention in Korea, Vietnam, Central America, the Persian Gulf, and other dangerous spots.

When focusing on Munich and World War II, that application of history has merit. An earlier and more forceful stand against Hitler might indeed have warded off the horrors that commenced in 1939. Perhaps a tougher stance against Russian or Chinese or indigenous Communism can serve the same purpose. But what "history shows" is more complicated than that. One has to go back no further than to the events that produced the 1914-1918 folly to discover that history may show, in the case of the First World War, quite the opposite "lesson" some claim to find in the Second.

In 1914, after the century of relative prosperity and peace that followed the conclusion of the Napoleonic Wars in 1815, a period in which Western civilization virtually took over the planet and seemed to possess all the answers as well as all the power, everything fell apart. We can now see that the West blundered into its catastrophe. There was no clear single force of aggression to parallel the Nazi phenomenon two decades later, despite Germany being forced to sign the "war guilt" clause at the Treaty of Versailles in 1919. Article 231 not only fails to represent an accurate rendering of history, but also stands as a major precipitant in Hitler's rise to power and the holocaust that followed.

Instead of the appeasement of aggression in 1914, we now see the Western world of the 19th century scrambling for colonies; replacing Christianity with the new religion of nationalism; dividing itself into two suspicious armed camps bent on protecting their colonies and championing their national glories; signing secret alliances; and altogether foreswearing compromise, negotiation, flexibility, and peace-making for national, militaristic chauvinism. When the Archduke Franz Ferdinand was assassinated in 1914, the secret treaty system plunged Europe into a war they could not believe was happening and which they were certain would be over by Christmas 1914. Their memories of war were of distant, heroic struggles waged by human beings. They failed to realize that this war would be fought by machines, of which humans were little more than spare parts.

For Europe, the world would never again be the same. For Americans the story was different. Profound domestic changes occurred in the New World after 1918, but except for combatants and the families of the dead, the War carried for most American citizens nothing of the shattering tragedy that it did for Europeans. Indeed, as the War slipped into history, it left behind memories of triumph, accompanied by a warning to Americans to separate themselves from the intrigues of the Old World. We forgot about the blunders and sanguine calculations of 1914. When later we drew "lessons" from history about how to avoid war, Munich had replaced Sarajevo.

Richard L. Rapson

So how dangerous is the United States? Could we really begin World War III because of our historical ignorance and selectivity? After all, the United States did lose the war in Vietnam. There have been strong anti-war movements within the country throughout our history. Americans now know that the Atlantic moat is beside the point in the nuclear age. Most people think of World War III as the final war and assume there will not be much of a world left for any survivors. But we are also violent; we can buy guns anywhere; crime runs rampant; we talk and walk tough; we act cocky; we sometimes seem to be spoiling for a fight. No industrialized nation in the world has streets as scary to walk upon at night as America's.

I do not know how to measure the quotient of danger of Americans, but I do know that the times themselves are frightening. And I think of Henry Adams, in 1862 during the Civil War, writing to his brother:

> Man has now mounted science and is now run away with. I firmly believe that before many centuries more, science will be the master of man. The engines he will have invented will be beyond his strength to control. Some day science shall have the existence of mankind in its power, and the human race commit suicide by blowing up the world.[52]

Americans and Russians are the major possessors of those destructive engines of science. The Russians, scarred as they are by their two ghastly experiences with wars this century, may be less dangerous than the Americans. Then again, their tens of millions of war dead may nudge them toward paranoia, while our more benign experience has led us toward casual arrogance. The combination is unsettling. Perhaps if Americans *felt* war in their bones as Russians do, we could do better together at backing away from the brink.

Americans have a special reason to calm down. The West has already won the Cold War. Or perhaps, more accurately, Communism has lost it. Evidence mounts daily that once people are fed and revolutionary fervor dies, they find freedom preferable to tyranny, democracy (not necessarily capitalism) to dictatorship. Unless we define capitalism rather than democracy as our cause, time is on our side; we can afford to be patient. In the West over the past 20 years, right-wing dictatorships have yielded to democracy in Spain, Greece, and Portugal. Communism has died in Italy and all over Western Europe. In Central and South America, Argentina, Brazil and a host of smaller nations have commenced the slow, uneven march toward democratic government.

In the East European Communist bloc, Russia's monolithic hold weakened long ago, and a loosening-up has taken place in Hungary, Poland, Yugoslavia, East Germany, and just about the whole region. The Soviet Union itself is beginning its experiment with "glasnost," or openness. And though it is too early to predict the consequences of Gorbachev's economic and political reforms, it seems that, barring war, the eventual opening of Russia is practically inevitable. The same experiment with freer enterprise, greater political expression, and openness toward the West continues in China and will soon spread to Vietnam and Laos, though it will be decades before they match the dynamism and democracy of Japan and some of its neighbors.

Right-wing tyrannies have recently fallen in the Philippines and Haiti, South Korea and Taiwan's dictatorships have begun to erode, and South Africa's society of apartheid cannot prevail any more than did Zimbabwe's or earlier colonial African regimes. As outside interference failed in Vietnam, so Russia failed to control events in Afghanistan. Afghanistan is not yet ready to emulate the democracy of its huge southern neighbor, India, but the first steps toward eventual democracy often start with self-rule followed by economic development.

Look around. Communist ideology does not work and gives way everywhere to a more pragmatic openness. The movement toward global glasnost, in the absence of war, seems inexorable. It may be difficult for Americans to feel the horrors of war because of their own history and because they know little of the history of others. But if we simply pay more attention to what's happening in the world *today*, we can perhaps learn to be more patient and remove our fingers from the triggers.

AFTERWORD

I've not repudiated much from American Yearnings. *I hoped that my effort to think historically in the late 1980's about many contemporary matters, to find long-standing historical and structural explanations for issues of the day, would stand some test of time.*

It's obviously too soon to claim that it has, but most of the negative tendencies I described two decades ago seem to have deepened in the ensuing years. Some of this may be attributed to the Bush administration, but it is important to remember that voting Americans (not a big percentage of eligible voters) elected W. two times. That suggests that the values he represented have genuine resonance with large portions of the nation and that more basic long-standing elements in the society tell us much more about the country than current politics.

Nowhere do I feel more like a soothsayer than in the conclusion to this chapter. My call for American patience in world affairs as I took the reader around the world—a trip taken before the end of the Cold War in 1989—worked out. My optimism about historical movements favorable to open, democratic, and free market societies eventuated in the breakup of the Soviet Union, the expansion of the European Union, the unification of Germany, the tearing down of the Berlin Wall, and a worldwide expansion of democracy—all without a global war.

While I was fairly prescient about the demise of the Soviet Union and the Cold War, which came about because of the fundamental weakness of Communism and the appeal of freedom (not because of Ronald Reagan's policies, as some claim), I had too little to say about the Middle East.

I make no claims to Middle Eastern expertise any more than I had special Cold War knowledge. But the historian's perspective may offer something of value to policy makers. In the case of the Cold War, I essentially proposed that Americans and their leaders be more patient. We're not a patient people. Note my comments in the chapter above: "We are . . . violent; we can buy guns anywhere; crime runs rampant; we talk and walk tough; we act cocky; we sometimes seem to be spoiling for a fight. No industrialized nation in the world has streets as scary to walk upon at night as America's."

But I urged removing our fingers from the triggers because large historical forces were moving in directions congenial to those of us who support open societies, We didn't need to force democratic values by military or imperial means on the Soviet Europe, Eastern Europe, China, and Latin America; indeed to do so would have set back those tendencies for a very long time. The end of the Cold War seemed to usher in times full of hope.

Before the American invasion of Iraq, I believe the same principles of patience would have worked as applied to the Middle East. I believe in these strategies, a sort of "Five-Point Plan". First, an aggressive campaign—military, informational, and economic—aimed at terrorists such as those who bombed the World Trade Center towers. Second, this would be action aimed at "criminals" not a "war on terror" or a "crusade," terms that suggest incorrectly that most Muslims are terrorists, terms that became something of a self-fulfilling prophecy; Third, unrelenting American efforts to broker an Israeli-Palestinian peace settlement of the sort that Bill Clinton came whisker-close to achieving before his Presidency ran out. Fourth, a long-range Marshall Plan to support those who wish to enter the world community, based on my conviction that if young people have a stake in life, they won't become suicide bombers: that they will wish to travel, attain knowledge, spend time on the Web, fall in love, be free, stay alive. And fifth, we should stop supporting corrupt and fundamentalist Middle East regimes. This can only be done by reducing our oil dependency, which pays the dollars that support madrasas (fundamentalist Islamist schools), violence, hatred of the West, denigration of women, terrorism, and potential mass destruction.

Ending our oil dependency is crucial, both for our foreign policy and for trying to reduce global warming and climate change. I place the fight against global warming and against nuclear proliferation as the most urgent goals of foreign policy, more urgent even than reducing terrorism. Less gluttony and the development of alternative sources of energy would take us a long way toward achieving those goals.

Before the American invasion and subsequent occupation of Iraq, I believed these long-range policies could work and could bring the Muslim world peaceably into the global village. That invasion has set the attainment of these goals back, perhaps, two decades, and may lead to horribly destructive events that make such attainment impossible.

The invasion moved us all exactly in the opposite direction from the ones I proposed. It has led to many, many more young people becoming terrorists than before we went into Iraq. It has isolated America from the rest of the world: never in my life has my country been so hated by the rest of the world. (The "coalition of the willing" has been, of course, a joke: this has been, for all intents and purposes, strictly an American operation.) It has resulted in serious assaults on American civil liberties in the name of security, further injuring our standing in the world and tarnishing claims of American freedom. It has destabilized the Middle East with consequences yet unknown. It has pushed Israeli-Palestinian peace talks off to the sidelines, making matters worse both for Israelis and the Palestinians. It has led to the deaths and maimings of tens of thousands of Iraqis and Americans. It has propped up radical Islamic regimes throughout the Middle East and isolated moderate Arabs. Our invasion has been stupid, historically uninformed, *and arrogantly ideological, leaving a host of calamities in its wake. It may be the biggest foreign policy disaster in American history.*

In the interests of full disclosure, I wish to note that I demonstrated, along with millions of Americans, against the impending invasion. Some people who now oppose it, four years on, say "how could we have known what would happen?" or "if I knew then what I know now . . ." But without having to know much about history or foreign policy, I and nearly everyone to whom I spoke did not believe:

That Saddam Hussein possessed weapons of mass destruction. *We trusted the U.N. inspectors rather than the claims of our government, based on cherry picked intelligence.*

That Saddam had anything to do with the 9/11 attacks. *Claims that he did were cynical manipulations of the truth, i.e. lies.[53]*

That we would be greeted with flowers as liberators when we marched into Baghdad. *We knew that Saddam was a vicious tyrant, but he was one among many in the world. Do we contain Iraq and its fellows or do we invade to bring about "regime change" in some or all of the countries ruled by dictators? The post-World War II policy of containment worked pretty well to bring about the downfall of the Soviet Union without the planet-wide war we all feared.*

That Shiities and Sunnis were prepared to get along and create a democracy. *Talk of a likely civil war was in the air as we marched in San Francisco that pre-invasion day. It did not take advanced knowledge to anticipate the dangerous insanity of the coming pre-ordained invasion.*

That the world would support the American invasion and that our "leadership" would be celebrated for it.

As I write this, we're still bogged down in Iraq's Civil War. We will get out of there someday, and when we do, there will likely be an escalated outburst of violence and killing. But the recent history of the Middle East has been filled with violence, and it could be argued that the American presence simply added another reason for more killing. So when we do get out, what next?

I would like to suggest that though the American invasion has made the world an even more dangerous place than it was before and set back the prospects of peace in the Middle East many years (with its spillover into other regions), we must once again endeavor to restore historical perspective. I still believe that the patient policies based on longer term perspectives that I proposed at the beginning of this Afterword (my "Five-Point Plan") offer us our best hope for bringing about a Middle East that lives peacefully with the rest of the world.

It will be harder now, and we've added to the dangers facing us all. But I still believe, as I said at the conclusion of this chapter 20 years ago, that the world would be better off if Americans would "remove our fingers from the triggers."

INGMAR SCENES FROM A
BERGMAN'S MARRIAGE

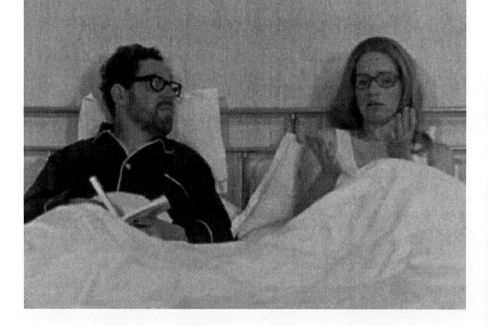

Scenes From A Marriage

9

For Love, For Money, Or For Myself?
Marriage and Individualism Since 1945

THE EXISTENTIAL CONTEXT

Historians find it convenient to divide up developments in the United States after the First World War into decades: The Jazz Age of the Twenties; the Depression of the Thirties; the Second World War extending into the beginnings of the Cold War in the 1940's; the Apathetic 50's; the Revolutionary 60's; the "Me decade" of the 1970's; conservative Reaganism in the 1980's. This periodization may be too neat, but it is revealing. It describes a half-century of fluctuating moods and circumstances with no apparent underlying unity. Such a notion requires closer scrutiny.

The disillusion which set in between 1918 and 1920 amounted to more than a new mood built upon weariness and disappointment. The cynical Treaty of Versailles, capped by the American refusal to join the League of Nations, speeded up the erosion of the older Faiths which had at different times in the past united Americans and shaped their sense of purpose: the 17th-century faith in the Christian God, followed by the commitment among 18th-century intellectuals and politicians to Reason, and finally taking a particularly American shape in the 19th-century experiment with Egalitarianism. (See Chapter Three for a fuller discussion of these broad themes.) Could any of these systems of belief stand up to the darker realities of the 20th century? Had they fallen short of their promise even before 1914?

The past century has been a time of spiritual retreat for Western civilization. Americans, in particular, who were swept along upon the tide of national success and 19th-century optimism, who believed in the Enlightenment, and who were amused by the world-weariness that some Europeans affected, felt the loss of faith with special dismay. What could sustain a life? Justify sacrifice? Rationalize long-range commitments?

The uncertainty about what to "believe in" has fostered that temperament which Existentialists call "alienation." We need to say something about Existentialism if we are to understand the modern sensibility. It is a commonplace that Existentialism is not so much a philosophy as an attitude. Still, the term needs definition, even if we cannot discern unity in the traditional sense by which philosophical schools are usually explained. Such definition may aid in the attempt to see the 20th century as something other than a state of miscellaneous disarray.

If judged by their own conclusions, the Existentialists seemed to be a scattered lot. One can talk of Protestant existentialists like Paul Tillich; Catholics such as Karl Jaspers and Gabriel Marcel; Jews, like Martin Buber, atheists or agnostics, such as Jean-Paul Sartre, Martin Heidegger (who dabbled with Nazism), and Albert Camus (who despised the Nazis). They did not often write formal philosophical treatises. Camus and Sartre did their best work as dramatists and novelists. The finest filmmakers of our time, masters of the most popular, life-imitating and revolutionary art form of the century, might well be called existentialists. These include such diverse figures as Ingmar Bergman, Federico Fellini, Luis Bunuel, Michelangelo Antonioni, Francois Truffaut, Lina Wertmuller, Eric Rohmer, Yasuhiro Ozu, Werner Rainer Fassbinder, Werner Herzog, Robert Altman, Stanley Kubrick, and Woody Allen. Their work would gain yet a further measure of understanding were film critics to point out their existential underpinnings.

The precursors of the movement labored in various forms of creative expression: the 19th-century novelist Feodor Dostoevsky; the 19th-century theologian Soren Kierkegaard; the 19th-century philosopher Friedrich Nietzsche; the late 19th-century composer Gustav Mahler; the 18th-century poet, visionary and artist William Blake; the 17th-century scientist Blaise Pascal. Some scholars trace existential roots in philosophy back to the confessing Augustine in the 4th century or even to Jesus, dying on the cross and crying out in fear and trembling his doubts about whether God exists.

That which unites the later Existentialists helps to define their movement. It is not their *conclusions* but their common *starting point* that brings them together. They start by assuming that people of the 20th century face life from a position of *not knowing* why we exist. The philosophers tend to agree that the condition of modern man is such that life no longer contains given truths, that one must find and create meaning by and for oneself. More than the omnipresence of technology, what differentiates the experience of living in the 20th century from past history is the absence of given meaning. In Sartre's famous definition, essence (handed-down, universally accepted truth) no longer precedes existence (life itself). Existence now precedes (forges) essence.

In the existential view, people of the modern era begin their philosophical quest not with sure answers but with confusion, with loss, alienation, aloneness, not-knowing. They function within an "absurd" universe, one in which one's birth, one's life, one's death fall into no Grand Design, indeed in which life and death may be quite random and devoid of meaning. In that universe of chance, the existentialists find themselves bound together by the fact that, one way or another, they depict man's efforts to try to *construct* some sort of meaning in life.

In such an endeavor they naturally find dramatic forms—fiction, movies, drama, music, art, poetry—as suitable for their purposes as the more traditional philosophical modes of essays and treatises. They are describing or even dramatizing life as a seeking process more than one based upon a set of delivered truths.

Some existentialists have concluded that no meaning in the usual sense can ever be found. In this vein, one can virtually feel Bertrand Russell's relish when he said that we are born for no particular reason and die for no particular reason.

> That man is the product of causes which have no prevision of the end they were achieving; that his origin, his growth, his hopes and fears, his loves and his beliefs, are but the outcome of accidental collocations of atoms; that no fire, no heroism, no intensity of thought and feeling can preserve an individual life beyond the grave; that all the labours of all of the ages, all the devotion, all the inspiration, all the noonday brightness of human genius are destined to extinction in the vast death of the solar system, and that the whole temple of man's achievement must inevitably be buried beneath the debris of a universe in ruins—all these things, if not quite beyond dispute, are yet so nearly certain that no philosophy which rejects them can hope to stand.[54]

Or as Carl Becker paraphrased and elaborated Russell's hymn to meaninglessness:

> The ultimate cause of this cosmic process of which man is a part, whether God or electricity or a "stress in the ether," we know not. Whatever it may be, if indeed it be anything more than a necessary postulate of thought, it appears in its effects as neither kind nor unkind, but merely as indifferent to us. What is man that the electron should be mindful of him! Man is but a foundling in the cosmos, abandoned by the forces that created him. Unparented, unassisted and undirected by omniscient or benevolent authority, he must fend for himself, and with the aid of his own limited intelligence find his way about in an indifferent universe.[55]

Existentialism originated primarily in Europe, but the circumstances that stimulated its development, especially the anguish between the two world wars, were also felt by American intellectuals and artists. However, when "the movement" crossed the Atlantic, such a stark view of the cosmos was softened somewhat. Americans had been *blessed* by history after all, so the universe could not be all that indifferent. Americans never quite took to heart that kind of pessimism. Existentialism may have furnished a backdrop for popular American thought, but it did not describe that thought. Americans continued to be both more optimistic and religious than Europeans. Yet old certitudes were nonetheless eroding even in the New World. How to shore them up? Old answers no longer seemed to work as well as they once had. So middle-class Americans came up with new ones.

Americans in the 20th century, as I see it, have guilelessly assembled an interesting alternative to philosophical emptiness. The American philosophy looks so simple (or simple-minded) that it has escaped the notice of many. While some Americans continue, with sincerity, to adhere fully to older beliefs, the public affirmations of most citizens—whether to Christianity, to Enlightenment Rationalism, to the Work Ethic, to the Nation, or to Technology—generally mask their deeper commitments.

The American solution to the question of Meaning possessed a disarming earthiness. If God had grown remote (!), and fulfillment in a Life after Death seemed too risky a proposition to justify the postponement of earth-bound pleasures, plain citizens would invent a pattern of meaning less grand, but more tangible. If people had grown skeptical about the extent of Humankind's capacity for rationality (a concept continually assaulted by the harsh realities of the 20th century) and if the belief in inevitable progress had begun to wear thin, then Americans would settle for more modest, intimate rewards. If anthropological relativism and too many experiences of injustice in the capitalist system had made people dubious about traditional moral certitudes which guaranteed money and an easy conscience to those who worked hard and possessed good character, if they were no longer even sure just what was meant by "good," then they would build a smaller universe of more solid materials.

ROMANTIC LOVE AND HAPPY MARRIAGE:
Through the 1950's

Increasingly as the 20th century wore on, Americans substituted for faith in God, faith in Reason, and faith in Egalitarian Virtue, a simpler, more manageable and less abstract hope. To gain some sense of what it might feel like, readers might try asking themselves this: when with your closest friend, engaged in your most intimate conversation, what do you talk about? When you fantasize about your deepest longings, what are they? Some will say: to have lots of money. More, especially women, will tout the pleasures of finding love.

Americans of the 20th century have until quite recently, in my opinion, placed their greatest hopes in finding the right person to love. Once having found that person, one then dreams of sharing a life with that person, most typically through marriage. Marry the right person and, it is believed, life will be lived at its sweetest . . . happily ever after.

Much of the energy expended in modern American life has focused on the personal task of each woman to find her Prince Charming and each man to find his Ideal Woman. When found, one would consummate the quest in the post-1750 invention—marriage for love. (Marriage before then most commonly joined people for practical, social, familial, political, and economic reasons—not for emotional ones. Families, more than individuals, married one another.) After marriage came children; the creation of a new family provided "a haven in a heartless world." Purpose, fulfillment, and happiness would presumably then follow.

Magical Thinking and The Decline of America

No matter how confused and chaotic the swirling external world of politics and philosophy appeared, no matter how distant and unanswerable the cosmic questions for which answers once had been known, within that disorder a family unit could construct its own smaller unit of meaning.

Modern husbands and wives had fairly fixed roles. They would love one another. The husband would earn the money, the wife would maintain the home ("the doctrine of the two spheres"). She would bring warmth to her husband who labored all day in the competitive factories and offices. Together they would have perhaps three children. By hard effort they would enclose themselves, their children, and a pet or two, in a home of their own (the "American dream"). And around the home, they could erect the symbolic white picket fence, walling off the family from many of the nameless, bewildering terrors loose outside. Within the walls women would have fixed responsibilities ("the feminine mystique"). There would be support, love, intimacy, serenity, purpose, and meaning. The family would be a place of refuge. By turning inward into the family, the middle class (where most people longed to be) could create modest pockets, miniaturized universes of clarity, order, happiness, love, and most important of all—security.

The 20th-century ideal of the one-to-one, heterosexual romantic relationship as the broadest path to salvation, institutionalized as marriage-for-love, today continues as the fondest longing for most Americans, though it staggers under new siege. It stands as an imaginative, superb, barely-conscious alternative to existential doubt, inventively designed to fill a void that, had it remained empty, could have led many people to despair. It had roots in the Victorian family that had achieved a sanctity in the popular culture of the 19th century and a solidity which the 20th century has not matched. The difference was that, in earlier periods, the family was buttressed by other more formidable beliefs and institutions. As those beliefs began to erode from within, the family had to fill in for them, aided only by a newer, narrower romanticism—that of a man and a woman "in love."

Romantic love became the staple for the makers of dreams, who reinforced the new mythology in myriad cultural expressions: films, novels, jokes, pop psychology, advertisements, radio and television programs, sermons, advice literature, school lectures, political speeches, family conversations, song lyrics. How many popular songs before 1960 have *not* been about romantic love, about falling in love in June beneath the moon while humming a tune to which we'll swoon/spoon/croon? Can one even count the number of movies where boy meets girl, boy and girl fall in love, trouble intervenes (usually as a third person or a horrible misunderstanding), trouble is overcome, boy and girl return to each others' arms, they kiss, marry, fadeout . . . THE END? The audience leaves the movie palace happy in the knowledge that after the Right One has been found and married, bliss follows: the modern American religion of happy endings.

Americans did not invent romantic love and marriage! But they may have been the first to make a religion of the trinity of passion, marriage, and the nuclear family.

121

The great mythic love affairs of the past, whether historically-based or literary—Pelleas and Melisande, Tristan and Isolde, Beatrice and Dante, Romeo and Juliet—had been viewed by their contemporaries as neurotic. Even God had never been very enthusiastic about the dalliance between Adam and Eve! These grand passions had always occurred within a climate of opinion that assumed the existence of yet larger truths about life. Meaning for most people still derived from those beliefs.

But in post-World War I America—with the force of these imposing systems of faith significantly diminished—romantic love, marriage, and even sex began to have to *mean* more, began to bear philosophical and spiritual burdens once borne by faith in God. One's life came increasingly to be measured by the extent to which one had made a happy, "successful" home life, had an attractive, companionable, reliable spouse, topped off by two or three "lovely" children who were to be given all possible educational benefits, and who inhabited a comfortable home filled with creature comforts. These bourgeois decencies furnished that secure refuge from a dangerous world.

As the 1950's—the heyday of the sanctification of marriage and family—gave way to the more turbulent 1960's, the divorce rate began to climb. Marriages began to collapse, partly because the institution had been asked to carry a heavier psychic freight than it could possibly bear. It had to mean practically *everything*. The pattern repeated itself as the culture expected recreational sex to carry some of this psychic load. Making love was not an exclusive modern American invention, either, but did it ever, anywhere, have to *mean so much?* The burden of meaning and emotional fulfillment in the second half of the 20th century became very heavy for romantic love, marriage, the nuclear family, and sex to bear.

The retreat into private lives reached its apotheosis in the 1950's. The forced gaiety of that decade can be deceiving, based as it was on the postwar anxiety about the return to normalcy. Anxiety can be seen everywhere in the 1950's. Men returning from the terror of war reasserted the ideals of the virgin-wife, the close family, the heartfelt religion, and the old-fashioned morality of previous generations. The cruel, unrelenting tensions of World War II and the ensuing Cold War fed the desire of people to hide in their tents. Pent-up people donned baggy, excessive clothing, wore ponderous and innocent ethics, and then stuck their heads into the sand. All this was evidence of a turnabout from the freer, more spontaneous 20's, 30's and 40's culture, a step in cultural development that turned backward in time. The religious revival of the period also represented an attempt to reassert comforting hopes in an anxious time.

The sacrilization of the domestic hearth had a strong negative impulse behind it. Americans tried to turn their backs on the grim, new truths of the period between World War I and the 1950's, including the cultural realities of liberation and hedonism. There was a tense determination to recapture the family, decency, God, religion, and the normal life of work and children, a determination reawakened by Ronald Reagan in the 1980's. It led to the abandonment of ethical imperatives announced by World War II, Buchenwald, and the Bomb. People lived silently, insecurely, in fear, and they resolved to ignore the shadows in the closet. All this helped to make the explosion of the 1960's so easy, swift, and spectacular. One casualty of that explosion was the sanctity of the traditional family and the "mystiques," masculine as well as feminine, which surrounded it.

INTO THE 1960'S: SHE'S LEAVING HOME

Personal Freedom

The family survived the 1960's, but not intact. Vietnam, the Civil Rights battles, the women's movement, ecological awareness, and the fear of an overly militarized world reawakened concern with public issues. A majority of people, however, still found enough to do in life without worrying about the human condition. The change in mood between one decade and another did not profoundly alter the rhythms of daily life for ordinary men and women. Most of them still worked hard to earn satisfactory salaries in order to maintain clean homes. Middle-class parents taught sons how not to be pushed around, daughters how to be popular. Families watched television a lot, traveled occasionally, voted periodically. Dads went bowling with the boys and on Sundays cheered on their favorite football teams. Moms shopped in convenient malls and tried to watch their weight.

The daily tasks were honorable, the rewards decent enough. The conventional wisdom went: "we ordinary folks cannot do much about the monumental problems of nation and world, so why spin our wheels uselessly? Those vague threats—a godless universe, global overpopulation, nuclear holocaust, thermal pollution, political corruption, racial injustice—leave them to the intellectuals, journalists, and politicians. As long as we can avoid these depressing subjects, life will be okay, if not always easy." Americans, the most optimistic people of the past two centuries, had not altogether forfeited their claim to that distinction. It was simply a matter of minding one's own business.

For ever-growing numbers of Americans, however, it became increasingly difficult not to think about some of these matters. Vietnam dragged on, black ghettos in large cities at home burned, young leaders were murdered, and many women, even at home, fiercely spoke their minds—and not always about political issues. The 1960's, as seen from the home looking outward, provides the perspective on the decade I should like to pursue.

The private 1960's start with private doubts, with feelings to which it was difficult to give voice. Misgivings were stirred in those who felt vaguely dissatisfied with their personal lives. They knew by heart the culturally defined bourgeois goals, rooted deeply in the Victorian era, which reached their apogee in the 1950's. But their hearts betrayed the empty feeling inside that came even when they achieved those goals for which they had worked so hard. The psychoanalyst Erich Fromm, writing in 1941, saw this happening to people everywhere. He wrote:

123

In school they want to have good marks, as adults they want to be more and more successful, to make more money, to have more prestige, to buy a better car, to go places, and so on. Yet when they do stop to think in the midst of all this frantic activity, this question may come to their minds: "If I do get this new job, if I get this better car, if I can take this trip—what then? What is the use of it all? Is it really I who wants all this? Am I not running after some goal which is supposed to make me happy and which eludes me as soon as I have reached it?" These questions, when they arise, are frightening for they question the very basis on which man's whole activity is built, his knowledge of what he wants.

People tend, therefore, to get rid as soon as possible of these disturbing thoughts. They feel they have been bothered by these questions because they were tired or depressed—and they go on in the pursuit of the aims which they believe are their own.

Yet all this bespeaks a dim realization of the truth—the truth that modern man lives under the illusion that he knows what he wants, while he actually wants what he is supposed to want.[56]

Fromm doubted the claims of happiness that many people made in defense of their lives, perhaps to shield themselves from the pain of reality. "Behind a front of satisfaction and optimism," he claimed, "modern man is deeply unhappy; as a matter of fact, he is on the verge of desperation."[57] The pursuit of commonly held goals proved disappointing, he thought, because the goals themselves did not develop spontaneously from within the person.

These shared aspirations were not forced upon people by an authoritarian government or an omniscient church. They came from anonymous authorities, from parents, teachers, preachers, television programs, movies, advertisements, from songwriters, presidents, friends—that is, from the general cultural milieu. Americans believed themselves to be individualists, but were in fact victims of whatever system of belief was in fashion at the time. But fashionable aspirations, even when achieved, rarely brought the lasting happiness that had been anticipated.

Nowhere was this truer in the 1960's than when it came to the ethic of happiness through marriage and family. In 1963, more men went off to fight in Vietnam's jungles, John F. Kennedy died bloodily in Dallas, and Betty Friedan's *The Feminine Mystique* was published. The society's placid surface rippled with change. A long history stood behind the agitations, but it took dramatic circumstances to make people notice.

Some writers who focused on the 1960's ignored that deeper psychological history. They looked at one generation and spoke of a fundamental "revolution" in political and cultural attitudes. They concentrated their attention upon young people, especially college students. Who were these young rebels? Some said: spearheads of a new consciousness. Others saw them as an atypical bunch of kids who would eventually be properly socialized, whereupon they would forget their wild ideas. Frightened critics characterized them as hunters after sensation, especially in sex and drugs. More modestly, some observers viewed "the revolution of the 1960's" primarily as a reaction to the war in Vietnam, especially the nightmare of being drafted and killed. When Vietnam faded away, they argued, so would the revolution. All saw the decade (1963-1974, really) as a special time and located the storm center on college campuses.

My own sense of the years was that the most interesting developments were those that happened, albeit differentially, to nearly *everybody*. The turbulence of the 1960's sprang from the same sources that had led the previous generation to seek shelter in marriage and family as the panacea for life's difficulties. The historical context was the violent, unpredictable 20th century itself. The emotions were shaped by uncertainty concerning the credibility of the grand systems of belief that had marked the long Christian era and, after 1750, of the shorter industrial period, with its sweet faith in inevitable progress.

From the emergence of the modern family early in the 19th century until well into the second half of the 20th, many Americans retreated into faith in marriage and family. That worked as long as the idealization of the nuclear family could be firmly buttressed by other, more substantial beliefs. But those beliefs faded under the onslaught of terrible events not easily explained by Christian or Enlightenment thought. Left relatively unsupported, there was no possibility that Marriage and Family as Religion could stand alone, especially in an era that also placed high value on individualism. As Carl Degler has argued, "the great values for which the family stands are at odds not only with those of the women's movement, but also with those of today's world. Democracy, individualism, and meritocracy, the values most closely identified with the last two centuries of Western history, are conspicuous by their absence from the family."[58]

Men and women in greater numbers in the 1960's began to notice if they felt unhappy in their marriages. If they did, many looked for ways out. They were willing to risk messy divorces in such numbers that by the end of the 1960's many States had legislated no-fault divorce laws, rendering a marital breakup potentially legally no more complicated than getting a driver's license. An uncontested divorce in those states came to cost little money and procedures for getting one were streamlined. Critics complain that divorce can be managed *too* easily. Sixty percent of first marriages currently end in divorce. Though the financial costs may be low and procedures simple, the emotional costs usually run high.

Among the current clichés attacking the belief in marriage, one hears, for example: "Two people cannot possibly satisfy one another for a lifetime." Some cite the burgeoning divorce rate as proof of this assertion. Marriage has come, for many, to represent a prison or a cage in which people are inhibited from personal growth and freedom. Further, it is a fashionable perception that when people do grow personally they will do so at different speeds and in divergent directions. While most divorces are followed fairly quickly by new marriages, indicating the resiliency of the institution, growing numbers wonder aloud if that road, whether taken once, twice, or thrice, leads into just another trap rather than to the good life. Millions of Americans now live alone, or unmarried with a lover (sometimes of the same sex), or in communal living arrangements. The nation today is experiencing a revolution in redefining what "family" means, with the nuclear model on its way toward becoming one among many.

The nuclear family has lost its sacrosanct position. Even when a man and woman marry, by no means do they assume that children shall inevitably follow. Many couples, particularly two-career couples, choose to remain childless. Having children can strike them as burdensome, or as self-indulgent in a world with too many people. Children are romanticized less than before. Couples know how difficult and time-consuming they are to raise. They recognize the loss in personal freedom that can ensue. They calculate how many tens of thousands of dollars it will cost to raise each child. Almost as often as children are celebrated as innocent carriers of a bright tomorrow, they are perceived as expensive burdens who exact a parental sacrifice.

Even that physical symbol of the national dream, the privately owned single-family home, has come under attack. Critics protest that it fragments society, eats up the countryside, and financially bleeds the middle class. People are being forced into high-rise apartments, few of which measure up as places for rearing children in the traditional suburban manner. For those who reject or seriously question the middle-class ideal of marriage and family, to what alternative can they turn in their pursuit of meaning? Millions of Americans have in fact come up with an answer.

Stated directly: the Self, being all that's left, has become the new center of faith for many people. All else seems external, abstract, illusory, unreal. If finding meaning through another person strikes some seekers as being no more solid than a bowl of jello, doubters will find being asked to live for either Yahweh or Rationality yet more insubstantial. One can at least see one's lover, hear his or her voice, touch and make love to the person. God and Reason speak, if they do, less obviously. However, though lovers are tangible, they have a way of entering one's life and leaving. They may be more substantial than will o' the wisps, but they can hardly be counted upon to hang around.

The self, whatever that is, at least stays. We remain with ourselves from birth to death. We must make some sort of peace with ourselves, for in a mobile, shifting world, the self and *only* the self, exists as the dominant continuing force in each person's mortal journey. Divorced or not, lots of people seek fulfillment through self-centered byways. A new hedonism has sprung up which has taken the bourgeoisie into many strange, novel places.

Though in one form or another, the Self or personal identity always informs any search for meaning, as with sex and marriage, never before has it been so consciously the object of scrutiny and regard. The vanguard of those whose energies go into "self-knowledge," "the search for identity," "self-actualization," "personal growth," (the phrases are numerous) may constitute a statistical minority of the country, but they are on the cutting edge and their numbers grow daily. They have helped make Psychology the popular discipline of our times.

Many practical consequences for a life well lived follow in the wake of faith in Self. "Freedom" replaces "security" as a holy word. A good life consists of individuals going through their "one existence on earth" thirsting to experience as much as possible, attempting everything, believing that the more one tastes of the world's inexhaustible delights the richer will be one's life: "You only come around once, so go for the gusto . . ."

The earlier era's fixation upon security seems, in this more dynamic setting, too stultifying. The search for experience, which springs from individual freedom, demands more of the individual but promises years or decades of adventure, risk, novelty, excitement, variety, and growth. Compared with the dubious security forged by marriage and family, the new freedom, say its proponents, offers the possibilities of much more fun.

Personal Freedom and Love

The major application of such a new strategy for living lives, paradoxically enough, in the old arenas: love, sex, marriage, and the family—the private sectors. Many single and divorced persons doubt that romantic love can last. Wary of marriage, many have come to view love in a serial fashion, as something one shares with many people during a lifetime.

It has become common for men and women to assume that they shall still fall deeply and passionately in love, but that such love probably will not continue "forever after." In this view each new encounter with a member of the opposite sex matters powerfully. The same assumptions apply to same-sex encounters. Homosexuality, naturally, becomes more culturally acceptable in the new self-oriented climate of opinion. Successful love-relationships in *any* form are rare and, thus, greatly to be treasured. If the partners in a gay couple can bring happiness to one another, more Americans than in previous times are inclined to applaud such good fortune. The enlarged tolerance probably does not yet extend to the majority of the American population, but with time and a successful battle against AIDS, one can imagine a generalized toleration eventually emerging toward homosexuality.

Whether homosexual or heterosexual, "modern" lovers believe they can and probably will repeat a romantic cycle many times with many different people. In that cycle, loneliness gives way as one meets the new person. The meeting is followed by interest, then the surprise of novelty, followed by the rush of anticipation fed by fantasy. If things go well, sex arrives (sometimes accompanied by intensity of feeling) and topped off by genuine love. From there some couples go into lasting connection. Far more often, the loss of novelty turns passion into warmth. The fear of commitment, combined with the fact that a huge number of variables have to come together to make a relationship work (particularly in an era in which personal fulfillment is valued so highly), leads to a diminution of good feelings. Constant contact leads to the ennui of habit. Feelings cool, bitter arguments ensue, leading to pain, boredom and finally, indifference. Sometimes the affair ends at the hating stage. The lovers part and loneliness returns . . . until the next person is met and the cycle recommences.

Richard L. Rapson

Such a love, it is believed, was not a waste of time just because it ended. Most relationships end. While it lasted it mattered, it was real. Its termination did not nullify the emotions that once existed, nor did its impermanence render the affair meaningless. Permanence does not measure the value of love. Many of these people will refer disparagingly to the lifetime of lovelessness experienced by their parents. Mom and Dad may have stayed together 50 years, but they were miserable most of the time. Time, their sons and daughters feel, needs to be lived in a different way, one in which the present counts for more, futuristic goal-orientation for less.

Each love-cycle might last for a decade, or it could go for several years, several months, a few days, or even just a couple of sexual hours. The dream of finding someone for a lifetime remains alluring. Yet the reality for many men and women is that they can count on one hand the number of marriages they truly envy. People experience the end of dozens of relationships; they know in their bones how easily and how often things can eventually go wrong. They have memorized Paul Simon's song about "Fifty Ways to Leave Your Lover." They sense that people who live alone may be happier than most of those who live with someone else.

They fear the final long stages of unhappy marriages with its life-depleting hatreds, and they look for ways to short-circuit them. One way is to avoid marriage or any serious commitment altogether. Most people find that alternative too categorical. Perhaps the agonies of the end game could be eliminated by a different set of expectations. For example, when the time came to part (as it most likely will), the "modern" couple about to break up would acknowledge the claims of transiency, note their gratitude for the good things they had shared, and express the wish that they would remain friends.

This sort of parting, they hope, would not involve the destructive mess of divorce, made more painful by the self-serving intrusions of lawyers and accountants: hence one reason why co-habitation often seems more desirable than marriage. Leave-taking would, with maturity and good will, be calm and sensible. Both parties could look forward to *new* partners who could speak to different sides of their personality. These new lovers would light up some hidden corner in that protean self which aches for expression and realization. And a new cycle begins with another person and then, perhaps another (sometimes overlapping) and yet another . . . until death parted them all.

I am talking more about city-dwellers than farmers, of a young generation more than the elderly, of whites more than blacks, of the middle-class more than the working-class, of Northerners more than folks from H.L. Mencken's "Bible Belt." I am describing a minority of the population. But without doubt it is a minority growing exponentially, and including Americans in ever-greater numbers who are middle-aged, who come from a variety of regions and ethnic groups, who live in suburbs or in the countryside, and who fit no stereotype. And I am describing attitudes toward questions of love and marriage that have entered the thoughts of most Americans, including those who think of themselves as traditional. The questions being raised would not be challenging more traditional views unless they were good questions. They have arisen because conditions have changed during this turbulent century. Even if some of the current answers to those questions are flawed, the queries themselves derive from genuine concerns.

Personal Freedom: At Work and In Love

A fairly similar pattern has operated with respect to work. In the age of marriage and family, a commitment to *vertical* mobility was the rule. The individual, usually a man, made a decision to stay in one type of job for life, just as he devoted himself to one spouse. He would then spend many years making his way into that vocation, whether it be through apprenticeship in the union, company, or office or else *via* graduate school for teaching, engineering, business, law, or medicine.

In those fields, especially the professions, he began the career at the bottom of the corporate hierarchy or the university or the law firm or the hospital. He would then spend his life climbing up the ladder of success in that institution, hoping not to die before the higher rungs had been attained.

For most women, the commitment was to the husband, the home, and the children. Having no "climbing" to do (except, perhaps, up the walls), frustration frequently developed, particularly for educated women. Though domestic life was central to men as well, the job furnished the husband the setting for his role as Provider. That work often turned out to be interesting in itself and it at least offered the challenge of trying to rise to the top.

In the 1960's, with its relative prosperity, *horizontal* mobility appealed to some people as an interesting alternative to the more traditional work pattern. When it came to making money, one would not make a long-term commitment to any one vocation. Rather one would do that which seemed stimulating at the time. As with a mate, when that job grew stale, the new "free" person left to find new work.

Women entered the job market in great numbers during the 1960's as part of their response to traditional roles and to weakened marriages. As did many of their male counterparts, many women worked at a well-paying, clearly temporary job (such as waiting tables) mainly to accumulate money. When they had saved enough, they could quit for a while in order to travel or play. Then they returned to a different job that seemed appealing at the time and would pay the bills. Then, when boredom set in, on to something else. No rising. Much movement and flexibility. This zigzag pattern yielded less long-term financial security and more short-term personal freedom. Horizontal mobility now looks to be a luxury affordable only during prosperous periods such as the 1960's or to privileged groups. The harder economic times of the 1970's forced a return to traditional career-consciousness—a return that, during the Reagan years, took on some obsessive qualities.

But if upward mobility on one career path has returned, transiency has continued in the arena of things and places. Americans still throw away material goods as they wear out, which happens often in an economy of planned obsolescence. And one out of five families moves every year, uprooting communities in the never-ending search for The

New Beginning. In the1970's and 1980's much of that movement transferred citizens from the Northeast and Midwest to the Sunbelt states of the South and West.

The same restlessness marks lifestyles and philosophies. The search for a particular, permanent religious or philosophical label, or for the proper style of living, strikes many people as unnecessary. Life may have no Meaning, some contend, but it may bring forth many meanings. So one tries on a variety of religions, philosophies, fads, friends, and identities just as one moves to new places to live every five years and buys new automobiles every four. When one tires of one's car, or city, or style of life, or system of belief, let alone one's current lover or spouse, one moves on to the next. Thus have things gone up to now in the final third of the 20th century.

What, then, of the rush to new Absolutes—meditation, drugs as religion, astrology, various mystery cults, Zen, the multiplying sensitivity groups, eastern religions, the variety of new Messiahs, Swamis, pop psychologists, psychics, gurus, and Shirley MacLaine? What about (among a different sector of the society) the resurgence of "born-agains," of the Moral Majority, of fundamentalism and Pat Robertson, of Tammy Faye and TV preachers?

The first group tends to gather under the umbrella name: "New Age" people. The latter group assembles under more conservative campground tents. Together with more mainstream Protestants and Catholics, they constitute a substantial majority of the population, proclaiming belief in God (variously defined) and some sort of an afterlife. The existentialists are barely audible in the United States. Does not this widespread pursuit of "answers" in fact signal a fear of the Self, a retreat from freedom, multiplicity, flexibility, openness, and complexity into a renewed search for Security?

This dash for certainty contains echoes of Ivan Karamazov's dream in Dostoevsky's *The Brothers Karamazov* wherein the Grand Inquisitor rails against Jesus. The Inquisitor condemns Jesus, telling him that people despise freedom and crave authority, fear questions and prefer answers, almost any answers, if only they are propounded rigidly, authoritatively, and unambiguously enough.

Intellectual openness has been buffeted by conservative Christianity, and even New Age mystics on the left do not go out of their way to put in kind words for secular humanism. All this underscores the fact that I am *not* associating the focus on self in the United States with existentialism or secular humanism or even intellectual openness. Americans shy away from such serious ideas. Throughout this book I have tilted toward Tocqueville in his depiction of the United States as the quintessential bourgeois society, little concerned with, and more than that, distrustful of, intellectuality and philosophy. Americans are, as Daniel Boorstin sees them, a "practical people," and I agree with Richard Hofstadter when he identifies a powerful *anti*-intellectual tendency throughout the nation's history.

The United States, when compared with the rest of the industrial world, still wears the robes of a religious, almost mystically-oriented society. But, characteristically, that religiosity runs quite shallowly. In 1986, a Gallup poll determined that 90% of Americans believed in the existence of a Supreme Being, and well over 70% proclaimed the reality of life-after-death, with the great majority of that 70% quite confident that they themselves were safely designated for Heaven. The National Opinion Research Center at the University of Chicago in that same year found that nearly a third of the population claimed a degree of clairvoyance. Traditional or New Age, most Americans cling to forms of mysticism, but also tend to take positions that they have not thought through in much detail or depth. They have better things to do with their time.

It is their *meta*-message that best reveals the emerging climate of opinion, more than answers to poll-takers' questions about a universe that works so nicely. "New Age" folks, in particular, shape and reflect that new spirit. When we examine their behaviors and deepest concerns it is evident that most of them belong well within the self-oriented milieu under discussion. How well do their communal affirmations fit with the individualistic mode? How does their spiritual quest comport with a lifestyle often regarded as hedonistic?

The key lies in the *proliferation* of mystical and psychological cults. There are thousands of them, and it is not uncommon for a New Age person to adhere to several different practices at one time, switching to new ones all the time. While the proliferation of New Religions superficially resembles a return to earlier ways of thought, the short-term hold they exert on their practitioners furnishes another sign that people desire to live multiple lives with multiple roles and beliefs. These various absolutes, though some are more serious than others, emit some of the evanescent flavor of fads, of hula hoops and saddle shoes. Most of them quickly appear and disappear, not only in our national life, but in people's personal routines.

New panaceas appear every few months. People often try them out with great zeal and sincerity, only to move on to something else when the value and novelty begin to wear thin. Converts embrace channeling, or they swear fealty toward Jonathan Livingston Seagull, the Moonies, primal screaming, kundalini yoga, Norman Vincent Peale, running as religion, physical fitness as salvation, Rajneesh, Maharaj-Ji, Tibetan Buddhism, Time Masters, tarot cards, psychic readings, re-birthing, Rolfing, bio-energetics, neuro-linguistic programming, dressing for success, or the hundreds of "how to get ahead and win and be number one" outfits that pop up daily. More often than not they know they will enjoy the new "Truth" and probably benefit from it for a while, but not forever. Instant, packaged salvation can—like new lovemates, jobs, hometowns, modular houses, and inflatable furniture—be savored while fresh and then replaced as they lose their tang. People try on and shed new faiths in much the same way they do lovers.

Even more to the point, the purpose of nearly all the current gospels is to put believers "in touch" with *themselves,* to aid in the establishment and affirmation of personal identity, to help them "get ahead" or "achieve that potential that lies within us all," to make people "feel good about themselves." The substance of the new programs reflects obsession with Self. Interestingly enough, one can make a case that even the right-wing evangelical faiths may have as much to do with self-help as traditional commitment. Many enthusiasts who raise their hands for Jesus and who contribute hard-earned dollars to millionaire TV preachers lose some of their zeal after relatively short periods of fervor. Many Americans try on Jesus for a while, but lose interest if and when the immediate burst of revelation ceases to make them feel better about themselves and life.

The cumulative effect of this variety of lives, wives, jobs, mates, places, things, lifestyles, identities, and faiths tends to be, in addition to novelty and renewal, a temporal disconnectedness. This makes existence take on the form, in William Irwin Thompson's metaphor, of television sets rather than novels: "No longer," Thompson wrote, "need a person carry the burden of a single identity from the cradle to the grave. He is free to change lives and wives as often as he has the energy. I imagine that the way Marshall McLuhan would describe this pattern is that the individual is no longer a novel, but a television set: at the flip of a channel he changes his program."[59]

In novels, Chapter Two follows from the first chapter in a linear fashion. Chapter Two then leads logically into Chapter Three. On television, Channel Two may carry a sitcom. Switch to Channel Four for news film of the latest bloody fighting in the Middle East. Flip to Channel Five to watch Larry Bird dunking the basketball and go on to Channel Seven which runs a commercial for the G.O.P. candidate for the U.S. House of Representatives in District X. Thompson, in using the novel/TV metaphor, had been sketching shapes of disconnectedness in Southern California, the place where the nation's future often germinates. He went on to note that now those patterns have leapt beyond the confines of Los Angeles:

> Disneyland itself is a kind of television set, for one flips from medieval castles to submarines and rockets . . . . But these discontinuities of history are no longer to be contained by Disneyland and Southern California . . . . Even now as one looks out the window of his Boeing 720 on the L.A.-to-Boston run, it seems as if he were flipping channels on a continental T.V. set: California tracts, Southwestern desert, a drink, and then it's Rocky Mountains, Green Iowa, the Finger Lakes, the Hudson, and then back, in time, as well as space, to Boston.
>
> Lacking the strong connective tissue of tradition, the individual can entertain in his fantasy life various possible identities. Since nothing is to stop him from acting out his fantasies, he can flip from identity to new identity, changing jobs and communities, as he makes his odyssey through the vast Mediterranean world of Southern California.[60]

Benjamin DeMott, in observing the apparent changes in people's lives at the beginning of the 1970's in *Surviving the Seventies,* rejected the notion that the developments of the previous decade were well-explained by notions of hedonism or those simply of a youthful rebellion. What was happening was happening in some degree to almost everyone: to wives contemplating divorce after a dozen years of marriage; to men leaving careers of 25-years duration in order to work at something which brought them pleasure and new challenge; to blacks daring to be themselves; to homosexuals and teenagers, to rich and poor, to men and women, to minorities and W.A.S.P.s, to young and old. In DeMotts' words:

Major changes have been occurring in our sense of self, time and dailiness. For one thing, we've become obsessed with Experience. (We behave, that is to say, as though we're determined to change our relation to our experience, or to have "usual" experiences in new ways.) For another, we've come to relish plurality of self. (We behave as though impatient or bitter at every structure, form, convention and practice that edges us toward singleness of view or "option" or that forces us to accept this or that single role as the whole truth of our being.) For yet another, we seem to be striving to feel time itself on different terms, anxious to shed ordinary linear, before-and-after, cause-and-effect understandings of events even in our personal lives. (We feel distaste for inward response that's insufficiently alive to The Moment, or that glides over each instant as a betweenness—in another minute it'll be time to go to work, go to dinner, write our brother, make love, do the dishes—rather than living into it, inhabiting it as an occasion, without the thought of antecedents or consequences.) And finally, we've conceived a detestation of the habitual. (We are seeking ways of opening our minds and characters to the multiplicity of situations. We hope to replace habit—"the shackles of the free," in Bierce's great definition—with a continually renewed alertness to possibility.)[61]

The open, flexible persons experience all conceivable variety on their free-swinging passages through life. They are without the traditional external anchors, signposts, and securities. Their baggage consists only of each individual self, which happens also to be considered multiple, a universe unto itself. They feel, in their journey of non-stop discovery, exhilaration or exhaustion, freedom or rootlessness. If we can invent the proper language with which to depict the realities of this emerging protean, often narcissistic, existence, then it may be easier to ask the right kinds of questions so as to make the prospects of this new way of living richer, happier, and stabler than, at first glance, it looks to be.

FOR LOVE, FOR MONEY, OR FOR MYSELF?

I have sketched a transition from a population seeking meaning through marriage and family to one increasingly looking for meaning through self-oriented experiences and awareness. If my vocabulary is useful it would suggest we ask at least this question: can we reconcile the goals of security (in the style of the 1950's and before) with those of personal freedom? Some cynics would contend that Americans have long found such reconciliation—in money. If you are rich, you have by definition purchased security *and* freedom. Americans believe above all else, they say, in money; the rest is psychological puffery.

This argument contains considerable truth. The desire for and belief in the value of material success has been a bedrock national religion for over 150 years. But the *uses* of money have in fact changed in accordance with the shifting climates of opinion, and these differences matter. Hence, in the 19th-century experiment with equality of opportunity, money furnished the measure of how well one did in the achievement-oriented competitive society; the things one could buy were secondary. Entrepreneurs relished the chase for wealth, but many who won the race, when they were certain of their victory, often disembarrassed themselves by giving their millions away.

Financially successful husbands during most of the 20th century (including those of modest means), poured their earnings into their families. As the age of marriage and the family gives way to the age of faith in the self, more people, men *and* women, spend their money on themselves. They buy fun, sexual appeal, and the immediate gratifications that they enjoy with less guilt than they ever did before. The desire for money may be fairly constant, but the changing climates of opinion within which the bourgeois, capitalist-thinking Americans have lived, have given texture both to their materialism and to much of their psychology. These climates have helped to shape their inner, emotional lives as well as their confrontation with the material world.

Finally, whether we talk about a population seeking meaning either through money, or through marriage and family, or through self-realization, it is clear that in all these circumstance we are describing a people fixed on their *private* needs. The divorce between public and private concerns has been more pronounced in this century than ever before. The implications for a nation whose citizens focus almost exclusively on the satisfaction of private desires, while in the pubic arena they keep themselves generally uninterested, ignorant, and impotent, do not add up, in this threatening age, to an altogether reassuring prospect.

AFTERWORD

When I ask my students to raise their hands if they consider themselves "feminists," almost no hands rise, including those of my women students. That is surprising and disconcerting for this feminist. But when I follow up with a second query to the effect that if feminism were defined simply as the belief that women should have the same choices and opportunities in life as men, would they then call themselves "feminists"? To this, nearly everyone raises his or her hands.

So what is going on here? I always defined feminism in that form—equal opportunity everywhere for women with men. In discussions of this paradox, it became clear that "feminism" had been made into a bad word in America. It was a sign of backlash and a victory for those who oppose the women's movement; the term had become associated with angry male-hating women, with bra burning, and hostility to sex, especially of the heterosexual kind. My young women did not clamor for those associations.

In further discussions, it became clear that most of my students, male and female, simply took for granted that equal opportunity for women was a reality, that it had been achieved. This was healthy for those of us who champion gender equality: these women would simply pursue whatever career or life (with our without marriage and children) they wished. In that sense the women's movement seems to have achieved major successes, and women were now doing everything: running for President, driving trucks, displaying athletic prowess, filling up the rosters of graduate schools of all kinds, running businesses, holding nearly 1/6 of the seats in Congress after the 2006 election (which is still far from 50%!), fighting in the military, and reporting news from the most dangerous hot spots in the world. It doesn't seem strange anymore to see women engaged in all kinds of activities.

On the other hand, such blithe indifference to the battles women have had to wage in the past, and to the continuing resistance to gender equality, may ill-equip them to recognize that resistance and be ready to do battle when called to the task. Whether from the right wing with its opposition to abortion rights, divorce, and even birth control to those at every point of the political spectrum who emphasize gender differences (Men Are From Mars, Women Are From Venus) or who promote premature reports about fundamental biological differences between the sexes (the real story is of tremendous variability within both genders), America is far from achieving gender equality and the forces arrayed against that remain formidable. Many northern European countries are far closer to achieving such equality than is the United States.

In the long run, gender equality will prevail. Once people experience choice, giving it up is a bit like trying to stuff toothpaste back in the tube after it has been squeezed out. But the long run may not be soon enough for all of my students, let alone the less educated. The final chapters in the battle for gender equality have not yet been written. As we approach the second decade of the new millennium in American, men continue to hold the vast majority of the keys to power.

Guess Who's Coming to Dinner

10

The Fate of Egalitarianism

CYCLES, SPIRALS, AND FORWARD MOVEMENTS

T he two largest groups generally excluded from the egalitarian experiment in opportunity have been women and blacks. This chapter looks at the overall direction of the nation's chief claim to value—the egalitarian experiment. It focuses particularly on the three major social revolutions of our time: the black struggle for equality, the women's movement, and the upheaval in sexual mores. All of them carry immense implications for the future of the nation and, because they generate so much heat, it has not always been easy to distinguish the durable elements from the sensational.

Background: The 1920's to the 1960's

After the First World War ended in 1918, changes in manners and ethical standards which had been building for several decades burst into the open. New norms overcame tradition, not only among progressive groups, but also with the conservative custodians of culture. The older rules insisted upon respect for parental authority; they cast the father as lord of the family, the husband as master of his wife; they insisted upon pre-marital chastity and fidelity in marriage for women. Men operated by different sexual standards.

The frequently successful assault upon this system manifested itself primarily in the 1920's. Much of it focused upon transformations in sexual norms and in the role of women in society. The following examples all fall into the period between 1918 and 1929:

1. The first conscious youth rebellion, with adolescents defining themselves as a group separate from the rest of the population, challenged old rules about sexual conduct.

2. The automobile enlarged chances for love-making far beyond what could be managed in chaperoned sitting rooms.
3. A distorted view of Freud gained popularity. Many believed that any suppression of sexual desires would cause an outbreak of mental illness, warts, and pimples.
4. There was a generalized obsession with sex. Promiscuity became a fact with college and even high school students. Confession magazines stormed the citadels of popular literature, telling shocking stories about "fallen women," many of them in their teens. The sexy Clara Bow—the "It" girl—replaced the demure Mary Pickford as the idol of the movies.
5. The fox trot and Charleston superceded the well-mannered waltz as the dance of choice.
6. Women gained the vote in 1920 with the ratification of the 19th Amendment to the Constitution.
7. Middle-class women increasingly took jobs in teaching, service industries and business. They also moved into the professions in larger numbers. Women in farming decreased while those in domestic service held steady.
8. Homemakers were aided by startling technological advances.
   As Arthur Link wrote:

> More readily available electrical appliances, central heat. and processed food products reduced the time and drudgery of housework for most urban women. Gas and electricity replaced wood and coal as primary sources of energy, and these fuels lessened or eliminated the tasks of chopping and carrying wood and cleaning the ever-present soot and dirt from fireplaces and stoves. Running water, hot and cold, freed housewives of other responsibilities, as did the widespread availability of refrigerators and gas and electric stoves. Equally significant were innovations in cleaning technologies: vacuum cleaners and washing machines resulted in tremendous reductions of human energy expended at home. These changes in the home environment added up to gains in productivity which matched those in industry. Housework, like factory work. entered an age of mechanization.[62]

9. Women gained power as they earned money. They married at an older age, bore fewer children, and more often than ever before divorced their husbands. Between 1914 and 1940, the divorce rate nearly doubled.
10. Women redefined what "proper" women could do. They smoked cigarettes and drank with men. Their fashions changed. "The average skirt was about six inches from the ground in 1919. From this time on the ascent was spectacular, until the skirt had reached the knees or even above by 1927."[63]
11. Families accelerated their movement from being units of economic production to collectives defined by love. Happiness became the chief object of marriage.
12. Women and children achieved more equality in families.[64]

These were changes of enormous consequence. They were accompanied by the more general cult of self that also had its clearest origins in the 1920's. Some of the reasons have already been discussed, but its strongest expressions can be found in the literature of the period. The spiritual vacuum left in the wake of the 1914-1918 War deprived writers of general philosophical reference points for their work. They had no choice but to turn inward and forge a subjective reality built around themselves. Howard Mumford Jones wrote:

> So far as I can remember, no literary period previous to ours has tried to establish the authority of art on the premise that the world of the spirit has vanished. The lonely writer of our time, however, having denied religion and having severed himself from virtually every other traditional function of the artist, is too often trying to produce an entire universe of discourse out of his own consciousness . . . .[65]

Jones arrived at this conclusion after analyzing the literature of the 1920's. He focused on Amory Blaine in F. Scott Fitzgerald's *This Side of Paradise* and noted that because "the existing order" did not give Blaine scope for his aesthetic perceptions and his emotional desires, "he found love, business, politics, and religion futile, and at the end of the novel falls back upon himself for the meaning of existence." What was true for Blaine/Fitzgerald "became the attitude of many writers in the twenties and since." Jones saw the cult of self in such works as *The Enormous Room* by E.E. Cummings, John Dos Passos' *Three Soldiers*, Thomas Wolfe's *Look Homeward Angel*, and *Main Street* by Sinclair Lewis. In fact, he concluded that "almost any anthology of recent and contemporary American poetry reveals the continuance of a solipsistic philosophy."[66]

In the 1970's, Robert Elias showed how the 1920's in all respects, not just the literary, was the seedbed for the general accelerated withdrawal from public to private concerns. Elias wrote in his aptly titled book, *"Entangling Alliance with None": An Essay on the Individual in the American Twenties*:

> If one undertakes to say what is historical about a period in which behaviorists, Freudians, and followers of John Dewey flourish, in which Andrew Mellon is thought to be the greatest secretary of the treasury since Alexander Hamilton, in which Calvin Coolidge is the representative president and Charles Lindbergh the ultimate hero, in which at the same time as Sinclair Lewis, Hemingway, and Eliot establish themselves as important writers, one must find some links. To put it simply, one must find out what John B. Watson, Coolidge, and Hemingway shared.[67]

The answer was "a commitment to discrete individuality—a commitment that gave the decade its distinctive mark." In all walks of life one could find overweening concern for the personal, a powerful privatization of interest, a fixation on:

the interested, selfish individual, with his secular concerns . . . . The Progressive Era, full of hope for a society dedicated to the general welfare, had culminated in American participation in a world war that many Americans felt subsumed the individual in abstractions and divorced the personal good from personal interest. The twenties exposed these slogans; those years reinstated the personal.[68]

Any close scrutiny of the 1920's demonstrates a striking connection between that decade and our own time, underscoring its decisive importance in shaping contemporary attitudes. The Depression of the 1930's and the World War of the next decade diverted attention from the basic privatization ushered in during the 20's, but only for a while. Elias pointed out:

After reading about the changes in marital relations and the arguments about education in the earlier decade, one looks at those of the sixties and seventies with a feeling of *déjà vu*. After immersing oneself in the feeling of political withdrawal that the earlier Republicans expressed, one wonders whether nowadays an old story is simply being retold.[69]

Arthur Schlesinger, Jr., modifying in 1987 his father's famous thesis, believes that old stories get told and retold many times. He has tracked a 30-year cycle during which issues of public purpose dominate and are then followed by years in which private interest takes over. This corresponds fairly closely to his father's description of shifts between liberalism and conservatism, each ruling the roost for an average of 16 years apiece. The newest formulation works slightly better. "People can never be fulfilled for long," says the younger Schlesinger, "either in the public or in the private sphere. We try one, then the other, and frustration compels a change in course . . . . Each phase breeds its distinctive contradictions."[70]

The periods of reform achieve most of their gains early and quickly. "Public action, in its effort to better our condition, piles up a lot of change in rather short order. Reform in the United States tends come in bursts." After the Hundred Days of Franklin Roosevelt, the momentum of change slowly subsided over a period of many years.

Sustained public action . . . is emotionally exhausting. A nation's capacity for high-tension political commitment is limited. Nature insists on a respite. People can no longer gird themselves for heroic effort. They yearn to immerse themselves in the privacies of life. Worn out by the constant summons to battle, weary of ceaseless national activity, disillusioned by the results, they seek a new dispensation, an interlude of rest and recuperation.[71]

The nation then moves on to the period of private interest. "Public action, passion, idealism, and reform recede. Public problems," writes Schlesinger, "are turned over to the invisible hand of the market." Social salvation now will be delivered by pursuing private interest. We enter times of privatization, "of materialism, hedonism and the overriding quest for personal gratification. Class and interest politics subside; cultural politics—ethnicity, religion, social status, morality—come to the fore." Often during these times innovations of the previous period "are absorbed and legitimized," so that consolidation can occur.

But the cycle continues on its way:

> Epochs of private interest breed contradictions too. Such periods are characterized by undercurrents of dissatisfaction, criticism, ferment, protest. Segments of the population fall behind in the acquisitive race. Intellectuals are estranged. Problems neglected become acute, threaten to become unmanageable and demand remedy. People grow bored with selfish motives and vistas, weary of materialism as the ultimate goal. The vacation from public responsibility replenishes the national energies and recharges the national batteries.[72]

In the Schlesinger model, the most recent epochs of private concentration have shown up in the 1890's, the 1920's, the 1950's, and the 1980's. Public concerns have dominated during the 1900's (the Progressive era), the 1930's (the New Deal), and the 1960's (the New Frontier and the Great Society). The next wave of reform, if on schedule, should appear by the 1990's. With the victory of the Democratic Party in the 1986 congressional elections, followed closely by the Iran-Contra exposures which dramatized a number of grotesqueries of Reagan's foreign policy and destroyed his shield from criticism, the next period of public interest—whether led by Republicans or Democrats is not the key variable—appeared to be on the way, Should that come about, the cyclical scheme would continue on track.

Because of its value, this model raises many questions. Does the nation, for example, move back and forth like a pendulum, oscillating between fixed points? No, said Schlesinger *pere*. A better image was the spiral, since the nation did not return, during the private interest epochs, to the same point as the public purpose era. The periods of privatization generally absorbed the legislation that preceded it. Schlesinger *fils* also employed the spiral image.

Between 1910 and 1950, the scholars who dominated the writing of American history not only adopted this view, but they also laced it with a judgment. The public interest periods were the "good" eras because they advanced the needs of the majority instead of the claims of capitalism (profit, property, free market, Social Darwinism). These were the liberal periods, and their leaders were seen as the nation's great Presidents: Jefferson in the 1800's; Jackson in the 1830's; Lincoln in the 1860's; Teddy Roosevelt and Woodrow Wilson for the 15 years which began this century; Franklin Roosevelt in the 1930's; and John Kennedy in the 1960's. This group of scholars, collectively called "Progressive historians"—both as a description of their political inclinations and in commemoration of the time of their historical school's birth (publication in 1913 of Charles Beard's extraordinarily influential *An Economic Interpretation of the Constitution*)—constituted a *Who's Who* of the profession: Beard, Frederick Jackson Turner, Vernon Parrington, Samuel Eliot Morison, Allan Nevins, Dumas Malone, Henry Steele Commager, and both Schlesingers.

The Progressive historians also postulated a tension between capitalism and democracy. Both systems began as allies against feudalism and monarchy. They share faith in majority rule, individual freedom, limited government, and equality before the law. But they differ after that. If capitalism places special value on profit maximization, competition, and the sanctity of property, proponents of democracy emphasize, in Schlesinger, Jr.'s words, "equality, freedom, social responsibility and the general welfare, ends to be promoted when necessary by public action regulating property and restricting profit."[73] While the overlap is considerable and most Americans would regard themselves as both capitalists and democrats, the Progressive historians underscore the conflict and ally themselves with the forces of democracy.

The cycle they describe possesses an inner dynamic that renders it independent of the unpredictable vicissitudes of economic and political life. Progressive reforms at the beginning of the 20th century, for instance, came during a period of prosperity, while the New Deal responded to the crash of the economy in 1929. Yet there is nothing inevitable in the cycles. Strong, able leaders must seize the moment. That is why these historians presented the nation with a roll-call of larger-than-life heroes who met their rendezvous with destiny straight on.

Between 1950 and 1970, a distinguished collection of historians challenged these views. They felt their predecessors had overstated the importance of conflict in American life; the younger scholars laid stress upon the agreements between so-called liberals and conservatives. These "consensus" historians included people like Richard Hofstadter (who, with good reason and without great success, resisted being placed in this camp), David Potter, C. Vann Woodward, Louis Hartz, Carl Degler, and Daniel Boorstin.

In *The American Political Tradition*, Hofstadter looked at the two political traditions—conservative (capitalist) vs. liberal (democratic)—that the progressives saw locked in conflict and see-sawing in ascendancy. He saw that the two traditions might, in reality, be just one; he discerned fake conflict full of sound and fury and signifying nothing where others described dramatic combat. In a famous passage, Hofstadter wrote:

> The fierceness of the political struggles has often been misleading; for the range of vision embraced by the primary contestants in the major parties has always been bounded by the horizons of property and enterprise. However much at odds on specific issues, the major political traditions have shared a belief in the rights of property, the philosophy of economic individualism, the value of competition; they have accepted the economic virtues of capitalist culture as necessary qualities of man. Even when some property right has been challenged—as it was by followers of Jefferson and Jackson—in the

name of the rights of man or the rights of the community, the challenge, when translated into practical policy. has actually been urged on behalf of some other kind of property.

The sanctity of private property, the right of the individual to dispose of and invest it, the value of opportunity, and the natural evolution of self-interest and self-assertion, within broad legal limits, into a beneficent social order have been staple tenets of the central faith in American political ideologies; these conceptions have been shared in large part by men as diverse as Jefferson, Jackson, Lincoln, Cleveland, Bryan, Wilson, and Hoover. The business of politics—so the creed runs—is to protect this competitive world, to foster it on occasion, to patch up its incidental abuses, but not to cripple it with a plan for common collective action. American traditions also show a strong bias in favor of equalitarian democracy, but it has been a democracy in cupidity rather than a democracy of fraternity.[74]

Hofstadter deplored this consensus and longed for rigorous, systemic political debate about genuine issues instead of the noisy but essentially empty carryings-on between Democrats and Republicans. The two political parties looked to consensus historians like Tweedledee railing against Tweedledum. The major historiographical debate of the post-World War II decades was over whether conflict or consensus shaped American public life.

That debate has always seemed to me another example of sound and fury. The Progressives were right in seeing turmoil and difference in society. But step back a few paces and compare the United States with European nations, and this country does appear to be significantly less divided and ideological than France or Italy or even Great Britain. "The consensus point of view is limited," wrote Hofstadter 20 years after the label of "consensus" historian was placed upon him, "in that it is only an assertion about the frame or the configuration of history and not about what goes on in the picture."[75]

Reconciling the consensus and conflict models still leaves unanswered the more interesting question of change. Whether through conflict or non-ideological consensus, where has the United States been headed? What transformations can be detected? Where is the nation currently headed? Can we discern any linear movement in our society?

Probably the only clear linear movement in modern history has been in technology. We are getting more technologically sophisticated all the time. Everything else seems to move in less consistent ways, back-and-forth, varying from class to class, region to region. But in both the Schlesinger and Hofstadter schemes, I think that certain fairly clear changes are discernible.

The one most pertinent for understanding this country involves its central theme: *equality of opportunity*. In the tension between capitalism and democracy, the bridge spanning the two is the idea of equality of opportunity. More opportunity in a capitalist world can lead to greater political participation in a democratic society. Has opportunity been expanding? Through the decades, have more groups been let in on the competitive scramble described by Hofstadter? Has each age of reform described by the Progressive historians left *permanently* a larger proportion enjoying the fruits of opportunity and democracy than before the reforms began?

The answers clearly seem to be "yes." Without plunging deeply into the past, and by looking only at two major dispossessed groups, blacks and women, important changes leap off the page. Blacks were better off in 1920, after the Progressive reforms, than in 1900; better off in 1940, after the New Deal and despite the Depression than in 1920; better off after the Warren Court decisions and the Civil Rights Act of 1965 than during the combat in World War II when the troops were racially segregated; better off today than they have ever been in this nation's sorry history of race relations. With great distances remaining to be traversed, it feels safe to predict that (backward steps notwithstanding) the march of blacks toward equal opportunity will continue to advance.

Women have reached a position of strength and possibility unmatched in the country's past, even after the unsympathetic years of the Reagan administration. It remains, though, to define "better off," to determine what steps or obstacles lie ahead, and what the general future of equality of opportunity might be in an age of limits.

Catalyst For Change: The Sixties

Between John Kennedy's campaign for the Presidency in 1960 and Richard Nixon's exit from office in disgrace in 1974 fell a period of intense social change. Those years ushered in great changes in white America. But add on the now-mythic struggles of blacks and one must mark the beginning of the era in 1954, when the Supreme Court outlawed school segregation in *Brown vs. Board of Education*. Between 1954 and 1974, an extra rush of emotion swept across the land in 1963 when President Kennedy was slain.

The outcry in the years after 1963 took most dramatic form in the street demonstrations against the war in Vietnam, in the various liberation movements, in calls for sexual freedom and the expanded use of drugs, in the rock music, the working class dress, and the new lifestyles that seemed concentrated on and near college campuses throughout the country. Men grew their hair long and some wore flowers. Women shed makeup (or obvious makeup), grew their hair not only long, but also limp, and straight, switched to blue jeans and men's clothes, frequently abandoned brassieres, and swore a lot. Working-class clothing and a nose-thumbing at fashion became fashionable. Food became more organic, music more electrified, beards bushier, language blacker.

Bob Dylan said it best when he mocked the middle class with his snarled nasal declaration that "something's going on here and you don't know what it is, do you Mr. Jones?" The across-the-board challenge hurled at nearly every middle-class dictum reached far and wide. Sexual prohibitions were flouted. Family was mocked. Institutional Christianity was rejected. Patriotism was scorned, universities closed down, career ambitions and achievements were ridiculed, capitalism reviled, the government abused, racial shibboleths flouted, marriage criticized, commercial sports challenged, America disliked.

Though some regarded the movement as dead by the 1970's, they often overlooked the continuity of change, taking the dramatic outward forms of the period to constitute its essence. When those forms faded, they wrote the obituary for a lost revolution. Yet when people joined together in communal living situations (and they were not all young, nor by any means were all the young involved), when they experimented with drugs, created counter-cultural commercial enterprises, and publicly demonstrated how to "make love, not war," they were proposing potentially invigorating living patterns. In the new order, love, spontaneity, freedom, mysticism, and sensuality would flourish where possessiveness, up-tightness, the need for security, the hang up on materialism, and the denial of the body had previously reigned.

In the context of the Reagan years, much of this sounded quaint. The deep, long-standing national commitment to materialist values resurfaced. Most Americans do love money and, structurally, ours has always been a business civilization. The phrase, popular in the 1980's—"I am into money"—demonstrated how traditional materialism can masquerade behind "groovy" language.

But some basic precepts of the 1960's have not died. As I said before, they *appear* to have done so only because the society has not been clear about what was fundamental and what was fluff. Fundamental was the sense that traditional external sources of meaning and happiness—the right marriage, the simple equation of wealth with happiness, once-a-week Christianity, male W.A.S.P. Americanism—might be inadequate strategies for a complicated world.

At bottom, lots of people—female and male, black and white, poor and rich, freaks and straights, old and young—began to feel that they had to rely more on themselves, on internal stabilities, on private strengths, on personally-derived truths in order to handle that difficult world. The realization affected some more than others, but in one degree or another it has affected the majority of citizens. Despite rejections of the flamboyant, ephemeral side of the Sixties, the deeper, slower, less flashy, and more diffused effort to redefine The Good Life has persevered. But it goes on without the ebullient sense of liberation and renewal that characterized the 1960's at their best, and made it such an exciting, if disorienting time. Gone is the sense of power, the general spirit of newness—new ideas, attitudes, and outlooks—that functioned as the engine of social change. Weakened is the passion and confidence behind reform. *Not* gone are the advances toward equal opportunity of the two most active reforming groups: blacks and women.

BLACKS

Arthur Schlesinger, Jr.'s cyclical theory postulated an era of public interest and reform dating from the end of the 1950's until the end of Richard Nixon's first term in

Richard L. Rapson

1972. The late years of the Eisenhower Administration were set against the movement for Civil Rights in the South—a movement sculpted chiefly by a remarkable group of black men and women. Schlesinger includes Nixon's first presidential years because Nixon then supported considerable far-reaching domestic legislation.

The commencement of the era of private concern coincided with Nixon's second term when his antipathy for political opponents led him to the Watergate debacle. The era includes the Democratic Administration of Jimmy Carter from 1977-1981, a man whom Schlesinger characterized as the most conservative Democratic President of the century. The Reagan years, apart from the disarmament agreements that followed, ground to a halt when the Democrats gained control of the Senate and the Iran-Contra deceptions surfaced, both in November 1986. And those two blows against Reagan no doubt contributed greatly to the President's interest in arms control.

While Schlesinger's theory makes sense, so does the proposition that the entire period from the late 1950's to the present saw, in periods of public interest *and* private obsession, gains unparalleled in the nation's history for blacks and women. The advance did not remain consistent during these decades and sometimes there were pauses and brief backward passages. But gains in the rights of these two huge groups moved fairly steadily and were of such significance that future history books could easily refer to the period 1954 *(Brown vs. Board of Education)* onward as the epoch of successful black and women's social revolution, indeed as the most revolutionary period in American history since the 1830's. This obvious point, not often made, needs to be stated in simple, undisguised words. It is a linear advance superimposed in bold relief upon any cyclical model.

The women's movement quieted during the 1970's chiefly because it had convinced people to listen during the previous decade and no longer needed to shout so insistently. Initial success permitted solid, if less spectacular work to continue, though there is a very long way to go. On the day when I composed the first draft of this essay, for example, the conservative Rehnquist Supreme Court in the seventh year of the conservative Reagan Administration ruled that affirmative action for women in hiring was the law of the land.

The cause of racial justice has also registered dramatic gains since the desegregation of the armed forces and the arrival of Jackie Robinson into baseball's big leagues in the 1940's, and especially since the boycotts and marches in Birmingham, Selma, and Montgomery in the 1950's. Though the Civil Rights movement sometimes seems to lack consistent direction, it continues to register gains. Institutionalized discrimination has been removed in myriad places. White stereotypes of blacks have become more varied and complex; perhaps the most popular American in the 1980's was Bill Cosby. Millions of blacks, as idealized by Cosby's TV family, have entered the middle class in recent decades. We sometimes forget just how far the United States has advanced beyond its nightmarish pre-1950's racism and widespread refusal among whites even to see blacks as human.

We forget because blacks and other minorities still suffer enormous injustices. But the movement of reform has not been reversed. New problems have surfaced, some

146

directly as a result of advance. We witness a widened gap, for instance, between the new armies of middle-class blacks and those who remain trapped in the ghettos.

Still it is no small accomplishment that large numbers of whites as well as blacks now believe that black can be beautiful, that black fashion, black music, black language, and a stunning array of black talent in entertainment and sports enrich white America. When whites begin also to recognize black achievement in science, literature, the professions, and in the academy, then integration could eventually replace the whitewashing process of assimilation as the strategy-of-choice for advancement.

But even that won't do much good if black unemployment runs three or four times higher than white, if the cities remain ghettoized, education unequal, crime not halted, and the drug traffic not strangled at the roots. If the "land of equality" fails to force the cancer of racism into remission, people someday will look back incredulously at United States history and wonder how humane, rational people could ever have let the disease begin, let alone proceed so far. The waste, not only of minds, but of generations of lives, has been a national tragedy.

Integration or Pluralism?

The greatest failure in the nation's past has been its inability to vanquish racism. Nearly all nations of the world, few of which are as heterogeneous as America, have similar histories of racial prejudice. Racism in this land stands out not by its existence but because of its special inappropriateness, thriving as it has in a society that boasted of making equality of opportunity its centerpiece. The egalitarian premise prompted some extraordinary innovation in the 19th century, but failure to extend the equal opportunities to non-whites, to women, and also to unassimilated Caucasian non-W.A.S.P. men (Irish, Italians, Catholics in general, Jews) profoundly marred some notable efforts.

Equality of opportunity in 19th-century America meant (in practice) equality of opportunity for W.A.S.P men and, by the end of the century, for many white men generally. Though the American experiment ran ahead of its time, the discrepancy that remained between ideal and reality has come home to roost.

Racism, a Civil War, and the continuing exploitation of Blacks, Indians, Chicanos, Puerto Ricans, Asians, and other ethnic minorities tell only part of the dismaying story. The tale must also include the psychic damage inflicted upon those who were brainwashed for more than a century to doubt their worth as human beings because their skin was darker than "white." The United States was no "melting pot"; it was a bucket of whitewash. In order to make it in America one had to deny one's blackness or ethnicity; one had to wash white.

Generations of immigrants, former slaves, and the true native Americans—the "Indians"—had to change their names, their language, and occasionally even their skin color, as when many Blacks tried to bleach their skin. They had to hide their customs and traditions, alter their beliefs and life-purposes if they chose to climb the red-white-and-blue ladder to success. They were required to assimilate, to disappear if they could, into the white mass. In the same way, non-Protestant Caucasians had to repudiate their past to look and act like any Fred Jones or Bill Johnson. W.A.S.P. values, styles, and attitudes became synonymous with "American," a tyranny of the majority which continued well into the 1950's.

Whitewashing (or assimilation, to use the politer term) has been publicly repudiated as a strategy for this heterogeneous polity. James Baldwin expressed reasons for this rejection eloquently when in *The Fire Next Time* (1962) he wrote:

> The white man's unadmitted—and apparently, to him unspeakable—private fears and longings are projected onto the Negro. The only way he can be released from the Negro's tyrannical power over him is to consent, in effect, to become black himself, to become a part of that suffering and dancing country that he now watches wistfully from the heights of his lonely power and, armed with spiritual traveller's checks, visits surreptitiously after dark. How can one respect, let alone adopt, the values of a people who do not, on any level whatever, live the way they say they do, or the way they say they should? I cannot accept the proposition that the four-hundred-year travail of the American Negro should result merely in his attainment of the present level of the American civilization. I am far from convinced that being released from the African witch doctor was worthwhile if I am now—in order to support the moral contradictions and the spiritual aridity of my life—expected to become dependent on the American psychiatrist. It is a bargain I refuse. The only thing white people have that black people need or should want, is power—and no one holds power forever. White people cannot, in the generality, be taken as models of how to live[76]

Well before the curtain came down on the 19th century, the explicit metaphor employed by white liberals to shape the racial future and to move it beyond assimilation was the "melting pot." In the melting pot, people from all over the world would mix together to produce a golden composite. Instead of whitewashing, whites would become darker and dark-skinned people lighter. This notion remained metaphorical; inter-racial marriage did not rank high on the list of many of the nation's most tolerant 19th-century reformers.

The strategy for achieving a color-blind society—one in which we would be judged for our character, intelligence, and talents long before skin color entered into the assessment—was integration. It became the means by which equal opportunity could be extended into the racial arena. Jobs, neighborhoods, schools, and, perhaps someday, even marriages would be racially mixed. The integrationists believed that when we were judged strictly on our merits, with no reference to skin color, the "race problem" would end. Integration, first through Constitutional amendment, then through legislation, and finally (with luck) through habit and preference would do the job. It has been the major liberal strategy for the past century, but race problems have not gone away. Some see this as proof of the poverty of an integrationist strategy. But, in fairness, it must be acknowledged that integration has not been fully or consistently tried.

The jury, by all rights, should still be out on integration. But some black (and other ethnic) leaders have already arrived at the firm verdict of "guilty." Instead of a melting pot, many prefer an American Stew or Mixed Salad, that is, an overtly pluralistic rather than integrated society. In the mixed salad the ethnic groups maintain their separate identity while presumably contributing to a rich, varied dish.

The Black Power movement and other group-conscious attempts at developing pride in one's race within a pluralist context have set off a yin-yang situation. They enhance the self-image of minority group members, but simultaneously pull them away from individuality by defining them firmly within the newly-vitalized ethnic group. Many racial leaders have, without irony, done just what they decry: they have carved racial niches for their followers on the dubious assumption that there exists some basic inborn racial/ethnic identity, the acceptance of which guarantees the emergence of intrinsic selfhood. The ensuing self-segregation of these groups distresses the white majority, and not only the racists among them.

The white liberals, those people who have long labored for racial harmony by means of integration, do not know what to do in this situation. They uneasily foresee a nation of separate tribes in which communication will be seriously circumscribed. They understand the need for blacks to join together without white participation or guidance, and so they watch uneasily from the sidelines, unpersuaded by the separatist approach.

The nation today seems uncertain whether to take a pluralistic or an integrationist tack. Some observers, however, believe that the dichotomy between cultural pluralism and integration may be more apparent than real, that they may stand in a potentially complementary relation to one another. Fifty years ago, Erich Fromm, the psychoanalyst, explained why individuals cannot love others without loving themselves, or at least possessing a degree of self-respect.

In certain ways the identification with the group, let us say a group that proclaims black as beautiful, enables a person to identify with his black sisters and brothers (an obvious, immediate outcome, widely understood and often feared), and to "feel better about himself" as well. Self-respect can then issue in comfortable personal relations with all kinds of people. This latter point has also been recognized, especially by black moderates, who rationalize exaggerated ethnic consciousness by regarding it as a necessary *interim* step on the road to a deeper societal integration.

These arguments have an unreal and abstract air to them. The United States may, demographically, resemble a mosaic composed of a multitude of many-colored, separate tiles. But the nation's moving force is and always has been centripetal, not centrifugal. Whatever one's original identity, the goal has always been to be an American. Whatever one's inherited class status, entrance into the middle class has been sought.

We return to equality of opportunity as the society's central strategy. We return to money as the chief way by which one measures whether entry into the Valhalla of bourgeois life has been attained. Blacks turn out to be little different in this regard from formerly excluded groups. Nor, I would argue, will other out-groups differ significantly. They will not resist the siren song of burgher respectability, whether they call themselves Chicano or Native American or boat people or feminists.

In viewing the last four decades of race relations, one is tempted, at first glance, to proclaim "there, it's happening again." The extraordinary creation of a large black bourgeoisie, including perhaps half of the nation's 25 million blacks, looks like a repeat of what occurred with Catholics and Jews, the Irish, Italians, Greeks, Poles, Hungarians, Russians, Japanese, Koreans, and Chinese. The black bourgeoisie took far longer to develop, but it had to overcome a heritage of slavery, lynching, segregation, and the most intense racial hatred and stereotyping imaginable. There can be no doubting an amazing black advance and a dramatic shift in white perceptions about blacks and what they can accomplish.

The white experience of the post-World War II era not only encompasses hero-worship of extraordinary athletes like Julius Erving, O.J. Simpson, Muhammad Ali, and Jackie Robinson—men who are honored for their character and courage as much as for their athletic skills. It not only includes entertainers of the same excellence such as Louis Armstrong, Billy Holliday, Diana Ross, Stevie Wonder, Sidney Poitier, Bill Cosby, along with perhaps hundreds of other entertainers and athletes in a culture which truly venerates these two professions. But it also must face the reality of a black Supreme Court justice, black Presidential candidates, black Nobel Prize winners, mayors of major cities, scientists, astronauts, doctors, entrepreneurs, professors, intellectuals, and writers and artists of genius—of both genders. Jesse Jackson's political successes in 1988 could not have been imagined even in 1978.

These black people, along with millions of their sisters and brethren of the middle class, rose because of their own efforts and are integrating fully into American society. They rose also because white America—finally and long overdue—permitted institutional integration. The majority did so reluctantly and under great pressure. But equality of opportunity in the guise of the integration of schools, neighborhoods, jobs, and the polling place stands as the law of the land. The blacks who have moved up will not only integrate publicly. They are and will date whomever they wish, fall into inter-racial love, engage in inter-racial sex, enter inter-racial marriage, and produce inter-racial children. Almost certainly in the long run they will be more American than black. Like other integrated ethnic and racial groups, their black identity, for better and for worse, will prove to be more ceremonial than fundamental: it will be celebrated on special occasions rather than incorporated into daily living.

One offshoot of this integration has been that the stereotype of blacks as inevitably shuffling, shifty, lazy, and incapable of rising mentally no longer defines the white consensus. The stereotype, however, has not disappeared, despite overwhelming evidence to the contrary. It remains, in modified form, alive and kicking. For when one looks at the recent black revolution, one difference from previous minority marches toward equality stands out. Left in the wake of the egalitarian advance is the other half of the black population, penned in ghettos, unsupported by traditional family structures, desperately poor, strung out on drugs, assaulted by violence, facing despair. Who are these people? What have they to do with equality of opportunity? What kind of future do *they* face?

For most Americans these are criminals; they fit the stereotype. They are worse than the old Stepin Fetchit image because they are not impotent. They can kill you. They frighten blacks almost as much as non-blacks. They are blamed for most of the nation's domestic maladies: unemployment, crime, urban blight, declining public education, teen-age pregnancy, and drugs. They seem to occupy a different physical, emotional, and moral planet from middle-class America. They are visible reminders of a terrible history of white racism. They appear beyond help. The claims of pluralism seem designed for them because they cannot be integrated. They are *them.*

But they are, in fact, us. A half-century ago 10 million of today's black bourgeoisie lived in poverty and near-hopelessness in Harlem, Watts, and on tenant farms in the South. Before that they were Jews on the lower East side of New York or Chinese in Chinatowns all across the continent. The evidence remains clear enough that integration as the expression of New World egalitarianism remains our best strategy and possesses the capacity for more advances.

WOMEN AND SEX

Many of these same issues haunt the movement for women's rights, but there are some crucial differences. White women were never literally slaves. British visitors to the United States after the Civil War often were struck by the freedom accorded women. They had never seen women so unshrinking back home. As early as 1867 the British observer Henry Latham, with a secret thrill, confessed he was "astonished at their touching without reserve upon all manner of topics which English ladies would ignore."[77]

Rudyard Kipling, making the same comparison in 1891, announced that "the girls of America are above and beyond them all. They are clever; they can talk. Yea, it is said that they think. Certainly they have the appearance of so doing. They are original, and look you between the brows with unabashed eyes as a sister might look at her brother."[78]

Lord James Bryce attributed to better educational opportunities for women the fact that "among American women an average of literary taste and influence prevails higher than that of women in any European country."[79] Even Matthew Arnold, who frequently chastised America as uncivilized, found that

> . . . there is a charm in American women—a charm which you find in most all of them, wherever you go. It is the charm of a natural manner, a manner not self-conscious, artificial, constrained. It may not be a beautiful manner always, but it is almost always a natural manner, a free and happy manner;

and this gives pleasure. Here we have, undoubtedly, a note of civilization, and an evidence, at the same time, of the good effect of equality upon social life and manners.[80]

These comments do not appear to accord with the current emphasis by some feminist scholars on the oppression of women in the American past. But both the travelers and the scholars are correct. Compared to conditions in the Old World, the emancipation of women had proceeded substantially since the 1830's. But compared to the opportunities afforded *American white males* during those same periods, women, rather than being afforded the full opportunities of citizenship, were treated more like pets; that is, they were pampered and kicked around, depending upon the moods and needs of their (male) owners.

While women in the United States today have risen to a more advanced state of emancipation than most of their sisters around the world, it is quite clear that they will settle for nothing less than complete equality of opportunity in the decades ahead. The reorientation demanded in the lives of just about every man and woman in this country will be more difficult—for some, agonizing—than that exacted by other movements for equal opportunity.

Machines have pretty nearly wiped away male advantages in manual strength over women, this superiority contributing to males gaining dominant status in the first place. Technology has placed a new premium on intelligence, a quality that appears to be unrelated to gender. If economic problems prove tractable, society should be able to adjust to an influx of women lawyers, doctors, professors, executives, journalists, politicians, and diplomats. At different class levels, dismaying though it will be for some men, we shall see many more women in the military, in the police and fire departments, in an array of security positions. And in more strictly physical jobs, women are infiltrating construction crews, doing carpentry, electrical work, delivering the mails, driving buses and trucks, flying airplanes, and making lots of money in professional sports. That adjustment is already well underway. The nation can also adapt to more men teaching in elementary schools, male nurses and secretaries, men shopping in the supermarkets and cleaning houses.

What the nation may resist will be deeper challenges to the "feminine mystique" and to the conventional nuclear family itself. The women's movement, despite its demurrals and its emphasis upon womens' *choice*, differs from other egalitarian movements in that it truly does challenge the sanctity of family, home, motherhood, the double standard of sexual morality, as well as the traditional roles of husband, wives, mothers, and fathers. That challenge occurs automatically when women feel they can enter the career world outside the home if they so desire.

The historian Carl Degler has squarely faced the fundamental, incompatibility of traditional family beliefs and attitudes with those which spur women to realize their full potential as persons. Near the end of *At Odds,* his comprehensive history of American women and the family, he says:

The central values of the modern family stand in opposition to those that underlie women's emancipation. Where the women's movement has stood for equality, the family historically has denied or repudiated equality. For even in the companionate family of the 19th and 20th centuries, hierarchy has prevailed among father, mother, and children. Few families have treated them equally or assumed them to be equal, even today. Where the women's movement has called for a recognition of individualism, the family has insisted upon subordination of individual interests to those of the group. Even fathers have been expected to share their earnings with the other family members and to shape their lives to such an extent as to provide a living for the whole family. And, finally, where the women's movement has asked for a person to be judged on merit, the family has denied merit as a basis of membership, approval or love. Indeed, the great appeal of the family has been that it accepts members simply because they are born into the group and not because of what they may achieve or contribute.[81]

Much experimentation with new family forms marks the lives of the middle and upper classes today. Most women in these groups desire both careers and families. Poorer married women have always had to work outside the home just to survive economically. But some magical reconciliation between female emancipation and the traditional, demands of family and home has not materialized.

Do we see Americans in significant numbers adapting to the phenomenon of househusbands? To lifelong, "swinging spinsters"? To communal families? To lesbians, homosexuals, and bisexuals? To women who are unmarried mothers by choice? To planned promiscuity in marriage? To traditional marriages in which it is assumed that the family moves from place to place to follow mother's work? These and other forms exist currently. There has been increased tolerance for some of these developments in segments of the population. But the majority of Americans, female and male, does not like most of them.

As long as women *need* men in order to survive or to lead a decent life, equality remains seriously impeded. But in the interplay between new technologies, new attitudes, and changing economic requirements, that dependence has been diminishing slowly since the onset of the Industrial Revolution about 250 years ago, and rapidly since the end of World War II. Nowhere has the dependence on men been eroded more dramatically than in the area one would think highly resistant to major alteration: sex.

The profound transformations in sexual relations between men and women over the last few centuries have been generally overlooked. A capsule history will seem oversimplified, but the rough outline of those changes is almost indisputable.

For the Western world in the first millennium-and-a-half of the Christian era, sexual relations were strictly for *procreation*. From the point of view of a woman, this meant that sex had nothing to do with her pleasure. She was supposed to make babies, and until little more than a century ago a major source of male power derived from the fact that wives were, from the onset of puberty until their generally early deaths, nearly always pregnant. Women, of course, required men for this form of sex and could find little cultural permission from Christianity or other institutions to enjoy sex for its own sake.

The Protestant challenge to Catholicism and the imperatives of various forms of Capitalism that began to develop 500 years ago slowly allowed the possibility of sex for *recreation,* surely one of the profoundest evolutions in human history. But for the bulk of these five centuries, the pleasure derived from sex was strictly for men. Women of most (though not all) social classes and in most regions were supposed to lie passively while the thrusting men achieved orgasms. But through primitive forms of birth control, some women were permitted escape from a life of unrelenting pregnancy and childbirth. As Peter Gay in *The Bourgeois Experience* and others have reported, they could occasionally, if surreptitiously, experience pleasure.

After Stage One (sex for procreation) and Stage Two (sex for masculine recreation as a second legitimized option), this century saw a dramatic enlargement of a third possibility: *sex for women's pleasure.* This was made possible chiefly by sophisticated technologies for birth control. In the middle classes of the West today, most men and women accept the notion that women should be able to enjoy sex. For the first time most women are not automatically punished for engaging in sex before marriage or even for adulterous affairs after marriage. Permitted now are the excitements of oral, manual, and other forms of non-coital sex—which cannot possibly lead to childbirth. Still, as in the first two stages, the norm is that women have their sex with men and associate it with love.

But that, too, is changing. Once sex for women's pleasure attained general acceptance, it was but a very short step to the next possibility: sex for women's pleasure *without men.* First came widespread acceptance by both genders that women could engage in sex for the fun of it and without emotional commitment. Second came the recognition that, like men, women could masturbate. Many women find it much easier to reach orgasm through masturbation than through intercourse. Third, and less generally accepted, is homosexual sex. But the increase in lesbianism renders it difficult to imagine that general tolerance will not eventually arrive. Women may now enjoy sex without the help of men. Each stage of this swiftly moving history allows women to experience more of the pleasures, responsibilities, and ordeals of life on their own.

New technologies are already making it possible for women to give birth to infants without heterosexual intercourse, As society witnesses ever-increasing numbers of women who, *if they choose,* can make it on their own financially, live comfortably alone or in an arrangement other than with a husband, and raise children outside the traditional nuclear family, new definitions of "family" will eventually gain common acceptance.

Lawrence Stone, in his path-breaking study of *The Family, Sex, and Marriage: England 1500-1800,* placed these epochal transformations on a large canvas. At the end of his work, as he peered into the unknown future, he saw the long rise of the nuclear family with its "intense affective and erotic bonding" as "no more permanent a phenomenon than were the economic ties of property and interest that united families in the past, even if this is the rough general direction in which Western society has been moving over the last three hundred years."[82]

Stone continued:

> Today parents can expect to live twenty or thirty years beyond the departure of the children from the home, the number of children is declining fast, and the numbers of mothers with small children who go out to work is rapidly growing. The separate economic preoccupations of each parent are beginning to detach them both from the home and from their dependence on each other. Already, moreover, the peer-group is almost as important as the family in the social life of the children. It therefore seems possible that a new, more loosely structured, less emotionally and sexually cohesive, and far more temporary family type is already being added to the number of options available. The frustrated and lonely housewife, the over-possessive mother and the Oedipal relationship of the son with the father may all be transient phenomena of a particular time, place and social class—to be replaced, no doubt, by a different set of pathological types. Furthermore, the historical record suggests that the likelihood of this period of extreme sexual permissiveness continuing for very long without generating a strong back-lash is not very great.[83]

Stone wrote that last sentence well before the onset of the AIDS epidemic of the 1980's. That disease has placed a chilling effect on anal, oral, and genital intercourse and on homosexual and heterosexual promiscuity. Whether it adds more emotional content to romantic relationships or makes people work harder at maintaining them remains to be seen.

Though devastating in its results, the AIDS plague will not last forever. It will not for long reverse the longer historical tendency toward greater independence for women.

That extraordinary development, so accelerated in the last half-century, is not an unmixed blessing, however. Single mothers make up a new poverty class. Many women have been cut off from kinship ties which once provided some external help in raising families, and many others face loneliness. Freedom can bring with it some loss of security.

But it will not do to idealize the life of pre-modern women. Their situation was worse by far even than the squalid life of most men before 1700. It will not do, despite the temptation in some quarters, to glamorize the life of wives and mothers in traditional nuclear families before 1960. Despite the bargain which promised them lifetime marital commitment and financial support, the price was very high. Women were expected to stay home and surrender all manner of freedoms that their husbands could enjoy. For millions it became a very bad bargain, and eventually the bargain itself collapsed. In the conventional nuclear family, the advantages were mightily skewed in favor of the men. The image of happy, protected, loved housewives and mothers in their single-family homes cheerfully washing the dishes and baking cookies for their children while their husbands labored wearily in the competitive, capitalist jungle belongs to romantic legend. Like most romances, that fairy tale is wishful and not faithful to reality. Men in fact had a better deal than women.

Economic inequality between husbands and wives fatally distorted millions of marriages. Women could not be psychological equals when they feared that speaking honestly might drive their husbands away. They could not make it in this society without money. So they held their tongues and stuffed their emotions: they could not risk intimacy because of their dependent status. When women achieve economic parity with men, they will be closer to psychological equality and to the rewards and risks of intimacy. Economic equality will always have to be a cornerstone of the women's movement in a culture of money.

The women's movement constitutes the major social movement of the 20th century. By making available the variable talents of more than 50 percent of the population—talents that were caged and circumscribed for nearly all of human history—society will gain immeasurably. And for the female half of the population the gains of increasing freedom must surely outweigh the burden of new responsibilities. I am glad to be alive while this revolution is taking place and delighted to witness its early returns.

Yet, as with any social revolution, all the gains bring new conundrums. Women are well-placed to ask the question which concerns those infused with the desire for autonomy: *after* liberation, what? Women aspire to fresh answers only to the extent they recognize the costs of imitating men. Replicating male patterns would resemble James Baldwin's concept of integration into a burning house. Men have laid traps for themselves in goal-oriented strategies for career and marriage which women might wish to avoid.

More sensitive than men to the *longeurs* of the bourgeois family, women may be specially motivated to lead society toward a reconciliation of freedom with security. The issues at stake are enormous and must not be understated for the sake of scholarly dignity. The feminist movement is among the significant reforms of history because of its implications for the propagation of the species; for its effects on the early imprinting of children; for its alteration of the fundamental economic relationship between mates, friends, and the sexes; for its redeeming of the emotional-cultural meaning of sexual identity; and for changing the cultural clothing of one of the strongest biological drives and socially subversive forces of humankind: physical sex. Most dramatically, the movement for female freedom raises for culture the ominous issue in the Age of Faith in Self: the possibility of ultimate social atomization. Today most women, in the effort to reconcile freedom and security, say they want career *and* family. But in the absence of definitive norms for successful careers and families, this reconciliation is easily said, not so easily done.

America's chief contribution to the advancement of civilization—the idea of equality of opportunity—has helped to foster the unfolding freedom of women and non-whites. I believe that the various forms in which that idea has been institutionalized have greatly contributed to the growing opportunities. Though there is a far distance to go, Americans have a right to feel proud. While the promise of the American experiment has fallen short in so many different realms, it is well to remember, celebrate, and thoughtfully enlarge its most auspicious, unsettling, and far-reaching achievement.

AFTERWORD

I should like to begin with two statistics, one about race, the other about marriage.

- *More African-American men spend time in prison than graduate high school.[84]*
- *More adult women are single than married.[85]*

The first statistic underscores a serious paradox that has developed in black-white relations over the past two decades. On the one hand, many of the major beloved icons of American life, more than ever before, are African-Americans. Most of them are in sports and entertainment, such as Michael Jordan, Tiger Woods, Oprah Winfrey, Muhammad Ali, Halle Berry, and Denzel Washington, just to name a tiny fragment of the total.

But many who come from the highest levels of government, intellectual life, and the highest arts are also familiar and celebrated: Colin Powell, Toni Morrison, Condoleezza Rice, Leontyne Price, Henry Louis Gates, and Barack Obama—again just to trace a trickle from an ever enlarging stream.

African-Americans in substantial numbers during the past two decades have entered the medical, legal, journalistic, and academic professions. Those men and women of achievement hardly raise an eyebrow anymore, where once their emergence would have been greeted with greater surprise and notice than today. Clearly, some of the walls erected against black achievement are crumbling, if not quite yet coming down. There is progress.

But for young African-American men in the urban and suburban ghettos, the story is horrific. They inhabit a world of violence, drugs, anger, unemployment, and hopelessness. They live on another planet not only from white Americans, but from the growing middle class of African-Americans. And it's getting worse. My update from 1988: it is the best of times, it is the worst of times.

As for changes in the life of women and the dramatic falloff in the marriage rate since 1988, some believe that decline presages the end of civilization. But the meaning behind the growing ranks of single women (and men) is more interesting and less distressing than the traditionalist would admit. First, marriage has always changed throughout history, and the chief reason that more women are choosing not to marry is that they don't have to. Historically, women were not allowed to work outside the home, except in a very limited way; they needed a husband to provide for them materially, to stay alive. They were dependent on a husband for survival, and there was little room for love.

Women now, more than ever, can support themselves materially, and so they can choose more carefully whom to wed, or whether to wed at all. That's much better than in the past, for men as well as women, and it increases the prospects for richer, happier marriages than those based on dependency and male domination.[86]

An interesting aspect of these changes involves educated women. Many who fret about the growing independence of women have argued that educated women have very little chance of marrying at all, and that careers and domestic happiness (to the extent it can be equated with marriage) do not go together like a horse and carriage. But the new fact is that women with college and advanced degrees are more likely to wed than those without. The historian of marriage, Stephanie Coontz, points out: "Many people claim men aren't willing to marry educated, independent women. But that's no longer true. Men are now much more likely to marry women who are their educational and economic peers."[87]

These marriages occur later in one's life than, say, the average age of 20 in the 1950's, "with the greatest single number of women [in that decade] marrying at 18." Today, women with a B.A. who decide to marry, do so at an average age of more than 27. That number goes up to 30 for those with advanced degrees. Not only do opportunities to wed not decline precipitously after age 30, but Coontz believes that "many of the older marriages being contracted now are between people who have the skills to construct those good marriages—more egalitarian men, more savvy women and lovers who have deeper friendships."[88]

There is no larger story since I wrote American Yearnings *than the rapid acceleration of the growing acceptance of a wide range of choices for how to live one's private lives: for all men and women, heterosexual, bi-sexual, and homosexual. More dramatic than the debate over same sex marriage has been the contested issue generally of what we mean by marriage, whether marriage is necessary, and how to arrange our love relationships. There is no single answer. The responses are multiple.*

And for those who bewail this multiplicity let me conclude here with the quite single-minded, famous, amazing, and now hilarious "Good Wife's Guide" from the 1950's—hilarious only because what once was taken with utmost seriousness now seems like a joke. I call this progress.

THE GOOD WIFE'S GUIDE

- *Have dinner ready. Plan ahead, even the night before, to have a delicious meal ready, on time for his return. This is a way of letting him know that you have been thinking about him and are concerned about his needs. Most men are hungry when they come home and the prospect of a good meal (especially his favorite dish) is part of the warm welcome needed.*
- *Prepare yourself. Take 15 minutes to rest so you'll be refreshed when he arrives. Touch up your make-up, put a ribbon in your hair and be fresh-looking. He has just been with a lot of work-weary people.*
- *Be a little gay and a little more interesting for him. His boring day may need a lift and one of your duties is to provide it.*
- *Clear away the clutter. Make one last trip through the main part of the house just before your husband arrives.*

- *Gather up the schoolbooks, toys, papers etc. and then run a dustcloth over the tables.*
- *Over the cooler months of the year you should prepare and light a fire for him to unwind by. Your husband will feel he has reached a haven of rest and order, and it will give you a life, too. After all, catering for his comfort will provide you with immediate personal satisfaction.*
- *Prepare the children. Take a few minutes to wash all the children's hands and faces (if they are small), comb their hair and, if necessary, change their clothes. They are little treasures and he would like to see them playing the part. Minimize all noise. At the time of his arrival, eliminate all noise of the washer, dryer, or vacuum. Try to encourage the children to be quiet.*
- *Be happy to see him.*
- *Greet him with a warm smile and show sincerity in your desire to please him.*
- *Listen to him. You may have a dozen important things to tell him, but the moment of his arrival is not the time. Let him talk first—remember, his topics of conversation are more important than yours.*
- *Make the evening his. Never complain if he comes home late or goes out to dinner, or other places of entertainment without you. Instead, try to understand his world of strain and pressure and his very real need to be at home and relax.*
- *Your goal: Try to make sure your home is a place of peace, order and tranquility where your husband can renew himself in body and spirit.*
- *Don't complain if he's late home for dinner or even if he stays out all night. Count this as minor compared to what he might have gone through that day.*
- *Make him comfortable. Have him lean back in a comfortable chair or have him lie down in the bedroom. Have a cool or warm drink ready for him.*
- *Arrange his pillow and offer to take off his shoes. Speak in a low, soothing and pleasant voice.*
- *Don't ask him questions about his actions or question his judgment or integrity. Remember, he is the master of the house and as such will always exercise his will with fairness and truthfulness. You have no right to question him.*
- *A good wife always knows her place.*[89]

Joseph Stalin, as husband, could not have said it better!

THREE: GLANCING AHEAD

Henry V

11

Toward The Future with Shakespeare

$\mathbf{M}$y 50th college reunion will convene in the year 2008. No one can foretell the future; anyone who claims to do so, whether an academic or a psychic, has no shame. But some possibilities on the way to 2008 are more likely than others. In this final chapter I should like to suggest, by way of conclusion, how America's recent history, as portrayed in these pages, adds up and to examine whether that sum may yield some hints about the future. While the topics I discussed have traversed a wide territory—marriage, war, celebrities, money, sex, race, the tension between equality and individualism, the resemblances between business and show business, and many others—certain larger patterns keep reappearing.

I have returned repeatedly to a triple vision of the United States. The three views are sometimes contradictory, sometimes complementary, always intertwined. That which seems most pertinent depends on what one wishes to look at and at what distant from America the observer stands.

When the frame of reference is national-comparative, that is, how one might best compare the United States with other countries, the most useful model still seems that associated with Alexis de Tocqueville in the 1830's. The United States by then was launched upon an experiment in equality of opportunity. Stripping away class privilege would enable a society of fluid classes to ensue. Life would be a competitive race in which one "rises." The measure of success would be money. Thus America would and, indeed, has become the quintessential middle-class society, valuing material achievement above the emotional, intellectual, spiritual, and aesthetic. In weakening the power of inherited aristocracy at the top and increasing opportunity at the bottom for people who had, in the Old World, known only peasantry and poverty as far back as memory could take them, America replaced ideology with pragmatism, and class conflict with consensus. The national consensus was this: that the name of the American game should be, both at the national and personal level, Upward Mobility.

In viewing this game from a sufficient distance, one sees order and patterns and rules: one also notices how different the English or the Japanese game is from the

American. Wheel the camera in closer, however, and the relatively clear shapes give way to a more chaotic hodge-podge. Conflict replaces consensus: the Schlesingers supercede Tocqueville. We see a much more fragmented society often waged in combat one group against another: whites and blacks, rich and poor, young and old, Protestants and Catholics, men and women, Northerners and Southerners. But if one doesn't get in too close it remains possible to discern pattern in the conflict. A periodic cycle becomes visible wherein private concerns and public interests vie for power; each gains ascendancy in roughly alternating 15-year cycles. Those associated with private satisfaction have been the "haves," the business interests, property holders, the East Coast, the conservatives—depending upon whose book you are reading. The combatants have been the "have-nots," citizens trying to gain a decent share of the American pie: farmers, factory workers, Catholics, Jews, Eastern Europeans, women, Latinos, blacks, and others. Theirs is the story of the ongoing efforts to enlarge opportunity, usually against considerable opposition. Those efforts have been generally, but neither universally nor inevitably, successful. And the battle is far from over.

Finally, pull the camera into position for a long-distance perspective, distant enough to pan around the globe over the past few centuries. A different picture emerges—one in which it is harder to distinguish the United States from other nations. From this view we see a world that, since the advent of recorded history, had explained nearly all events in supernatural terms. It was also a world that found the huge majority of its inhabitants living on farms and at the edge of survival. A remarkable transformation reshaped the planet in the last three or four centuries. Scientific thinking rose in importance, usually at the expense of the religious. An increasingly urbanized, crowded world was marked by greatly improved living standards. In the West, Christianity gave way for many 18th-century thinkers to a rationalistic view, which in turn over the next two centuries evolved into an individualistic outlook.

From the second and third vantage points—the close-up view of political and economic combat and the distant perspective of global transformation—the United States resembles other societies. But American uniqueness becomes more visible when we focus on its experiment with equality of opportunity. That experiment has significantly colored the nation's socio-economic conflict on the one hand and its changing *mentalités*, generally shared with the rest of the world, on the other.

By and large, America's experience with fluid classes operating within an ethos of equal opportunity has been successful. Each cycle of reform has witnessed new groups being allowed access to the nation's wealth. This advance has been halting, uneven, and always short of political claims; nothing like across-the-board fairness yet exists. But the advance has been unmistakable. Compared to most of the people of the world, Americans have lived materially well for the past 250 years—*and they know it*. This knowledge has resulted, along with the prosperity itself, in perhaps the most far-reaching legacy of upward mobility: Americans have generally been the most *optimistic* people on the face of the Earth.

This optimism has cast politico-economic conflicts and the approach to life's larger questions in a particular light. A high percentage of Americans believe they can and will be rich. They often think about being rich and are willing to work long hours to attain wealth. They scramble ceaselessly to come up with money-making ideas, and they believe it is within their power to succeed. Even when they fall short (as they are practically bound to do in the face of reality), they keep plugging, in the meanwhile identifying closely with celebrities who personify the glorious rewards of "making it." These vicarious joys keep alive the functional Religion of America: *The Power of Positive Thinking*.

By turning attention on the individual rather than the system, positive thinking helps dampen class conflict and even the most primitive discussion of socialism. If a person does not succeed, the fault lies squarely with him. He simply has to try harder.

The long tradition of self-help goes back to Benjamin Franklin and has been carried on by Andrew Jackson, Horatio Alger, Jr., Emil Coué, Bruce Barton, Dale Carnegie, Norman Vincent Peale, Werner Erhard (E.S.T.), and a battalion of others who have taught Americana how to "win," to seize responsibility for their own actions, and not only "dream the impossible dream," but make the dream come true by believing in it hard enough.

A cursory glance at the lists of books that have been bestsellers ever since such lists began demonstrates this. Look at this Sunday's *New York Times* bestseller list, watch Oprah and *Good Morning, America*, examine the list of seminars and workshops available this week in your hometown. Everywhere Americans are making money by teaching millions of other Americans how to make money—or, on the way to wealth, gain an appealing personality, look attractive, lose weight, become sexually devastating, develop a happy marriage, achieve true potential, or win friends and influence people. But the bottom line for most of these efforts is "success," whether preached by salesmen, pop psychologists, or people of the cloth. As the evangelist Jim Bakker put it, while quoting no less an authority than God Almighty Himself: "Poverty sucks!"

Most of these preachers do not advocate the quicker fixes against poverty: lotteries, prize sweepstakes, and gambling. Yet millions of Americans believe they will strike it rich in one sudden moment. If that fails, drug-dealing and crime offer tempting possibilities for a frighteningly substantial number of the citizenry.

European critics (many of them jealous) have long said that Americans are materialists. But it is important to note that Americans are also optimistic individualists. Happily, many Americans have been "self-made." Most of them have lived happier lives than had they remained in poverty. The model they represent has drawn millions of immigrants to the United States and made it the most admired, envied, and popular country in the modern era. Even the lingering hope of wealth has energized Americans who have not yet achieved it. Studies show that Americans as a whole are far less emotionally depressed than the populations of Asia and Africa. Table One indicates that their self-perception is comparatively upbeat.

Richard L. Rapson

Table One: Percentages "Very happy" in North America, Africa, and the Far East[90]

Highly Satisfied With:

	Very happy	Standard of living	Housing	Family life
North America	40	46	55	73
Africa	18	5	14	18
Far East	7	8	14	18

But there is a down side to positive thinking simply because: *it is not always accurate thinking.* The energy released by expectations that are not met turns to disappointment that can border on despair. False hope that cannot be fulfilled often becomes depression. Erich Fromm once wrote that "behind a front of satisfaction and optimism modern man is deeply unhappy; as a matter of fact, he is on the verge of desperation."[91]

In studies designed to measure anxiety, figures for the United States tend toward the high side, lending some statistical support to Fromm's impressionistic observations. In a recent survey of 18 industrialized nations which attempts to measure "happiness and well-being," the United States had the seventh highest ranking in the key "anxiety index." Assuming, that is, the preference for calm over agitation, the United States came in 12th place among the 18 in turning away anxiety. With rankings ranging from the least anxious (Ireland: 31.4) to the most anxious (Austria: 66.3), the United States (51.6) scored better only than Belgium (51.7), Italy (57.1), West Germany (60.9), France (61.5), Japan (61.7), and Austria (66.3). After Eire, the least anxious, in order were: Great Britain (40.3), Sweden (43.0), New Zealand (44.4), Netherlands (44.5), Denmark (44.9), Norway (45.0), Finland (46.9), Australia (47.6), Canada (50.8), and Switzerland (51.5).[92]

More telling perhaps are the data derived from the three major combined indices that seek to compare the "quality of life" of the world's nations from quantifiable variables. In all these the United States does pretty well, but never approaches the ratings of the highest-ranked countries. The most elaborate measure, for example, is the Index of Net Social Progress compiled in 1983 by Richard Estes. Based upon 11 sub-indexes (education, health, women's status, defense, economic, demographic, geographical, political stability, political participation, cultural diversity, and welfare effort) and 44 indicators for a total of 55 variables, it rates 107 nations. The United States comes in 23rd place, far behind the Scandinavian countries (which usually do best on these comparisons) but also well behind most of the nations of Western Europe.[93]

The United States fares better on the Physical Quality of Life Index (1981—only three variables: life expectancy, infant mortality, and literacy), coming in 11th place out

166

of 164 nations. (The drought-ridden nations of Africa come out poorest on all these scales.)[94] Finally, on the Combined Index of Social and Economic Indicators the United States is rated seventh, behind (in order) Sweden, Denmark, Norway, France, Iceland, and Australia, slightly ahead of Canada, West Germany, and Switzerland.[95]

There is a silly quality to these numerical rankings reminiscent of Garrison Keillor's spoof on America as "Number One" (Chapter Eight). I mention them only as a counterpoint to exaggerated American self-regard and boosterism. We need to distinguish between the simplicities of our extravagant fantasies and the richer textures of reality. Life in the real world may be finite, but in the long run it is more interesting than Disneyland.

Despite our will to believe, most people lose in lotteries and most Americans are not millionaires. That does not stop people from trying again, but there remains an internal life of Americans behind the veneer of optimism that needs to be explored. My guess, both as a therapist and an historian, is that when that detailed exploration takes place we shall gain some measure of how high the cost of unrealistic optimism runs. I think that it produces a peculiarly American and as-yet unnamed mental affliction. It affects people who get high on instant religious conversion, who truly feel they will win the sweepstakes by hoping for it strongly enough, who get "born again," who "re-birth," who start anew with fad diets, fitness as religion, or faith-healing, who actually believe that "today is the first day of your life," who always "think positively."

Sadly, after the instant highs, they experience deep, often lasting lows in a pattern like that induced by cocaine and cocaine withdrawal. They sink down not only because lows usually follow artificially-fabricated highs, but also because, unfortunately, not everyone can win. The following statement almost sounds un-American, but the charge of being unpatriotic might as well be faced: there simply are limits to the possible, limits which are produced by biology, history, culture, and everyday reality. One does not have to be an historian to realize that today is *not* the first day of the rest of our lives.

Unfounded optimism may be America's chief mental disease. Its main cause—and here I walk on even more treacherous, untrod terrain—may be that we Americans are simply, quite possibly, not smart enough. The chief cure, it follows, would require the creation of a more intelligent population, a goal whose attainment would require a formidable effort.

I am not just talking about the lower test scores achieved by American schoolchildren when compared with West Europeans or Japanese. That is part of the problem and we most certainly do need to elevate our educational standards. Nor am I referring to the powerful strain of anti-intellectualism in American culture, though its hard to see much value in that sort of discrimination, either. Citizens who prefer Mozart to Twisted Sister or Bellow to Rambo need not be put down (or reviled) as snobs. Nor am I using the term "intelligence" in a biological sense, though neurological research suggests we may find that intellectual laziness and ignorance can produce actual physiological changes in the brain. My main interest for now is in learned rather than genetic intelligence.

The conundrum at issue here goes more deeply into cultural attitudes and frames of mind. Americans do not much care about history, know very little, and, more dismaying, feel they are better off for their ignorance. They verge with pride on the provincial, knowing next to nothing about the rest of the world. Qualities such as irony, detachment, or a sense of tragedy border on heresy compared to more American ideals such as "believing in yourself" or assuming that problems only exist in order to be overcome.

In *The Great Cat Massacre* (1984), a brilliant study of the *mentalité* of the French during the Old Regime, Robert Darnton tried to describe what he meant by "Frenchness." He deemed the term as "a distinct cultural style [which] conveys a particular view of the world" that included:

> A sense that life is hard, that you had better not have any illusions about selflessness in your fellow men, that clearheadedness and quick wit are necessary to protect what little you can extract from your surroundings, and that moral nicety will get you nowhere. Frenchness makes for ironic detachment. It tends to be negative and disabused. Unlike its Anglo-Saxon opposite, the Protestant ethic, it offers no formula for conquering the world. It is a defense strategy, well-suited to an oppressed peasantry or an occupied country. It still speaks today in colloquial exchanges like: *Comment vas-tu?* ("How are you?") *Je me défends.* (*"I* defend myself").[96]

I do not propose to turn Americans into French peasants; the gains would not be greater than the losses. I do mean to raise the possibility that a greater sophistication about the workings of the world might be a more valuable aide for dealing with complicated reality than that offered by simple faith and looking on the bright side.

Some years ago I delivered the keynote address at a conference of educational, vocational, and psychological counselors, lecturing on how Americans have leapt from one set of certitudes to another during an enthusiastic and quixotic national lifetime (as described in Chapter Three). The first settlers during the 17th century embraced God; the Founding Fathers, during the Enlightenment, served the Deity of Rationality. In the 19th century, humbler citizens found themselves beneficiaries of the Age of Reason and were caught up in the egalitarian experiment, swearing fealty to the Work Ethic. As Christianity, Liberalism, and Capitalism tried to fight off a series of 20th-century challenges, many people, in the confusion, fled and hid behind the picket fences of Family. Many of these folks are now exploring worship of The Free Self. Each successive Faith promised "answers"; Americans flocked enthusiastically to every new system, holding only to skeletons of their previous faith. And we keep rushing to new salvations if they are marketed well enough: primal screaming, TV evangelism, channeling, getting rich. We look for guidance from health nuts, gurus, psychics, drug dealers, child preachers, and movie and TV stars, few of whom have much time for complication.

Magical Thinking and The Decline of America

The tendency of Americans, marginally more pronounced than for Europeans, to embrace simple-mindedly one form of salvation after another reveals a past strength and a current liability in the national character. The optimistic faith in a reliable future founded upon secure beliefs, changeable though they were, supplied the people with unquenchable vigor, hope, and the willingness to attempt nearly anything. As long as the United States continued its march to prosperity and strength, as it has for most of its history, these upbeat faiths were tenable. And, up to a point, the energy released by them helped to provide evidence for their prophetic promises, whether as harbingers of Heaven, Progress, wealth, family bliss, or self-actualization. Each of the world-views cherished by the people contained admirable, enduring elements, and none has been fatally discredited: though weakened, they all survive today. The nation, all in all, can be fairly proud of its past commitments; other societies have worshipped lesser, meaner gods than did the Americans. Still . . .

So went my talk. It held the audience, but the surprise for me came afterward when I was assigned to "enliven" a series of small group discussions. As I went from room to room, the first question the counselors invariably asked was: "Well, what are *you*?" That is, how might I label myself? In what did I believe? After describing various popular philosophies, I was asked for more "guidance" than my mildly ironic style afforded. The counselors were mostly Americans, and characteristically enough they wanted answers.

My initial response to their queries was to remain mysterious. I rejected their wish that I pigeonhole myself. I chose to remain enigmatic, unfathomable, superior to the constrictions of classification, larger than any label! But as they kept repeating the question, they reminded me of the wish, even amongst society's professional advisers, to get things down pat. In order to address these earnest needs, I began seriously to assay some sort of reply to a question I did not like. *Was* there a particular body of insights that had touched me considerably more than had any other? Was there a special fount of wisdom from which I knew I must drink, and to which I must return frequently? Had I a guru? I thought intently while my audience waited silently. After an uncomfortably long pause, I finally mumbled: "I think, uh, maybe, uh, well perhaps I could call myself a Shakespearean."

My confession appeared to disappoint absolutely everyone. It evoked no huzzahs, no wild applause of gratitude, no signs of admiring, amazed recognition. Nothing. After a heavy silence I was asked, without much enthusiasm, what I meant. Just what were Shakespeare's views on life, human nature, and purpose anyhow? What, if anything, was I talking about?

That disappointed puzzlement made a point for me. Over these past few years, I have liked my answer/non-answer to the question I did not like. There is, of course, no simple way to categorize Shakespeare's views of existence, humanity, and purpose. There is no system of thought, no church called "Shakespearean." The Bard's conceptions of life and meanings are difficult to paraphrase. They cannot be reduced enough to fit into neat categories.

The best way to understand him is to go to the plays. Shakespeare did not diminish to stereotypes the characters he created. King Lear can be plausibly played in a thousand different ways by as many different actors; the play can be staged in multifold varieties and still emerge credible and moving. At his best, which happened often, Shakespeare brought to life a universe of uncaricatured individuals, revealed in their full complexity, inhabiting richly textured worlds. Whether in comedy, history, or tragedy he saw, in ways surpassed by no one, the *many* sides of life, the *many* meanings, the *many* unknowables, the full range and depth of humanity. Appreciation of his rich insights, expressed through cascades of beautiful poetry and a gaudy assemblage of characters about whom we continually discover more, grows with time.

To talk of being a Shakespearean carries some other overtones: he is not a contemporary; human nature has not metamorphosed over time nor has human wisdom deepened; there exists no Shakespearean epistemology. I use the Shakespearean label paradoxically, to cast doubt upon the assumption that mental health requires faith in something, preferably a well-articulated and firm set of beliefs, a system of answers. I'd like to side with readers who do *not* envy those who drive around with bumper stickers declaring "I've found it!" or "I've got it!" I'd like to put in a good word for the sticker that reads: "I'm not so sure."

Actually, I am most alarmed by those who claim certainty. Ideology and blind faith have historically been used to justify killing others in order to appease one's own god or version of the truth. In a nuclear age, ideology can rationalize the destruction of the human race itself, whether in the name of Allah, the Dialectic, or The Second Coming. So, my Shakespearean metaphor is meant to infer the possibility of pleasure in the inordinately rich textures of life. It suggests that one can relish uncertainty, fullness, complexity, and ambiguity. It questions the necessity of flight from doubt into certainty, and it asks whether the immediate security is worth the pain of failed panaceas and disappointed illusions. Less fancily, I would be happy if only we would clearly value life itself and recognize the worth of survival even though imperfection surrounds us.

In the final analysis I hope we Americans will work to be smarter. I hope we will learn more about the world, become less needful of simple answers, and inch our way toward greater detachment, tolerance, and an appreciation for complexity. The long American tradition of optimism can still serve us well, but I do not equate it with cheerful, mindless, positive thinking. We need not become French, but it is worth revisiting the words of one modern-day Frenchman, Albert Camus, who at the end of his novel of successful resistance against *The Plague*, explained why his "unphilosophical hero" had to tell the world about his town's battle against evil:

> Dr. Rieux resolved to compile this chronicle so that he should not be one
> of those who hold their peace but should bear witness in favor of those
> plague-stricken people; so that some memorial of the injustice and outrage

done them might endure; and to state quite simply what we learn in a time of pestilence; that there are more things to admire in men than to despise.

Nonetheless, he knew that the tale he had to tell could not be one of a final victory. It could be only the record of what had had to be done, and what assuredly would have to be done again in the never-ending fight against terror and its relentless onslaughts, despite their personal afflictions, by all who, while unable to be saints but refusing to bow down to pestilences, strive their utmost to be healers.

And, indeed, as he listened to the cries of joy rising from the town, Rieux remembered that such joy is always imperiled. He knew what those jubilant crowds did not know but could have learned from books: that the plague bacillus never dies or disappears for good; that it can lie dormant for years and years in furniture and linen-chests, that it bides its time in bedrooms, cellars, trunks, and bookshelves; and that perhaps the day would come when, for the bane and the enlightening of men, it would rouse up its rats again and send them forth to die in a happy city.[97]

The United States, with its benign view of war, its sense that it has escaped history and need not know about the past, its belief that mobility is always upward, and its relentless insistence on the power of positive thinking has nearly gotten away with it all because of lucky historical timing, fortunate geography, and some brave and genuine creativity.

Without foreswearing the sweet American habits of optimism, friendliness, a sense of fun, and idealism, it may be time to add to those estimable qualities something harder to associate with the American character: respect for subtle, rigorous, informed, and accurate thinking. With that respect, the future—with an its complex challenges of overpopulation, resource depletion, environmental deterioration, nuclear proliferation, global interconnectedness, and technological possibility—may not prove overwhelming to currently unprepared Americans. The prospect before us, being not unrelievedly bleak, means that knowledge can sometimes be grafted upon optimism, that we need not altogether abandon our upbeat historical faith if we decide to strive, as I hope we will, to become smarter.

AFTERWORD

In recent years, for obvious reasons, the media have rediscovered Richard Hofstadter's great Pulitzer-Prize-winning book, Anti-Intellectualism in American Life *(1963). It offers deep structural and historical reasons for the phenomenon described in his title and explored throughout this book; and it speaks to today's America more than any book I know. When I was his graduate student I thought it was the most penetrating book about this country since Tocqueville's* Democracy in America. *I have not changed my mind and happily acknowledge my intellectual debt to it and its author, who died way too soon, in 1970, at the age of 54.*

A Beautiful Mind

12

Toward The Future with Molecular Biology: A Coda

One particular area in which I hope Americans will get smarter fast is in what cognitive scientists are learning about the brain. In the past decade, scientists have developed explanatory models for the brain that work and are testable. This achievement ranks on a par with the paradigms of Newton, Darwin, and Einstein, and the implications for personal lives, cultural tendencies, and the future itself are at once breath-taking and minimally understood by the public.

I shall not here try to describe neurotransmitters, receptors, neurons, synapses, axons, and dendrites.[98] That new vocabulary does suggest the following propositions.

- The brain is a biological computer.
- The brain is best understood not as some spiritual essence but as a bio-chemical machine.
- The brain and the mind are one and the same.
- Psychology is moving from being an impressionistic enterprise toward becoming a science.
- Since the physical configuration of the brain is shaped not only genetically but by one's life events, the nature *vs.* nurture debate is resolved; i.e. the *interaction* between heredity and environment accounts for our emotions, thoughts, and behavior.

Other less abstract consequences and questions pour out at this point. If the mind is a machine, it can be fixed by psychic engineering. Just as we now see that insanity is not a moral or spiritual failing but a physical disease amenable to physical treatment, so too may the following be "mental illnesses" subject to similar amelioration: depression, anxiety disorders, personality disorders, addiction to drugs, alcohol, and tobacco, aspects of criminality, and perhaps a whole order of milder dysfunctions currently labeled imprecisely as "neuroses." While that sentence is easy to write, the adjustments required by society in the economic, political, and, moral realms will be enormously difficult. What happens, for example, to the concepts of "blame" and "responsibility"?

More: immortality may come to mean that after death we live on in the altered brain receptors, neural pathways, and dendritic clusters of those whose lives we have touched. That may not be much consolation when we consider the likelihood, assuming that "mind" or "soul" really equals "brain," that we ourselves may have no consciousness of anything after we die. If the brain is a bio-chemical computer, brain-death may be the same as the death of the soul.

Still more: Shakespeare's complex portrayals of people seem more pertinent than ever to the new discoveries about the incomparably complicated brain. As Jon Franklin, a science writer, observed: "The brain . . . was every bit as complex and delicate as poets had surmised. It was a churning cauldron of fluctuating metabolic rates, squirting neurotransmitters, oscillating receptor sensitivities . . . ."[99] Not so pertinent are the simplicities of the evangelical mystics on the right, or the New Age mystics on the left. Their vocabularies, questions, and conclusions seem wildly off the mark now and (unless we willfully ignore knowledge of the neurological research—work which advances in major ways with each passing month) they are likely to become even more pointless in the years ahead. Anyone in search of awe and wonder mixed with testable hypotheses would do well to foreswear crystals, channels, and speaking in tongues for the grander, stranger, and more useful delights of neurotransmitters.

The notion of the brain as machine may raise fears of mechanistic determinism and genetic engineering run amok. We need to face squarely the myriad of social, cultural, and ethical issues raised by our new understanding of the brain. But we cannot suppress the truth simply because it forces us to ask discomfiting questions.

I ended the previous chapter with the wish that Americans try to become generally smarter (that is, more knowledgeable). I conclude the book with the proposal that as these final words are read the reader will resolve to discover all he or she possibly can about what scientists now know about the brain. That unfolding knowledge is, after all, *our* story, the story of what it means to be human and, barring the real possibility of self-annihilation, the tale of where our futures might be headed. We are reminded yet again, at the end, of the awesome power of ideas.

AFTERWORD

Anyone with the faintest knowledge of research into the brain will recognize how far neuroscience has advanced since the pretty primitive stuff I wrote above in this Coda. My heart was in the right place, but I had no real idea how fast and far this research would travel in 20 years. The American Psychological Association has named the first years of the 21ˢᵗ century: The Decade of the Brain. And with much reason!

Scientific discoveries are far more thrilling than the penny-ante stuff of astrology and New Age mysticism, the medieval religious myths that still define the world's major faiths, and the banal proclamations of "psychics" and "healers." Alas, I fear that Americans are more scientifically illiterate than ever, and the cost of that ignorance is high.

I recently asked one of my classes this question: if you were a parent and did not wish your children to get infantile paralysis, would you: 1) have them take some herb recommended by your auntie? 2) have them pray not to get polio? or 3) have them take the Salk or Sabine vaccine? Would you have any way of knowing which would offer the best chance for your children to avoid catching this crippling and often fatal disease?

I thought this was a "who's buried in Grant's tomb?" sort of question. No such luck. A young man raised his hand and said that there was "no way of knowing which of the three alternatives would be best. Whatever you believe is true." The idea that claims can be tested and that evidence exists for making wise decisions simply was not part of his intellectual repertoire. My heart sank.

Some claims are more valid than others, but that is not an idea expressed by the catchword of our times: "whatever." Science has not only marched way beyond my descriptions of the brain in this chapter; new and remarkable knowledge has emerged in almost all realms under study. The discoveries everywhere are astonishing.

Happily, scientific understanding is no longer beyond the grasp of normally intelligent citizens, as accessible science writing now abounds. I've begun asking my students, as a starter, to read Bill Bryson's delightful summary of the current state of knowledge in a wide variety of scientific areas: A Short History of Nearly Everything *(2003).*

But perhaps it will do to conclude the coda to my book with this, from the astronomer Carl Sagan, reminding us that "science is a way of thinking much more than it is a body of knowledge." He continued:

> *The truth may be puzzling. It may take some work to grapple with. It may be counterintuitive. It may contradict deeply held prejudices. It may not be consonant with what we desperately want to be true. But our preferences do not determine what's true. We have a method, and that method helps us to reach not absolute truth . . . never there, just closer and closer, always finding vast new oceans of undiscovered possibilities.* [100]

POSTSCRIPTS

13

The Psychological Revolution[101]

A revolution is sweeping the world, a revolution perhaps more powerful than the economic, political, and material transformations that make up the most obvious elements of "globalization." I refer to the Psychological Revolution that, at the deepest level, has altered the character of Western civilization over the last 500 years. And now it may be sweeping the rest of the world as well.

At the core of the Psychological Revolution is the general tendency toward individualism—the idea that we as individuals are entitled to personal happiness in life and that we may take actions to try to increase that happiness. In many traditional religious and authoritarian cultures this belief is the profoundest heresy.

Individualism manifests itself most powerfully in continually changing notions as to the purposes of sex and when we might engage in it,[102] what we mean by family, the very nature of marriage, the rules for divorce, the role of women in society, the nature of relationships, and how we think about love itself.

Marriage, for example, not very long ago had nothing to do with love. Tina Turner had it right: "what's love got to do with it?" The answer was nothing. Arranged marriages were the norm; marriage was strictly a practical, economic matter. How many social changes run deeper than the transformation of marriage into an institution based on love?

And marriage itself continues to change and be contested. Does one—particularly a woman— have to marry in order to achieve fulfillment in life? As women need depend less and less on men for material survival, the answer to that question is increasingly "no." Is marriage an institution only between a man and a woman? Is it about raising children? Should it possess a sacred quality and last for a lifetime no matter what? Should divorce be made difficult to attain? These are not settled matters, and it's hard to imagine a unitary answer in the future.

Marriages used only to terminate at death, no matter how much violence and cruelty (almost always toward women) they involved. The historian Lawrence Stone thinks the most important social alteration of the last few centuries has been from what he called "a non-separating society" to "a separating society." Not being condemned to spend one's life in a miserable (frequently arranged) marriage, the possibility for a second chance in life, has expressed itself in ever-changing rules for divorce, mostly in the direction of increased permissiveness. This, too, is contested and the battle is hardly over.

Richard L. Rapson

Sex in the West was, for a very long time, permissible only for procreation. Over the centuries the justifications for sexual activity have expanded to include today sex for love, for fun, for curiosity, for self-esteem, for revenge, for stress reduction, and for scores more reasons. Serious study of the consequences of the growing multiplicity of sexual motives has only recently begun.

These psychological transformations that took place in the West over a 500-year period and continue to do so at an ever-accelerating rate are also occurring with breathtaking speed nearly everywhere else on the planet as well. The speed of these changes in the role of women, the nature of marriage and divorce, and the rules for sexual behavior, varies with the region of the world in question and in urban-rural differences. It is slowest in the Middle East and Africa, more rapid in much of urban Asia, and explosive in Latin America and the rest of the West. And the overall movement toward individualism itself may tell the biggest global story of all.

Among the Western countries, the resistance to change is greatest in the United States. It's not hard to understand why the evangelical and political family values crowd longs to return to a time when the rules for love, sex, and marriage were clear and universally accepted. But it has been a very long time since that was the case; the historical story of love, sex, marriage, divorce, and the desire for personal fulfillment, tells of constant and accelerating transformation.

Perhaps rather than futilely resisting it, we should try to make ourselves smarter and better informed about the manifold choices we now have about how to live our private lives. Perhaps we should know more, not less, about sex. Perhaps our politics should adapt to the reality of consensual unions, multiple family forms, un-closeted homosexuality, the multiplicity of sexual motives, and the many ways of loving.

Though it can cause confusion and lead to stupid decisions, I think there is much to be said in behalf of personal choice. I wouldn't bet on authoritarians and reactionaries successfully reducing those choices in the name of order, tradition, or religion for very long. The historical tide has for 500 years generally been sweeping us away from uniform cultural stipulations and toward personal freedom. I regard that psychological revolution as, by and large, a great (though not unalloyed) triumph over authoritarianism and its quenching of the human spirit. The trick is not to flee from or waste the opportunities of private freedoms, but to manage them with informed knowledge, bravery, and good sense.

14

New College: 1968-1973[103]

I think it safe to say that New College stands as the most ambitious and far-reaching educational experiment in the history of the University of Hawaii. Nothing before its creation in 1968 presaged its emergence. Since its demise in 1973, no comprehensive structural reconsideration of the nature of University undergraduate education has even been attempted.

Educational reform has taken place in the last two decades separately in a hundred different classrooms, shaped by an array of imaginative professors. That sort of reform undoubtedly remains the wellspring of the educational enterprise, and is alive and well at this University. But such innovation and energy prospers better when there exists an architecture to protect and nourish it. The University of Hawaii has been, in my opinion, a distinctly lesser place since the death of New College.

If success were measured by longevity, New College would have to be accounted a disappointment. If success were gauged by the scope of its ambitions, by the loyalties it engendered among its students and faculty, by the kind of teaching and learning it promoted, and by the energies it sent off into the community—campus-wide and beyond—it would probably have to be adjudged a triumph. If measured by how close it came to achieving its own goals, the verdict would be complex, mixed, and uncertain.

THE NATURE OF NEW COLLEGE

Just what was New College? Essentially it was a four-year liberal arts College that functioned within and as a part of the University of Hawaii. When would-be freshmen applied for admission to U.H., they were given a chance to choose New College (also known as The Experimental College of Humanistic Studies) as their program, the application forms being accompanied by a College brochure. We received many more applications than we had places, and experimented with different admissions criteria.

New College required all students to take the same two courses each semester for the first two years. The courses were multidisciplinary and related one to the other sequentially; they covered large areas in the social sciences, humanities, and physical sciences. There was a strong emphasis on methodology, process, and critical thinking. They were also taught in a cross-cultural way whenever possible. They were designed to form a true, integrated core, but also be innovative, team-taught, rigorous, and flexible; written evaluations replaced formal grades.

Since all students took the same courses at the same time with all their classmates, we hoped to foster an intellectual community. We hoped students would talk among one another about the questions raised in their classes; by and large, that seemed to have happened. The courses, being team-taught by faculty from different disciplines, led to conversations in our faculty that rarely took place at the larger University, with its large specialized Departments. And students and faculty regularly talked with one another more than they ever did across the street.

For the final two years, students were freed from the highly-structured lower-division curriculum to work in Oxbridge style tutorials, culminating their college careers with major creative projects: a series of scientific experiments, an art show, a scholarly thesis, a novel, a musical performance, a mathematical treatise, or the like.

The College was housed across from the main campus in a stately Victorian mansion. It rested on spacious grounds and the classes were held inside and in wooded nooks within its own campus. It invited a sense of community far more intense than common in the far more atomized University. Meals were cooked at New College, events took place on the campus, day and night—ranging from Ravi Shankar recitals to non-credit workshops for the community to lectures and social gatherings. These brought students and faculty onto the premises long after the classes were done for the day.

I got to know more faculty from other departments in the five years of New College's existence (two years to create it, three years of actual life) than in my other two-plus decades at the University proper. I think most of our remarkable faculty had the same experience. Students got to know other students, because they hung around the place; New College did not follow the commuter pattern of the larger University. And faculty and students did truly talk together.

We sought democratic governance and a full feeling of participation and identity, and I think we went a far distance in achieving it. Our major instrument toward that end was the All-College meeting (all students, staff, and faculty with one vote), which we held weekly at a large, yet intimate room designed to promote conversation for large groups at the East-West Center.

The Faculty

The College attracted a veritable Who's Who of the regular University faculty plus a distinguished handful who came to Hawaii specifically to teach with us. Those in the first camp were given released time by their own Departments, most of which cooperated handsomely with us. The visitors, including Paul Goodman, Theodore Brameld, Mary Gayle Bitterman, and Donna Haraway, taught full time with us. I was proud to be able to help assemble the entire group, perhaps as fine a faculty as could be found anywhere . . . .

How New College Came To Be

I came to the University of Hawaii in 1966, following teaching stints at Amherst College (my alma mater) and Stanford University. I was not yet 30. It was a time of great growth and hope at

U.H. (and across the Mainland as well). Much national talent poured into the Islands during that period, even at the Administrative level, and expectations ran high that the University could become a serious national and international educational and research force.

I was asked in 1968 by Harlan Cleveland, the new President and former Ambassador to N.A.T.O., to generate new ideas to further the Humanities on campus. A group of students and I decided, rather than putting together a one-shot festival or series of workshops, to create something that could last and could address fundamental questions of education. By 1969 we had forged the framework of New College, and with Cleveland's support we circulated our proposals to a faculty which raised hardly any objections but which was largely apathetic. I was given permission by Cleveland to find a campus, gather a faculty and staff, seek out students, and begin. We were ready to open our doors in time for the Fall semester, 1970. Nothing in my professional career ever came close to generating the joy that came from giving birth to New College and bringing in dozens of other midwives; it was a singularly gratifying enterprise—and a lot of fun.

Cleveland and I actually thought New College could be one of many colleges at U.H. We had the vision of converting a mass university into a series of separate colleges and programs, each possessing their own physical home, student body, faculty, curricular emphasis, and identity. The idea was not new; Oxford and Cambridge had been doing it for 700 years. The five-college nexus around Amherst, Smith, Mount Holyoke, Hampshire, and the University of Massachusetts wasn't as old, but it worked on and off, and I knew it well, having taken undergraduate courses at Smith and Mount Holyoke. California's Claremont colleges derived from the same principle. But, as far as we knew, no public university in America had on its own gone this route, although the college system of the University of California at Santa Cruz lay just around the corner.

That was a dream for the future (unrealized), one that could bring the intimacy, sense of student and faculty identification and community, and emotional involvement of the small college in concordance with the great resources of the large university. Our first job, however, was to make New College work.

THE PHILOSOPHY

At my opening speech on September 8, 1970, I offered the following remarks:

> *. . . From the beginning we have rejected the spurious dichotomies which are frequently given us: freedom vs. structure, feeling vs. thought, creativity vs. discipline, the heart vs. the head. We are testing out the proposition that freedom, structure, feeling, thought, creativity, and discipline are, when properly conceived, intimately bound together, indeed necessary to each other.*

We thought we just might be on to that proper conception, but from Day One we operated within a very difficult historical context of which we were acutely aware. The 1960's of liberation, counter-cultures, and untrammeled freedom were actually at their peak in the early 1970s, and most of us over-30 faculty (the age at which trust from the rebels was supposed to terminate!)

were largely excited by the times. Most of us were against the Vietnam War, for the Civil Rights and Women's movements, and supportive of a good deal of the political and social agenda of the 1960s. But, while we occasionally inhaled some pot and wore jeans and were not unmoved by the new sexual permissiveness, we were professors not hippies. We were interested equally in rigor as in freedom, and we adhered to an educational model more complex than the "do your own thing" ethos of some of our students. My own major model was Amherst, which consciously prepared us, through a tremendously demanding curricular experience, for the freedom of choosing our own honors project.

Because we were not simply following the fashion of some of the other do your own thing experimental programs popping up across the nation in the 1960's, our more complex approach engendered a fairly substantial literature about New College, both locally and nationally. It also fed our most difficult political dilemma: the high-wire act between a sometimes radical student body (joined by some professors) and a wary and suspicious, far more conservative community, legislature, and university administration (the latter groups all paying our bills). Our strategy was tirelessly to try to explain, persuade, and communicate a message that was true to our complications; and this was no simple or easy task, either with politicos or with ourselves. We all experienced many unquestioned delights during our New College days, but there came one unmitigated disaster: our termination in November 1973.

THE DEMISE

Much has been written about our death at the hands of the Regents, especially in light of official faculty recommendations, after exhaustive evaluation, that we be permitted to continue indefinitely to exist. How did it happen? There were local, political causes centering upon the choice of my successor. I had announced from the first day that I would step down the summer of 1973 because I believed we needed constant infusions of new ideas in order to be truly experimental.

We followed our usual democratic procedures (everyone in the community received one vote), and chose an eminently qualified person to take over from me. But she was also controversial to the powers that be and had the University in the courts. Some believe her election forced the hand of the Regents and that we thus committed suicide. Many experimental programs did (and do) have a certain moralistic self-righteousness and perhaps our idealism contributed to our demise.

Some in the Administration claimed we fell because of our own deficiencies. Flawed we were, but the faculty report recommending that we be allowed to go on led me then (and still does) to doubt that explanation.

I felt at the time (and now blessed with hindsight feel it with more certainty) that the largest cause of our end was that which terminated nearly every experimental program in the nation at about the same time. I speak here of large cultural and economic forces, national and international in scope, that brought about a cultural sea change at about this time.

I refer generally to the swing to conservatism and right-wing attitudes that swept this nation for almost three decades. It began with revulsion against the 1960s, with its challenge to all middle-class verities, all the way into the big chill of the Reagan-Bush years. The immediate catalyst came with the OPEC crisis and long gas lines of 1973. Money was drying up; America was losing independence and confidence; it was time to retreat. States decreased their largesse to universities almost in unison with the OPEC scare, and the first programs to go—everywhere—were the newest and most experimental. New College was an easy, vulnerable target and proximate rationalizations for killing it were easy to find.

And so New College died, and with it went most innovation at the University of Hawaii (and elsewhere) for more than a quarter of a century. We still find a lot of good teaching; worthy programs to foster it are still extant. Various "studies" programs have come into being, but most of them focus on the substantive challenge to received ideas rather than rethinking the process of thinking and learning itself. They sometimes have a political rather than educational agenda. Further, New College never really died. Many of its faculty still teach here and have exercised signal influence on the life of this University. Many students have gone on to wonderful things and have spread the news. The spirit of New College remains alive for its participants and for its large cadre of supporters, and I would like to think that such a legacy has enriched this University.

The hard fact remains, however, that New College itself does not exist, that it did not last long, and that nothing remotely like it has replaced it; nor do I see anything out there on the horizon. Yet there is no reason that this need remain the case. The political and cultural times are a-changin' again even as I write this piece (at the end of the first year of the Clinton Presidency). There are a lot of new, young faculty out there with pedagogical passion and personal energy, and perhaps someone reading this little piece will be stimulated to get something started. I hope so and would encourage the effort.[104]

As may be seen to be implicit here, I am not by nature a nostalgic person with a longing for imagined good old days. My personal and professional life has gotten better and better with the passage of the years; and no time has been better for me than now. But, it is my opinion that the University of Hawaii became a less lively and interesting place for teaching and learning in the years after New College died than it was during the ferment of the late 1960s and early 1970s. In looking back to those days, particularly when it comes to excitement, idealism, and commitment to the educational enterprise, I believe we might have been younger and wiser then.

The Evolution of Dumb.

DUMBAND
DUMBERER
WHEN HARRY MET LLOYD

Before the first movie, there was high school.

 www.whenharrymetlloyd.com

Dumb and Dumber

15

America The Ignorant[105]

I think I know the precise moment when America's world dominance began to erode. It was in December 2000, when the Supreme Court gave the Presidential election to George W. Bush, despite Al Gore's lead in the popular vote and despite widespread voting irregularities in Florida. The hit to American hegemony has taken place on the two key fronts: military/political and cultural/moral.

The military/political represents the form by which power is most often perceived. While clearly THE military superpower in the world, we have discovered that such predominance still could not prevent the U.S. from losing its war in Vietnam, and now failing to secure the peace in Iraq. Overpowering military force guarantees nothing against guerilla tactics and a motivated adversary. Further it invites suspicion and fear from the rest of the world, feelings profoundly aggravated by the arrogant and bullying foreign policy of the current Bush Administration. It has assumed a dismissive attitude towards the U.N., the European Union, Russia, China, or anyone who dared to question the merits of the Iraq invasion. Has any American Administration, in the entire history of this nation, ever been so universally despised and distrusted as is the current one?

In less than four years, and only three years after the rush of sympathy evoked by 9/11, this Superpower has overreached, like the Spanish, French, British, and Russian Empires before them. The American economy has been stretched thin and the nation finds itself isolated in the world—clear signs of Imperial Decline.

Though the dislike of America around the world focuses on George W. Bush and his appointees, and while former allies try to distinguish Americans generally from their President, there has been some inevitable overlap. After all, Americans elected him, and no one else would. What does that say about the nation and its culture overall?[106] It raises disturbing questions for many about Americans, about their judgment and their knowledge.

These questions serve as reminders of the appalling ignorance of Americans about the world, the past, and serious questions generally. We recall how miserably our students perform on tests of history and much else. It is noted how America stands alone among industrialized nations in its near-majority belief in creationism over evolution, the majority beliefs in the existence of angels, the Devil, Hell, Heaven, and magical thinking generally, combined with its scientific illiteracy.

We also see a popular culture that exalts stupidity and triviality—on TV, in movies, and in its music. We recall the long history of anti-intellectualism in this nation, never stronger than today. We should shudder at the attacks on the best thing about America—its Universities and Colleges, not long ago admired nearly everywhere on the planet. Now these formidable institutions are losing students from abroad in the name of "national security," are finding their budgets cut to the bone everywhere, the research enterprise threatened, and interest in what they do waning.

Thus American culture, even of the popular brand, has begun to lose its cachet. What industrialized nation today really wishes to emulate American society? And with the old charges of its overweening materialism and its relentless banality gaining force, who can regard America as the moral beacon for the world? When the culture and its claims for moral superiority fade and are combined with its military limitations, economic vulnerabilities (note the colossal budget deficits), and political isolation, an inescapable conclusion emerges. Just when America became the world's only superpower, its power began to wane.

And to what extent need we mourn for the beginnings of this descent from singular eminence?

16

America The Rightwing

*A*merica, *I fear, really is—clichés notwithstanding—too much about the making of money. It's not enough, for my tastes, a nation that honors the life of the mind or of the arts or of the senses. It allows too many of its citizens to live in poverty and despair, homeless, unable to afford to go to the doctor, struggling unnecessarily to raise children—all this while some of its citizens enjoy obscene riches. It is a violent place where anyone can own a gun. Yet the culture drips with sanctimony, and it gives credence to creationism, psychics, and Satan. It guzzles oil and energy heedlessly, putting the rest of the world at risk. It devours its once plenteous pristine lands with economic development. It creates a cheesy popular culture and disdains knowledge of societies beyond its borders. I feel at home only in a few of its more cosmopolitan cities, primarily on the two coasts.*

A main problem in my view is Capitalism run rampant, the same Capitalism that, until a decade or two after the end of World War II, afforded me—and millions like me—more opportunities to put together a better life than I could have had anywhere else. Capitalism has proved itself the best engine of economic growth and for creating wealth. The world acknowledges that and few societies in the early 21ˢᵗ century stand outside that system. Capitalism has succeeded as the way to manufacture goods and wealth, and when we talk about free markets and globalization, we are really talking about Capitalism. Capitalism has won most of the world.

But there is more to life than the generation of wealth, and here America shows its deficiencies. Many elements of life have little to do with profits or markets but they go a long way toward defining a civilized society. The question that truly faces us revolves around matters of balance. What is the best balance between the money-generating power of free market Capitalism and that of social justice? How much governmental involvement (through taxation, regulation, and public investment) is appropriate? When is too much? When too little? This leads us inevitably to questions about the Good Society and about life itself; it leads to debates concerning those activities that are not about profit.

Clean air does not make a lot of money, but shouldn't citizens of a worthy society breathe clean air? Who will provide that, if not the government? The same goes for medical care that everybody can afford; inexpensive medical care does not lend itself to vast profits. Should the society, through its taxes, provide good, affordable education for all? That would not be a snappy moneymaker. Nor would open lands, parks, and conserved nature.

Richard L. Rapson

Clean water, no one living on the streets because they can't pay for a roof over their heads, keeping competition fair and open, protecting worker safety and health—how to make money on that? Additionally, perhaps an enlightened society should help its artists, writers, musicians, scholars, and scientists survive, free of market pressures. Or shall we let the market or private philanthropy rule in the arts and sciences?

Different societies have arrived at different answers and the balances keep shifting. The Industrialized World is Capitalist; all the nations of the world regulate that Capitalism to varying degrees and invest in public expenditures in varying amounts. Democratic elections are, to a great extent, actually about which balances are preferred by the public at the moment. Capitalism in the West is nowhere laissez-faire; Welfare Capitalism prevails everywhere.

But a disquieting pattern appears to have developed since the end of the Second World War. The differences have come down to those between the United States, which stands on the capitalist, unregulated end of the continuum versus everyone else. Substantially to the left lies "the rest of the West" (the Western European societies, Japan and the remnants of the British Empire—Canada, Australia, New Zealand); these nations tend to believe far more deeply in the concept of guaranteed (or at least protected) social and economic rights for all. And they are willing to tax themselves at a far higher rate than Americans to assure these rights.

In fact, the mainstream Conservative parties of Western Europe at the turn of the 21st century accepted far more government intervention in the economy and supported guaranteed social rights (medical care, childcare support, unemployment protection, pensions, publicly supported radio, TV, and the arts, worker vacations, mass transit, and more) than did the Democratic "left" in the United States. That is, Rightists like Jacques Chirac, Helmut Kohl, and John Major supported expenditures on social rights more than did the Democratic Party of Bill Clinton and Al Gore. As for the American Republican Party of Reagan and the Bushes, they were off the charts, far to the right, standing alone in the Western World—unless you count the Far Right extremist fringe in Europe. They wished to underwrite practically no social rights.

I prefer the balances struck by Western Europe, Canada, and Oceania to the American form—though the great productivity of the American economic system cannot be gainsaid. But wealth doesn't always trickle down from the wealthiest. I enthusiastically appreciate the public amenities of Europe, Canada, and Australia. By European standards I would probably be regarded as a mainstream moderate on these issues; in America I stand pretty far out on the left. By my own standards, I consider my views unexceptional and rooted in common sense.

17

America The Resilient?

I bring this book to a close 18 months before an election that, at the moment, looks to bring to the White House in March 2009, a less ideological President and Administration than that of George W. Bush. This seems true whether Americans choose a Republican or a Democrat. I look for better governance than we've had at the commencement of the new millennium.

But the historian's observations shouldn't bounce around, depending on the latest election results. Even though the updates in this book have been shadowed by recent developments, I've always sought deeper and more fundamental historical and cultural realities to explain how America functions.

So, while I look for improvement ahead, a new President will not be able profoundly to alter America's suspicion of: national health insurance; higher taxes to pay for it and other social programs; environmental sacrifices; much more money for schools and teachers, much less for military spending. Suspicion also of: enlarged support for the arts; Darwinian evolution; people who don't believe in God; non-magical thinking; much of the rest of the world; diplomacy and patience over force and anger; the life of the mind; and relaxed attitudes toward sex. The country will remain conservative and religious, relative to the rest of the developed world, no matter who sits in the White House—at least for the next years.

Still, two of the best things about America have been its willingness to be self-critical and its capacity for a degree of pragmatic flexibility. Though its period for bestriding the globe like a colossus is likely to give way to a multi-polar world in which American power declines and Chinese and European power, relative to America, grows, America will certainly still continue to be a serious player. It's a big country (a continent, really). It has wealth, power, and dynamism. It has, at its best, improved the lot of mankind. In my lifetime, it has afforded me more opportunities to write the script of my own life than I could have found anywhere else. It has resilience.

So while I doubt that a new President can change the nation's fundamental nature, he or she might be able to encourage in its people greater knowledge and less fantasy, and muster a greater display of its finer qualities. Fingers crossed!

BOOKS OF INTEREST IN PSYCHOLOGICAL HISTORY:

Love, Marriage, Emotions, Divorce, Child-Rearing, Sex.

(Starred books denote excellent overviews. Note that most of the books on this and the following Cultural History list are those that have been particularly helpful to me, do not represent an exhaustive list, and are mostly of recent vintage.)

Elizabeth Abbott, *A History of Celibacy* (Scribner: NY, 2000)

Patricia Anderson, *When Passion Reigned: Sex and the Victorians* (Basic Books: NY, 1995)

Natalie Angier, *Woman: An Intimate Geography* (Houghton Mifflin: NY, 1995)

Philippe Aries, *Centuries of Childhood* (Vintage: New York,1965)

Beth Bailey, *From Front Porch to Back Seat: A History of Courtship in America* (Johns Hopkins U. Press: Baltimore,1988)

Lois Banner, *American Beauty* (U. of Chicago Press: Chicago and London, 1983)

Susan Bordo, *Unbearable Weight: Feminism, Western Culture, and The Body* (U. of California Press: Berkeley, 1995)

Susan Bordo, *The Male Body: A New Look at Men in Public and in Private* (Farrar, Straus & Giroux: NY, 1999)

John Boswell, Christianity, *Social Tolerance, and Homosexuality: Gay People in Western Europe from the Beginning of the Christian Era to the Fourteenth Century* (U. of Chicago Press: Chicago, 1981)

John Boswell, *Same-Sex Unions in Premodern Europe* (Vintage: NY, 1995)

John Boswell *The Kindness of Strangers: The Abandonment of Children in Western Europe from Late Antiquity to the Renaissance* (U. of Chicago Press: Chicago, 1998)

Janet Brodie, *Contraception and Abortion in Nineteenth-Century America* (Cornell U. Press: Ithaca, N.Y., 1994)

Judith Brown, *Immodest Acts: The Life of a Lesbian Nun in Renaissance Italy* (Oxford U. Press: NY and Oxford, 1986)

Patricia Fortini Brown, *Private Lives in Renaissance Venice: Art, Architecture, and the Family* (Yale U. Press: New Haven, 2005)

Joan Jacobs Brumberg, *The Body Project: An Intimate History of American Girls* (Random House: NY, 1997)

Vern Bullough, *Science in the Bedroom: A History of Sex Research* (Basic Books: New York, 1995)

George Chauncey, *Gay New York; Gender, Urban Culture, and the Making of the Gay Male World, 1890-1940* (Basic Books: NY, 1995)

Candace Clark, *Misery and Company: Sympathy in Everyday Life* (U. of Chicago Press: Chicago, 1997)

John R. Clarke, *Looking at Lovemaking: Constructions of Sexuality in Roman Art, 100BC-AD250* (University of California Press: Berkeley, 1998)

Hera Cook, *The Long Sexual Revolution: English Women, Sex. And Contraception* (Oxford U. Press: London, 2004)

*Stephanie Coontz, *The Social Origins of Private Life: A History of American Families, 1600-1900* (Verso Books: NY, 1988)

*Stephanie Coontz, *The Way We Never Were: American Families and the Nostalgia Trap* (Basic Books, NY: 1992)

Stephanie Coontz, *The Way We Really Are: Coming to Terms with America's Changing Families* (Basic Books: NY, 1997)

*Stephanie Coontz *Marriage: A History* (Viking: NY, 2005)

Nancy Cott, *Public Vows: A History of Marriage and the Nation* (Harvard U. Press: Cambridge, 2001)

Louis Crompton, *Homosexuality and Civilization* (Harvard U. Press: Cambridge, 2004)

Gary Cross, *Kids' Stuff: Toys and the Changing World of American Childhood* (Harvard U. Press: Cambridge, 1998)

Natalie Zemon Davis, *Women on the Margins: Three Seventeenth-Century Lives* (Harvard U. Press: Cambridge, MA., 1996)

*Carl Degler, *At Odds: Women and the Family in America from the Revolution to the Present* (Oxford U. Press: Oxford, 1980)

Joan DeJean, *The Reinvention of Obscenity: Sex, Lies, and Tabloids in Early Modern France* (U. of Chicago Press: Chicago, 2002)

*John D'Emilio and Estelle B. Freedman, *Intimate Matters: A History of Sexuality in America* (Harper & Row: NY, 1988) Second edition: (U. of Chicago Press: Chicago, 1997)

Emma Donoghue, *Passions Between Women: British Lesbian Culture 1668-1801* (HarperCollins: NY, 1996)

Catalina de Erauso: *Lieutenant Nun: Memoir of a Basque Transvestite in the New World* (Beacon: NY, 1996)

Joanne Ferraro, *Marriage Wars in Late Renaissance Venice* (Oxford U. Press: London, 2001)

Anthony Fletcher, *Gender, Sex, and Subordination in England 1500-1800* (Yale U. Press: New Haven, 1996)

Peter Gay, *The Bourgeois Experience,* vol. 1: *Education of the Senses* (Oxford U. Press: Oxford, 1984)

Peter Gay, —————————, vol. 2: *The Tender Passion* (Oxford U. Press: Oxford, 1986)

Peter Gay, —————————, vol. 3: *Hate and Aggression* (Oxford U. Press: Oxford, 1993)

Peter Gay, —————————, vol. 4: *The Naked Heart* (Norton: NY, 1995)

Peter Gay, —————————, vol. 5: *Pleasure Wars* (Norton: NY, 1998)

*John Gillis, *For Better, For Worse: British Marriages, 1600 to the Present* (Oxford U. Press: NY and Oxford, 1985)

John Gillis, *A World of Their Own Making: Myth, Ritual, and the Quest for Family Values* (Basic Books: NY, 1996)

Richard Godbeer, *Sexual Revolution in Early America* (Johns Hopkins Press: Baltimore, 2002)

Julia Grant, *Raising Baby By the Book* (Yale U. Press: New Haven, 1998)

Robert L. Griswold, *Fatherhood in America: A History* (Basic Books: NY, 1993)

Carol Groneman, *Nymphomania: A History* (Norton: NY, 2000)

Elizabeth Haiken, *Venus Envy: A History of Cosmetic Surgery* (Johns Hopkins Univ. Press: Baltimore, 1998)

Barbara Hanawalt, *Growing Up in Medieval London: The Experience of Childhood In History* (Oxford U. Press: London, 1993)

Barbara Harris, *English Aristocratic Women, 1450-1550: Marriage and Family, Property and Careers* (Oxford: London, 2003)

Hendrik Hartog, *Man and Wife in America: A History* (Harvard U. Press: Cambridge, 2001)

Elaine Hatfield and Richard L. Rapson, *Love, Sex, and Intimacy: Their Psychology, Biology, and History* (HarperCollins: NY and London, 1993)

Elaine Hatfield and Richard L. Rapson, *Emotional Contagion* (Cambridge U. Press: London and New York, 1994)

Elaine Hatfield and Richard L. Rapson, *Love and Sex: Cross-Cultural Perspectives* (Allyn & Bacon: NY, 1996)

Christian Henriot, *Prostitution and Sexuality in Shanghai: A Social History, 1849-1949* (Cambridge U. Press: London, 2003)

Marianne Hirsch, *Family Frames: Photography, Narrative, and Postmemory* (Harvard U. Press: Cambridge, 1998)

Martha Hodes, ed., *Sex, Love, Race: Crossing Boundaries in North American History* (NYU Press: NY, 1999)

Ann Hulbert, *Raising America: Experts, Parents and a Century of Advice About Children* (Knopf: NY, 2003)

Helen Lefkowitz Horowitz, *Rereading Sex: Battles Over Sexual Knowledge In Nineteenth-Century America* (Knopf: NY, 2002)

Lynn Hunt, ed. *The Invention of Pornography* (Zone Books: NY, 1993)

Margaret Hunt, *The Middling Sort: Commerce, Gender, and the Family in England, 1680-1780* (University of California Press: Berkeley, 1996

*Olwen Hutton, *The Prospect Before Her: A History of Women in Western Europe. Volume 1, 1500-1800* (Knopf: NY, 1996)

Betsy Israel, *Bachelor Girl: The Secret History of Single Women in the Twentieth Century* (William Morrow: NY, 2002)

James H. Jones, *Alfred C. Kinsey: A Public/Private Life* (Norton: NY, 1998)

Charles Kaiser, *The Gay Metropolis: 1940-1996* (Houghton Mifflin: NY, 1998)

Paula Kamen, *Her Way: Young Women Remake the Sexual Revolution* (NYU Press: NY, 2001)

Ruth Karras, *Common Women; Prostitution and Sexuality in Medieval England* (Oxford U. Press: London, 1996)

John Kasson, *Houdini, Tarzan, and the Perfect White Man: The White Male Body and the Challenge of Modernity in America* (Hill & Wang: NY, 2001)

Gary Kates, *Monsieur d'Eon Is a Woman: A Tale of Political Intrigue and Sexual Masquerade* (Basic Books: NY, 1995)

Jonathan Ned Katz, *The Invention of Heterosexuality* (Dutton: NY, 1995)

_____, *Love Stories: Sex between Men before Homosexuality* (U. of Chicago Press: Chicago, 2002)

Michael Kimmel, *Manhood in America: A Cultural History* (The Free Press: NY, 1996)

Emmanuel Roy Ladurie, *Montaillou: Promised Land of Error* (Vintage: NY, 1978)

Thomas Laqueur, *Making Sex: Body and Gender from the Greeks to Freud* (Zone Books: NY, 1990)

Thomas Laqueur, *Solitary Sex: A Cultural History of Masturbation* (Zone Books NY, 2003)

John Loughery, *The Other Side of Silence: Men's Lives and Gay Identities—A Twentieth-Century History* (Holt: NY, 1998

Lynne Luciano, *Looking Good: Male Body Image in Modern America* (Hill & Wang: NY, 2001)

Karen Lystra, *Searching the Heart: Women, Men, and Romantic Love in Nineteenth-Century America* (Oxford U. Press: NY and Oxford, 1989)

Michael Mason, *The Making of Victorian Sexuality* (Oxford U. Press: Oxford, 1994)

Elaine Tyler May, *Barren in the Promised Land: Childless Americans And the Pursuit of Happiness* (Basic Books: New York, 1995)

Alan Macfarlane, *Marriage and Love in England: Modes of Reproduction, 1300-1840* (Blackwell: London, 1986)

Lara Marks, *Sexual Chemistry: A History of the Contraceptive Pill* (Yale U. Press: New Haven, 2001

James McMillan, *France and Women 1789-1914: Gender Society, And Politics* (Routledge: London, 2001)

Sara Mendelson and Patricia Crosby, *Women in Early Modern England, 1550-1720* (Clarendon Press: Oxford, 1999)

Jeffrey Merrick and Bryant Ragan, *Homosexuality in Modern France* (Oxford U. Press: London, 1996)

Joanne Meyerowitz, *How Sex Changed: A History of Transsexuality in the United States* (Harvard U. Press: Cambridge, 2002)

*Steven Mintz and Susan Kellogg, *Domestic Revolutions: A Social History of American Family Life* (Free Press: NY, 1988)

*Steven Mintz, *Huck's Raft: A History of American Childhood* (Harvard U. Press: Cambridge, 2004)

George Mosse, *The Image of Man: The Creation of Modern Masculinity* (Oxford U. Press: London, 1996)

Mary Beth Norton, *Founding Mothers & Fathers: Gendered Power and the Forming Of American Society* (Knopf: NY, 1996)

Catherine Orenstein, *Little Red Riding Hood Uncloaked: Sex, Morality and the Evolution of a Fairy Tale* (Basic Books: NY, 2002)

Nicholas Orme, *Medieval Children* (Yale U. Press: New Haven, 2002)

Steven Ozment, *Flesh and Spirit: Private Life in Early Modern Germany* (Viking: NY, 1999)

Steven Ozment, *Ancestors: The Loving Family in Old Europe* (Harvard U. Press: Cambridge, 2002)

Grace Palladino, *Teenagers: An American History* (Basic Books: NY, 1997)

Daphne Patai, *Heterophobia: Sexual Harassment and the Future of Feminism* (Rowman & Littlefield: Lanham, MD, 1999)

Kathy Peiss, *Hope In a Jar: The Making of America's Beauty Culture* (Metropolitan Books: NY, 1998)

R. Phillips, *Putting Asunder: A History of Divorce in Western Society* (Cambridge U. Press: Cambridge and NY, 1988)

Sarah Pomeroy, *Goddesses, Whores, Wives, and Slaves: Women in Classical Antiquity* (Schocken: NY, 1999)

Teresa Riordan, *Inventing Beauty: A History of the Innovations That Have Made Us Beautiful* (Broadway Books: NY, 2005)

Graham Robb, *Strangers: Homosexual Love in the Nineteenth Century* (Norton: NY, 2004)

Michael Rocke, *Forbidden Friendships: Homosexuality and Male Culture in Renaissance Florence* (Oxford U. Press: NY, 1998)

Sheila and David Rothman, *The Pursuit of Perfection: The Promise and Perils Of Medical Enhancements* (Pantheon Books: NY, 2004)

E. Anthony Rotundo, *American Manhood: Transormations in Masculinity from the Revolution to the Modern Era* (Basic Books: NY, 1993)

Guido Ruggiero, *Binding Passion: Tales of Magic, Marriage, and Power at the End of the Renaissance* (Oxford U. Press: London, 1993)

Steven Seidman, *Romantic Longings: A History of Love in America: 1830-Present* (Routledge: NY and London, 1991)

Merril Smith, ed., *Sex and Sexuality in Early America* (NYU Press: NY, 1998)

Christine Stansell, *American Moderns: Bohemian New York and the Creation Of a New Century* (Henry Holt: NY, 2000)

Peter N. Stearns, *American Cool: Constructing A 20th-Century Emotional Style* (NYU Press; NY, 1995)

Peter N. Stearns, *Battleground of Desire: The Struggle for Self Control In Modern America* (NYU Press: NY, 1999)

Peter Stearns and Jan Lewis, eds., *An Emotional History of the United States* (NYU Press: NY, 1998)

Brenda E. Stevenson, *Life in Black and White: Family and Community in the Slave South* (Oxford U. Press: NY, 1997)

*Lawrence Stone, *The Family, Sex and Marriage: In England 1500-1800* (Harper: NY, 1977)

*Lawrence Stone, *The Road to Divorce: England 1530-1987* (Oxford: NY, 1990)

Frank Sulloway, *Born to Rebel: Birth Order, Family Dynamics, and Creative Lives* (Pantheon Books: NY, 1996)

John Tosh, *A Man's Place: Masculinity and the Middle-Class Home In Victorian England* (Yale U. Press: New Haven, 1999)

Andrea Tone, *Devices and Desires: A History of Contraceptives in America* (Hill &Wang: NY, 2001)

Randolph Trumbach, *Sex and the Gender Revolution, vol. 1 Hetero-Sexuality and the Third Gender in Enlightenment London,* (U. of Chicago Press: Chicago, 1999)

Sharon Ullman, *Sex Seen: The Emergence of Modern Sexuality in America* (Univ. of Calif. Press: Berkeley, 1999)

Georges Vigarello, *A History of Rape: Sexual Violence in France from the 16th To the 20th Century* (Polity Press: London, 2002)

Marilyn Yalom, *A History of the Breast* (Knopf: NY, 1997)

Marilyn Yalom, *A History of the Wife* (HarperCollins: NY, 2001)

BOOKS OF INTEREST IN CULTURAL HISTORY

Bonnie Anderson and Judith Zinsser, *A History of Their Own: Women in Europe from Prehistory to the Present*, 2 vols. (Oxford U. Press: London 1999)

Philippe Aries, *The Hour of Our Death* (Knopf: NY, 1981)

William F. Baker & George Dessart, *Down the Tube: An Inside Account of the Failure of American Television* (Basic Books: NY, 1998)

Jacques Barzun, *From Dawn to Decadence: 500 Years of Western Cultural Life—1500 to Present* (HarperCollins: NY, 2000)

J.M. Beattie, *Policing and Punishment in London, 166-1750: Urban Crime and the Limits of Terror* (Oxford U. Press: 2002)

Rudolph Bell, *How To Do It: Guides to Good Living for Renaissance Italians* (U. of Chicago Press: Chicago, 1999)

Renate Bridenthal and Susan Mosher Stuard, eds., *Becoming Visible: Women in European History* (Houghton Mifflin: NY, 1997)

Daniel Boorstin, *The Discoverers: A History of Man's Search to Know His World and Himself* (Random House: NY, 1983)

Daniel Boorstin, *The Creators: A History of Heroes of the Imagination* (Random House: NY, 1992)

Daniel Boorstin, *The Seekers: The Story of Man's Continuing Quest* (Random House: NY, 1998)

David Bordwell, *On the History of Film Style* (Harvard U. Press: Cambridge, 1998)

Fernand Braudel, *The Mediterranean: and the Mediterranean World in the Age of Philip II*, 2 vols. (Harper & Row: NY, 1966)

Fernand Braudel, *Civilization and Capitalism: $15^{th}h$-18^t Century*, 3 vols. 1. *The Structures of Everyday Life* (Harper & Row: NY, 1981); 2. *Wheels of Commerce* (1982); 3. *Perspective of the World* (Harper & Row: NY, 1984)

Leo Braudy, *The Frenzy of Renown: Fame and Its History* (Oxford U. Press: NY, 1986)

Michael Brown, *The Channeling Zone: American Spirituality in an Anxious Age* (Harvard U. Press: Cambridge, Mass., 1997)

Patricial Cline Cohen, *The Murder of Helen Jewett: The Life And Deathof a Prostitute in Nineteenth-Century New York* (Knopf: NY, 1998)

Gail Collins, *America's Women: Four Hundred Years of Dolls, Drudges, Helpmates and Heroines* (Morrow: NY, 2003)

Michael Cook, *A Brief History of the Human Race* (Norton: NY, 2003)

Robert Darnton, *The Great Cat Massacre; and Other Episodes in French Cultural History* (Basic Books: NY, 1984)

Robert Darnton, *The Kiss of Lamourette: Reflections in Cultural History* (Norton: NY, 1990)

Robert Darnton, *The Forbidden Best Sellers of Prerevolutionary France* (Norton: NY,1995)

Robert Darnton, *George Washington's False Teeth: An Unconventional Guide to the Eighteenth Century* (Norton: NY, 2003)

James N. Davidson, *Courtesans & Fishcakes: The Consuming Passions of Classical Athens* (St. Martin's Press: NY, 1998)

Natalie Zemon Davis, *The Return of Martin Guerre* (Harvard U. Press: Cambridge, 1983)

Natalie Zemon Davis, *The Gift in Sixteenth-Century France* (U. of Wisconsin Press: Madison, 2001)

Joan DeJean, *The Essence of Style: How the French Invented High Fashion, Fine Food, Chic Cafés, Style, Sophistication And Glamour* (Free Press: NY 2005)

Carl Degler, *In Search of Human Nature: The Decline and Revival of Darwinism in American Social Thought* (Oxford U. Press: NY, 1991)

John Demos, *The Unredeemed Captive: A Family Story from Early America* (Knopf: NY, 1994)

Jared Diamond, *Guns, Germs, and Steel: The Fates of Human Societies* (Norton: NY, 1997)

Ann Douglas, *Terrible Honesty: Mongrel Manhattan in the 1920s* (Farrar, Straus: NY 1995)

Barbara Ehrenreich, *Blood Rites: Origins and History of the Passions of War* (Holt: NY, 1997)

Cynthia Eller, *The Myth of Matriarchal Prehistory: Why an Invented Past Won't Give Women a Future* (Beacon Press: Boston, 2000)

Richard Evans, *Tales from the German Underworld* (Yale Univ. Press: New Haven, 1999

Felipe Fernandez-Armesto, *Food: A History* (Macmillan: NY, 2002)

Sheila Fitzpatrick, *Everyday Stalinism: Ordinary Life in Extraordinary Times: Soviet Russia in the 1930s* (Oxford U. Press: London, 1999)

Judith Flanders, *Inside the Victorian Home: A Portrait of Domestic Life in Victorian England* (Norton: NY, 2004)

Estelle Freedman, *No Turning Back: The History and the Future Of Women* (Profile: NY, 2002)

Lawrence Friedman, *The Horizontal Society* (Yale U. Press: New Haven, 1999)

Peter Gay, *Schnitzler's Century: The Making of Middle-Class Culture, 1815-1916* (Norton: NY, 2001)

Carlo Ginzburg, *The Cheese and the Worm: The Cosmos of a Sixteenth-Century Miller* (Johns Hopkins U. Press: Baltimore, 1980)

Jonathan Glover, *Humanity: A Moral History of the Twentieth Century* (Yale U. Press: New Haven, 2000)

Ann Goldberg, *Sex, Religion, and the Making of Modern Madness: The Eberbach Asylum and German Society, 1815-1849* (Oxford U. Press: London, 1999)

Beatrice Gottlieb, *The Family in the Western World from the Black Death to the Industrial Age* (Oxford U. Press: London, 1993)

Hans Ulrich Gumbert, *In 1926: Living On the Edge of Time* (Harvard U. Press: Cambridge, 1998)

Barbara Hanawalt, *The Ties That Bound: Peasant Families in Medieval England* (Oxford U. Press: London, 1986)

Deborah Hayden, *Pox: Genius, Madness and the Mysteries of Syphilis* (Basic Books: NY, 2003)

Paul Heelas, *The New Age Movement: The Celebration of the Self and the Sacralization of Modernity* (Oxford U. Press: London, 1997)

Arthur Herman, *The Idea of Decline in Western History* (The Free Press: NY, 1997)

David Hollinger, *Post-Ethnic America: Beyond Multiculturalism* (Basic Books: NY, 1997)

David Hollinger, *Transvaluations: Science, Jews and Secular Culture—Studies in Mid-Twentieth-Century American Intellectual History* (Princeton U. Press: Princeton, 1997)

Ralph Houlbrooke, *Death, Religion, and the Family in England, 1480-1750* (Oxford U. Press: London 1998)

Rhys Isaac, *The Transformation of Virginia, 1740-1790* (U. of North Carolina Press: Chapel Hill, 1982)

Susan Jacoby, *Freethinkers: A History of American Secularism* (Metropolitan Books: NY, 2004)

Pat Jalland, *Death in the Victorian Family* (Oxford U. Press: London, 1996)

Jenna Weissman Joselit, *A Perfect Fit: Clothes, Character, and The Promise of America* (NY: Holt, 2001)

Wendy Kaminer, *Sleeping with Extra-Terrestrials: The Rise of Irrationalism and Perils of Piety* (Pantheon: NY, 1999)

Michael Kammen, *American Culture, American Tastes: Social Change and the 20th Century* (Knopf: NY, 1999)

Paul Kennedy, *The Rise and Fall of the Great Powers: Economic Change and Military Conflict from 1500-2000* (Random House: NY, 1987)

Bettyann Kevles, *Naked to the Bone: Medical Imaging in the 20th Century* (Rutgers U. Press: NY, 1997)

Mary Laven, *Virgins of Venice: Enclosed Lives and Broken Vows in The Renaissance Convent* (Viking: NY, 2002)

Emmanuel Le Roy Ladurie, *The Beggar and the Professor: A Sixteenth-Century Family Saga.* Translated by Arthur Goldhammer. (U. of Chicago Press: Chicago, 1997)

Jackson Lears, *Fables of Abundance: A Cultural History of Advertising in America* (Basic Books: NY, 1995)

Gerda Lerner, *The Creation of Feminist Consciousness: From the Middle Ages to 1870* (Oxford U. Press: NY, 1993)

Richard L. Rapson

Seymour Martin Lipset, *American Exceptionalism: A Double-Edged Sword* (1996)

Alberto Manguel, *A History of Reading* (Penguin: NY, 1997)

Darrin McMahon, *Happiness: A History* (Atlantic Monthly Press: (NY, 2006)

Regina Morantz-Sanchez, *Conduct Unbecoming A Woman: Medicine on Trial in Turn-of-the-Century Brooklyn* (Oxford U. Press: NY, 1999)

Charles Murray: *Human Accomplishment: The Pursuit of Excellence In the Arts and Sciences—800 B.C. to 1950* (HarperCollins: NY, 2003)

Stephen Oates, *The Approaching Fury: Voices of the Storm, 1820-1861* (HarperCollins: NY, 1997)

Steven Ozment, *The Burger-Meister's Daughter:Scandal in a 16th-Century German Town* (1996)

Richard Pells, *Not like Us: How Europeans Have Loved, Hated, and Transformed American Culture Since World War II* (Basic Books: NY, 1998)

Roy Porter, *London: A Social History* (Harvard U. Press: Cambridge, 1995)

Stephen Prothero, *American Jesus: How the Son of God Became A National Icon* (Farrar, Straus: NY, 2004)

Richard L. Rapson, *American Yearnings: Love, Money, and Endless Possibility* (University Press of America: Washington, D.C., 1988)

Daniel Roche, *France in the Enlightenment* (Harvard U. Press: Cambridge, 1999)

Simon Schama, *The Embarrassment of Riches: An Interpretation of Dutch Culture in the Golden Age* (Collins: London, 1987)

Simon Schama, *Dead Certainties: Unwarranted Speculations* (Knopf: NY, 1991)

Simon Schama, *Landscape and Memory* (Knopf: NY,1995)

Carl Schorske, *Fin-de-Siecle Vienna: Politics and Culture* (Knopf: NY, 1980)

Richard Sennett, *Flesh and Stone: The Body and the City in Western Civilization* (W.W.Norton: NY, 1994)

Matthew Stewart, *The Courtier and the Heretic: Leibniz, Spinoza, and the Fate of God* (W.W. Norton: NY, 2006)

Patricia Meyer Spacks, *Boredom: The Literary History of a State of Mind* (University of Chicago Press: Chicago,1995)

Rebecca Spang, *The Invention of the Restaurant: Paris and the Modern Gastronomic Culture* (Harvard U. Press: Cambridge, 2000)

Jonathan Spence, *The Question of Hu* (Knopf: NY, 1988)

Jonathan Spence, *God's Chinese Son: The Taiping Heavenly Kingdom of Hong Xiuquan* (Norton: NY, 1996

Jonathan Spence, *The Chan's Great Continent: China in Western Minds* (Norton: NY, 1999)

Peter Stearns, *Fat History: Bodies and Beauty in the Modern West* (NYU Press: NY, 1997)

Liselotte Steinbrugge, *The Moral Sex: Woman's Nature in the French Enlightenment* (Oxford U. Press: London, 1995)

Gary Taylor, *Cultural Selection: Why Some Achievements Withstand the Test of Time—and Others Don't* (Basic Books: NY, 1997)

E. Fuller Torrey, M.D., and Judy Miller, *The Invisible Plague: The Rise of Mental Illness from 1750 to the Present* (Rutgers U. Press: New Brunswick, NJ, 2002)

Laurel Thatcher Ulrich, *The Age of Homespun: Objects and Stories in the Creation of an American Myth* (Vintage: NY, 2002)

Glenn Wallach, *Obedient Sons: The Discourse of Youth and Generations in American Culture, 1630-1860* (Univ. of Massachusetts Press: Amherst, 1998)

Marina Warner, *From the Beast to the Blonde: On Fairy Tales and Their Tellers* (Chatto & Windus: London, 1995)

Garry Wills, *Inventing America: Jefferson's Declaration of Independence* (Mariner Books: NY, 2002)

Garry Wills, *John Wayne's America: The Politics of Celebrity* (Simon & Schuster: NY, 1997)

Garry Wills, *Lincoln at Gettysburg: The Words That Remade America* (Simon & Schuster: NY, 1992)

Theodore Zeldin, *An Intimate History of Humanity* (HarperCollins: NY, 1995)

FOOTNOTES

1   Tom Wicker, "Not So Bright a Future," *New York Times*, February 23, 1988, p. 25.

2   *Ibid.*, p. 25

3   Edward Luttwak, quoted in *Newsweek*, February 22, 1988.

4   Lewis Lapham, *New York Times,* July 24, 1987.

5   Robert Darnton, *The Great Cat Massacre* (New York. 1984). p. 64.

6   Richard Hofstadter. "History and the Social Sciences." in Fritz Stern, ed., *The Varieties of History: From Voltaire* to *the* Present (New York, 1972), p. 370.

7   Quoted In Robert Kelley, *Reviews in American History*, vol. 15, no. 2 (June, 1987). p. 213.

8   T.S. Eliot, *Four Quartets. Little Gidding, IV.*

9   Maureen Dowd, "A Giant Doom Magnet," New York Times, February 17, 2007.

10   *Ibid.*

11   'Carl Degler, *At Odds: Women and the Family in America from the Revolution to the Present* (Oxford, 1980), pp. 8-9.

12   Morgan Philips Price. *America After Sixty Years: The Travel Diaries of Two Generations of Englishmen* (London, 1936), pp. 107-08.

13   Henry Latham, *Black* and *White. A Journal of a Three Months' Tour in the United States* (London, 1867), p. 251.

14   Alexander Mackay, *The Western World* (London, 1849), vol. I, pp. 137-138.

15   Alexis de Tocqueville, *Democracy in America* (New York: Modern Library College Editions, 1981), vol. 1, p. 3.

16   Pollingreport.com, February 11, 2007.

17   Author's note: since writing the above, there has been a huge accumulation of reliable data that TV, video games, and movie violence begets more violence. They also make people very fearful.

18   David Potter, *People of Plenty: Economic Abundance and the American Character* (Chicago, 1954), p.177.

19   John Kenneth Galbraith, *Economics and the Public Purpose* (Boston, 1973), pp. 30-33.

20   America's celebrities are shooting stars. As I reel off the names of the famous in 1988, it may be interesting as readers go through these paragraphs in later times, to note which of them remain stars, who are remembered, who have faded, who have disappeared altogether, and who are the replacements. It is also interesting that, though some are not officially American, they become so by their media style.

[21]   Russell Baker, "The Price of Liberty," *New York Times,* July 5, 1987.

[22]   John Lahr. *Harper's* (January, 1978).

[23]   Barbara Goldsmith. "The Meaning of Celebrity." *New York Times.* December 7, 1985.

[24]   Warren I. Susman, *Culture As History: The Transformation of American Culture in the Twentieth Century* (New York, 1984), p. xxii.

[25]   *Ibid.,* p. xx.

[26]   *Ibid.,* p. xxiv.

[27]   *Ibid.,* p. xxv.

[28]   *Ibid.,* pp. xxv-xxvi.

[29]   *Ibid.,* p. xxix.

[30]   Goldsmith, *op. cit.*

[31]   As quoted by Goldsmith, *op. cit.*

[32]   Richard Schickel, *Intimate Strangers: The Culture of Celebrity* (New York, 1985), pp.viii-ix.

[33]   Randy Cohen, "The Ethicist," *New York Times,* March 11, 2007.

[34]   D. H. Lawrence, *Studies in Classic American Literature* (New York, 1923), p. 20

[35]   E. L. Doctorow. *Ragtime* (New York. 1975). p. 44.

[36]   Peter Gay. *The Bourgeois Experience, Victoria to Freud: Education of the Senses* (New York 1984), p. 5.

[37]   Anthony Trollope, *North America* (London. 1862). vol. 2, p. 74.

[38]   E. L. Doctorow, *op. cit.,* pp. 153-54.

[39]   F. Scott Fitzgerald, *The Great Gatsby* (New York, 1925), p. 174.

[40]   *Ibid.,* p. 182.

[41]   John Kenneth Galbraith, *The Affluent Society* (New York, 1958), pp. 199-200.

[42]   Barbara Ehrenreich, "Is the Middle Class Doomed?" *New York Times,* September 14, 1986.

[43]   *Ibid.*

[44]   *Ibid.*

[45]   David Brooks, "The Triumph of Hope Over Self-Interest," *New York Times,* January 12, 2003.

[46]   Hannah Fairfield, "America: Not Their First Choice," *New York Times,* July 3, 2005.

[47]   *Ibid.*

[48]   Garrison Keillor, *Happy To Be Here* (New York, 1981), pp. 150-52.

[49]   David M. Kennedy, "War and the American Character," *The Stanford Magazine* (Fall 1984), p. 17.

[50]   This statement forms the frontispiece to C. Vann Woodward's *Origins of the New South.*

[51]   See Kennedy, *op. cit.,* for the best-developed statement of this general theme.

[52]   W.C. Ford, *A Cycle of Adams Letters, 1861-1865* (Boston, 1920), vol. 1, p. 135.

[53]   One of the grave historical distortions of the period is that which led many Americans to divide history into the "pre-9/11 world *vs.* a post-9/11 world." The assumption that the world changed forever on 9/11 reveals the provincialism of Americans (and cynicism of some of its leaders) and assumes that the horrific 9/11 attacks constituted the beginning of violence in the world, and that nothing would be the same thereafter. I don't believe 9/11 is anything of a historical watershed other than reminding Americans that they are

not exempt from outside violence. It constitutes terrible and misleading history. It may be worth remembering that those two towers with its nearly 3,000 deaths would have had to be bombed every day, without exception, for *six years* to equal the deaths brought about by the Holocaust against the Jews and *nine* years when we include the gypsies and others! And it would take *50 years* of daily World Trade Center bombings to come close to the death count brought about by the Second World War. History did not significantly change on that awful 9/11.

54 Bertrand Russell, *Mysticism and Logic* (London, 1918), p. 47.

55 Carl Becker, *The Heavenly City of the Eighteenth-Century Philosophers* (New Haven, 1932), pp. 14-15.

56 Erich Fromm, *Escape From Freedom* (New York: 1964 edition), pp. 277-78.

57 *Ibid*, p. 281.

58 Carl Degler, *At Odds, op.cit.* p. 471.

59 William Irwin Thompson, *At the Edge of History* (New York, 1971), p. 19.

60 *Ibid.*

61 Benjamin De Mott, *Surviving the Seventies* (Baltimore, 1971), pp. 19-20.

62 Arthur S. Link. William A. Link, William B. Catton. *American Epoch* (New York: Sixth edition, 1987), p. 189.

63 *Ibid.* p. 190.

64 *Ibid.*, pp. 188-90.

65 Howard Mumford Jones, *The Bright Medusa* (Urbana, Ill., 1952), pp. 63-64.

66 *Ibid*, p. 65.

67 Robert H. Elias, *"Entangling Alliances with None": An Essay on the Individual in the American Twenties* (New York, 1973), p. xiii.

68 *Ibid.*, p. 203.

69 *Ibid.*, pp. xiv-xv.

70 Arthur Schlesinger, Jr., *The Cycles of American History* (Boston, 1986), p. 28.

71 *Ibid.*

72 *Ibid.*, pp. 28-29.

73 *Ibid.*, p. 26.

74 Richard Hofstadter, *The American Political Tradition and the Men Who Made It* (New York, 1948: First Vintage edition, 1974), p. xxxvii.

75 *Ibid.*, p. xxix.

76 James Baldwin, *The Fire Next Time* (New York, 1962), pp. 129-131.

77 Henry Latham, *Black and White: A Journal of a Three Months' Tour in the United States* (London, 1867), p. 251.

78 Rudyard Kipling, *American Notes* (New York, 1891), p. 55.

79 James Bryce, *American Commonwealth* (London, 1888), vol. 3, p. 521.

80 Matthew Arnold, *Civilization in the United States: First and Last Impressions* (London, 1988), p. 168.

81 Carl Degler, *At Odds, op. cit.*, p. 471.

82 Lawrence Stone, *The Family, Sex and Marriage: In England 1500-1800* (New York, 1979), p. 427.

83   *Ibid.*

84   Erik Eckholm, "Plight Deepens For Black Men, Studies Warn," *New York Times*, March 20, 2006.

85   Kate Zernike, "Why Are There So Many Single Americans?", *New York Times*, January 21, 2007.

86   In 1986, a *Newsweek* story claimed that "a single 40-year-old woman had a better chance of being killed by a terrorist than getting married." Such a claim was nutty then and is no less crazy now. Though there were no data to back it up, the story received a great deal of attention and no little credulity. Social conservatives used it to deplore the decline of "traditional" marriage. On June 5, 2006, twenty years on, *Newsweek* finally publicly apologized for its laughable, bogus fairy tale.

87   Stephanie Coontz, "Three 'Rules' That Don't Apply," *Newsweek*, June 5, 2006, p. 49.

88   *Ibid.*

89   *Housekeeping Monthly*, May 13, 1955.

90   Michael Argyle, *The Psychology of Happiness* (London, 1987), p. 103.

91   Fromm, *Escape From Freedom, op. cit.*, p. 278

92   Argyle, *op. cit.* p. 105.

93   Richard J. Estes, *The Social Progress of Nations* (New York, 1984), pp. 91-122.

94   George Thomas Kurian, *New Book of World Rankings* (New York, 1984), pp. 331-332.

95   *Ibid.*, pp. 437-483.

96   Robert Darnton, *The Great Cat Massacre, op. cit.*, pp. 61-62.

97   Albert Camus, *The Plague* (New York, 1948), p. 278

98   My favorite non-technical books which do this are Oliver Sacks, *The Man Who Mistook His Wife for a Hat* (New York, 1985) and Jon Franklin, *Molecules of the Mind: The Brave New Science of Molecular Psychology* (New York, 1987).

99   Franklin, *Molecules of the Mind, op.cit.*, p. 146.

100   "Wonder and Skepticism", Skeptical Enquirer Volume 19, Issue 1, (January-February 1995).

101   During the years of writing *American Yearnings*, my chief scholarly interests swerved gently toward what I call "psychological history." This is the study of the emotional life of the 99% of our sisters and brothers of the past who did not make it into the dominant top-down mode of previous historical study: political and military history. History had generally focused on the powerful, rather than the majority. When one switches to the private lives of "the people," the topics become more psychological in nature: love, marriage, divorce, relationships, emotions, child rearing, family, sex. Hence, "psychological history." My brief essay below hints at the richness of the field, while the first of the two bibliographies at the back of this book points the way to further study. The second bibliography in the new cultural history includes additional titles that have greatly influenced my recent work and thinking.

102   See E. Hatfield and R. Rapson, "Love and Passion," in Irwin Goldstein, Cindy M. Meston, Susan R. Davis, & Abdulmaged M. Traish (Eds.) *Women's sexual function and dysfunction: Study, diagnosis and treatment* (London: Taylor and Francis, UK., 2006), pp. 93-97.

103   While I always had an interest in moving beyond political history into the study of the lives of the many, my focus on psychological history got a boost from my becoming a co-

therapist with my psychologist-scholar wife, Elaine Hatfield, and from the series of books we subsequently wrote together. But I had another career interest before Elaine: educational reform. The reader of this book will surely note that one of its major themes is my continuing concern about the low level of education in America and the society's anti-intellectualism, as expressed bluntly by the title of the next Postscript: "America the Ignorant."

My main attempt to do something to enrich education on a personal level is in my teaching. But my broadest effort came when I founded and led an experimental college some 40 years ago. Below are excerpts from a piece I wrote a decade ago about that college for a history of the University of Hawaii. I include it here to illustrate some of my ideas about how to stimulate, at least in my profession of higher education, a love of the life of the mind. Short of that, I'll settle for an uptick of informed thinking in our society.

104   Alas, as of 2007, nothing like New College, has returned to campus, despite much talk and several committees designed to explore the idea. Universities in America generally have shied away from educational experimentation and are increasingly run more like businesses. Like much else in the nation, the bottom line tends to rule.

105   The final Postscripts unfold in three acts: Act One—America the Ignorant; Act Two—America the Rightwing; and Act Three—America the Resilient?

"America the Ignorant" was written before the 2004 Presidential election, when George W. Bush was returned for a second term. Sadly, I feel that my observations there have grown in pertinence.

"America the Rightwing" is a brief excerpt from a book I wrote in 2003 called *Amazed By Life: Confessions of a Non-Religious Believer.* This book was a bookend to *American Yearnings.* Metaphorically, *Yearnings* was 20% personal and 80% cultural and historical analysis. *Amazed* was a memoir of ideas, 80% personal and 20% cultural/historical.

I look ahead with "America the Resilient?" The words in it are the last ones written for this book, composed 18 months before the 2008 Presidential election. They reflect briefly on what may lay in the future for my country. I am not without some modest hopes.

106   And then—a second time!